CENTRAL AND EASTERN EUROPEAN MEDIA IN COMPARATIVE PERSPECTIVE

T0304126

Central and Eastern European Media in Comparative Perspective

Politics, Economy and Culture

Edited by

JOHN DOWNEY
Loughborough University, UK

SABINA MIHELJ
Loughborough University, UK

Routledge
Taylor & Francis Group

LONDON AND NEW YORK

First published 2012 by Ashgate Publishing

Published 2016 by Routledge
2 Park Square, Milton Park, Abingdon, Oxfordshire OX14 4RN
711 Third Avenue, New York, NY 10017, USA

First issued in paperback 2016

Routledge is an imprint of the Taylor & Francis Group, an informa business

British Library Cataloguing in Publication Data
Central and Eastern European media in comparative perspective : politics, economy and culture.
   1. Mass media policy – Europe, Central. 2. Mass media policy – Europe, Eastern. 3. Mass
   media – Political aspects – Europe, Central. 4. Mass media – Political aspects – Europe,
   Eastern. 5. Mass media and culture – Europe, Central. 6. Mass media and culture – Europe,
   Eastern. 7. Mass media – Economic aspects – Europe, Central. 8. Mass media – Economic
   aspects – Europe, Eastern. 9. Mass media – Social aspects – Europe, Central. 10. Mass media
   – Social aspects – Europe, Eastern.
   I. Downey, John. II. Mihelj, Sabina.
   302.2'3'0943-dc23

Library of Congress Cataloging-in-Publication Data
Central and Eastern European media in comparative perspective : politics, economy and culture
/ edited by John Downey and Sabina Mihelj.
      p. cm.
   Includes bibliographical references and index.
   ISBN 978-1-4094-3542-6 (hardback : alk. paper)
   1. Mass media – Political aspects – Europe, Central. 2. Mass media – Economic aspects –
   Europe, Central. 3. Mass media and culture – Europe, Central. 4. Mass media – Political
   aspects – Europe, Eastern. 5. Mass media – Economic aspects – Europe, Eastern. 6. Mass
   media and culture – Europe, Eastern. I. Downey, John. II. Mihelj, Sabina.
   P92.E93C47 2012
   302.230943–dc23

                                                                            2011037039

ISBN 13: 978-1-138-25693-4 (pbk)
ISBN 13: 978-1-4094-3542-6 (hbk)

Contents

Contents

List of Figures

List of Tables

Notes on Contributors

John Downey is Reader in Comparative Media in the Department of Social Sciences at Loughborough University, UK. He was educated at Cambridge University and has taught at universities in Germany, the UK and the USA. He has published books and articles in the fields of new media, European media, and comparative media. He has conducted research for the *Guardian* newspaper in the UK, the UK Electoral Commission, the Commission for Racial Equality, the BBC Board of Governors, the Economic and Social Research Council, and the UK Department of Health. He recently completed a project analysing public debates about the national DNA database in the UK, funded by the Economic and Social Research Council.

Alison Harcourt is Senior Lecturer in Politics and Jean Monnet Chair in the information society at the University of Exeter. She is a specialist in European integration and public policy. Her primary focus of research is regulatory change in communications markets. She has written on the regulation of traditional and new media markets at European and EU Member State levels contributing to the literature on regulatory competition, committee governance, Europeanization, policy transfer and policy convergence. Originally from Chicago, Alison has a PhD from the University of Manchester and has worked at the universities of Warwick, Oxford, and the European University Institute before joining Exeter in 2004.

Karol Jakubowicz worked as a journalist and executive in the Polish press, radio and television for many years, and has also taught at universities in Poland and abroad. He is now senior adviser to the Chairman of the National Broadcasting Council, the broadcasting regulatory body of Poland. In 2008–2010 he was Chairman of the UNESCO Intergovernmental Council of the Information for All Programme. In 2007–2008 he was member of the Council of the Independent Media Commission of Kosovo. He has also been active in the Council of Europe. His publications include the books *Rude Awakening: Social and Media Change in Central and Eastern Europe* (2007), *Public Service Broadcasting: The Beginning of the End, or a New Beginning?* (2007, in Polish); *Media Policy and the Electronic Media* (2008, in Polish), and *The EU and the Media: Between Culture and the Economy* (2010, in Polish).

Sabina Mihelj is Senior Lecturer in Media, Communication and Culture in the Department of Social Sciences at Loughborough University, UK. Prior to coming to Loughborough, she worked as a researcher at the Ljubljana Graduate School of the Humanities and taught in the Sociology Department at the Faculty of Arts,

University of Ljubljana. She is the author of *Media Nations: Communicating Belonging and Exclusion in the Modern World* (2011) and has published a wide range of journal articles and book chapters on media and nationalism, religion and the new media, cosmopolitanism, European communication, comparative media research, Cold War culture and television history.

Mojca Pajnik is Assistant Professor at the Faculty of Social Sciences, University of Ljubljana, and Senior Research Associate at the Peace Institute, Institute for Contemporary Social and Political Studies in Ljubljana, Slovenia. She is the author of *Prostitution and Human Trafficking: Perspectives of Gender, Labour and Migration* (2008) and co-author of *Where in the Puzzle: Trafficking from, to and through Slovenia* and of *Immigrants, who are you? Research on Immigrants in Slovenia* (2002). She has (co)edited several books, among them *Alternative Media and the Politics of Resistance: Perspectives and Challenges* (with J.D.H. Downing, 2008) and *Precarious Migrant Labour across Europe* (with G. Campani, 2011). In recent years she has been a guest lecturer at the University of Florence, the University of Helsinki and the Central European University in Budapest. She acted as a project coordinator for several international research projects on citizenship, gender and migration and has published widely on these topics.

Colin Sparks is Professor of Media Studies in the School of Communication at Hong Kong Baptist University. He previously taught at the University of Westminster, where he was Director of the Communication and Media Research Institute (CAMRI). He has written extensively on various aspects of the media but today his main interest is in the comparative study of media in societies undergoing rapid social and economic change.

Václav Štětka is Senior Research Fellow at the Department of Politics and International Relations, University of Oxford, where he works on a comparative research project 'Media and Democracy in Central and Eastern Europe' (2009–2013). He holds a PhD from Masaryk University in Brno, the Czech Republic, where he was Assistant Professor at the Department of Media Studies and Journalism from 2006 to 2009. His publications include a range of articles and book chapters on media, nationalism and globalization, public service television, European campaign strategies, media ownership and autonomy, and children and the media.

Acknowledgments

This book started as a conversation among participants of the COST A30 action *East of West: Setting a New Central and Eastern European Media* (2004–2009), chaired by Miklós Sükösd. The *East of West* action aimed to increase the understanding of media landscapes in Central and Eastern Europe, examine the applicability of Western European and American concepts and theories, and develop novel conceptualizations.

Thanks to the support of the *East of West* action we were able to meet several times to discuss our preliminary ideas and drafts, and we also benefited from exchanges with other participants of the network.

We owe special thanks to Karol Jakubowicz for his contribution to the early stages of the book planning.

Introduction
Comparing Media Systems in Central and Eastern Europe: Politics, Economy, Culture

Sabina Mihelj and John Downey

Typologies designed to account for the diversity of media systems around the world have been a recurring element of communication research for well over half a century. Yet, in common with comparative endeavours in other areas of social scientific inquiry, the analysis of media systems has long been plagued by simplistic, teleological and ethnocentric understandings of social change. The four-fold typology of press models proposed by Fred Siebert, Theodore Peterson and Wilbur Schramm in 1956 – which distinguished between the authoritarian, libertarian, social responsibility, and Soviet communist concepts of the press – was designed from the normative perspective of classical liberalism, and ranked the four types of the press on an evolutionary scale culminating in the press model promoted in the West. The analytical framework used was too narrow to capture the varied social and political theories underpinning media policies around the world, and left little scope for acknowledging the unequal distribution of economic, political and communicative power on a global scale (Christians et al. 2009: viii). In this sense, the title of the book – *Four Theories of the Press* – was a misnomer: instead of offering four theories of the press, it offered 'one theory with four examples' (Nerone 1995: 18).

Nonetheless, it is worth acknowledging that the *Four Theories* also put forward a key argument that remains a valid starting point for comparative inquiries into mass communication to this day. As the authors stated in their introduction, any systematic understanding of the press has to proceed from the recognition that 'the press always takes the form and coloration of the social and political structures within which it operates' (Siebert et al. 1956: 1). To put it differently, the key contribution of the *Four Theories* was not merely the typology itself, but rather its attempt to avoid media-centrism, and construct an explanatory framework that acknowledges the importance of factors external to the media system. In subsequent decades, this key lesson was often forgotten, sometimes even by the authors themselves. Especially when examining the link between mass communication and processes of social change, media and communication scholars have time and again fallen pray to technological determinism, abstracting the media from the context in which they operated and treating them as an autonomous modernizing force. Mass media were thus expected to lay the groundwork needed for successful modernization, namely to: inculcate modern work routines and health habits, instil cultural attitudes favourable to innovation, promote cooperation and long-term effort for the common good, and lure the population away from traditional customs, fatalism and superstitions that were seen to stand in the way of progress. Wilbur Schramm was notoriously infatuated with the transformative potential of communication technologies and the good it could bring to the 'undeveloped' countries of the world. In his characteristically prophetic and moralistic *Mass Media and National Development*, the radio receiver figures as an object of almost supernatural qualities: in the hand of inhabitants of remote villages in the Middle East, it becomes 'a magic carpet' capable of carrying them 'beyond the horizons they had known' (Schramm 1964: 20).

Similarly as the general theories of media and modernization developed at the time, *Four Theories* was of course an intellectual child of the Cold War. Shaped by the global competition for influence over former colonies, these new typologies and theories provided not only description and explanation, but also offered normative and practical guidelines that would help justify and preserve the leading role of the US on a global scale, and most of all its advantage over the rival project of modernity advanced by Soviet communism (Letham 2000, Gilman 2007). Given their embeddedness in Cold War politics, it is of little surprise that the theories developed by US scholars such as Walt Withman Rostow, Lucien Pye, Daniel Lerner and Wilbur Schramm shared many of the weaknesses of the nineteenth-century evolutionist theories. Although they have shed the racist assumptions of their nineteenth-century predecessors, these post-World War II theories of modernization were still premised on a black-and-white opposition between 'tradition' and 'modernity', and saw modernization as a uniform process culminating in the forms of society, economy, politics and the media known from the industrialized West, and the United States in particular.

These approaches to modernization came under severe criticism already in the 1960s, and were to a large extent discredited by the 1970s (Gilman 2007: 203–40). The early theories of media and development, along with the four-fold typology proposed by Siebert et al., were no exception. From the 1970s onwards, several attempts have been made to construct alternative typologies, or to correct the original typology by adding additional comparative dimensions. For example, Ralph Lowenstein (1970) revised the original criteria for describing world press systems, and developed a typology that categorized different press models not only with regard to their relationship with the political system, but also with regard to different types of media ownership and different levels of economic development of the media. Herbert Altschull's (1984) typology was similar in this respect, but put even more emphasis on the economics of the media as the key basis for describing world press systems. In contrast, William Hachten (1981) retained the original focus on the media-politics relationship, but suggested two additional concepts of the press – the revolutionary and the developmental – and merged the libertarian and the social responsibility models into a single 'Western' model of the press. Finally, Dennis McQuail (1983) proposed a slightly different alternative to the original typology. While retaining the four media theories discussed by Siebert et al., he added two further ones: the development media theory, and the democratic-participant media theory.

These alternative proposals – and many others not mentioned here – brought significant new insights into the diversity of public communication around the world. However, many of them failed precisely where the *Four Theories* succeeded – namely in avoiding a media-centric approach, and in offering an explanation rather than merely a description of different media systems. The first decisive break with this tradition of comparative media analysis came with the publication of Daniel Hallin and Paolo Mancini's *Comparing Media Systems* (2004), which opened with a seemingly simple question, posed also in the *Four Theories*: Why are the media as they are?

To answer this question, Hallin and Mancini proposed to examine the relationship between media systems and political systems, and their primary focus is on the news media, journalism and media policies. Their threefold typology, based on empirical data drawn from eighteen West European and North American countries, essentially distinguishes the different media models with respect to their relative proximity to, and type of involvement with, two key factors: the market and the state, or economy and politics. At one end of the spectrum is the liberal media model, which finds its best approximation in the media systems of the US and Canada and is characterized by: a) medium-sized press markets, b) low politicization, c) a high level of journalistic professionalism, and d) the dominance of market principles. In contrast, the polarized pluralist model, exemplified in the states of Southern Europe, is marked by a) small press markets, b) high politicization, c) a low level of professionalism, and d) strong state intervention. The third media model identified in their scheme, the democratic corporatist model, dominant in Central and Northern Europe, falls mid-way between the two on all four counts. The roots of each of the three media models can be traced back to the key characteristics of the political systems in which they operate: the historical trajectory of democratization, particularly with regard to the patterns of conflict and consensus (polarized vs. moderate pluralism), the role of the state (the strength of the welfare state), the type of government (consensus or majoritarian) and the development of rational-legal authority.

While we welcome this explanatory turn in comparative media analysis and the increased interest in the field in recent years, we believe that much of the research inspired by Hallin and Mancini's framework has yet again lost sight of the key question – namely, why the media are as they are – and reverted back to a predominantly media-centric and descriptive approach that is largely content to locate a particular media system in one of Hallin and Mancini's ideal types. In contrast, we propose to go back to the main coordinates of Hallin and Mancini's explanatory model, and expand them not only empirically, but also theoretically. The empirical limitations of Hallin and Mancini's work are easy to pinpoint – geographically, their analysis is restricted to Western Europe and Northern America, and historically, it deals primarily with the post-World War II decades up to the end of the Cold War. From this point of view, focusing the analysis on recent media developments in Central and Eastern Europe (hereafter CEE) seems a logical first step. How do the media in the region fare with regards to the key dimensions of media systems identified by Hallin and Mancini, such as political parallelism, professionalization or types and degrees of state intervention? And, more generally, is their explanatory framework capable of accounting for the particular trajectories of media transformation in the region, and thereby explaining why the CEE media are as they are? If not, how should it be amended?

This volume is not the first one to raise these questions – the applicability of existing models and theories is a central concern in much of the recent research and writing on CEE media (Jakubowicz 2007, Dobek-Ostrowska and Głowacki 2008, Jakubowicz and Sükösd 2008, Dobek-Ostrowska et al. 2010). Yet while providing valuable empirical insights into media developments in the region, this body of work has not offered much in terms of theoretical innovation. Although some authors have put forward suggestions for theoretical improvements to existing comparative frameworks, these have yet to be implemented empirically. The same is true also of many recent comparative studies of the media beyond CEE. Drawing on an ambitious study spanning eighteen countries and four continents, Thomas Hanitzsch and his colleagues (Hanitzsch et al. 2010, Hanitzsch 2011) have developed a rich and truly global typology of journalistic cultures, but have not yet delved into the various explanatory factors that may have shaped them – although they argue that this is exactly where future comparative efforts need to go. On the other hand, studies concerned with causal relationships are often mediacentric. They stay within the remit of media systems themselves, and pay little attention to extra-media factors. A recent study of political information flows in six countries, for instance, focuses on the relationship between media coverage of current affairs on the one hand, and different media system types and varying levels of media commercialization on the other, without considering the role of extra-media factors (Aalberg et al. 2010). In a similar vein, another study argues that the supply of political information and public awareness of political issues are both influenced by the properties of national media systems, but pays no systematic attention to links with, for example, political systems or economic indicators (Iyengar et al. 2010). Without considering such external factors, it is impossible to ascertain whether and to what extent media systems are indeed an independent causal variable in the supply of political information, and how exactly they relate to other potential explanatory factors. Many studies of media systems share this fundamental design flaw.

More decisive steps beyond media-centric research designs can be found in recent cross-national research on media attention and news values. Though this body of work is not specifically concerned with advancing the comparative understanding of media systems, it is worth briefly surveying some of the recent studies to highlight the explanatory potential of extra-media factors. For instance, in her comparative analysis of media coverage of 9/11 in four countries, Cristina Archetti (2010) develops an explanatory framework that includes not only factors internal to the media system (national journalistic cultures and editorial policies of individual media organizations) but also factors pertaining primarily to the political system (national interests). Drawing on a comparative study of news coverage of earthquakes in three countries, Ruud Koopmans and Rens Vliegenthart (2010) propose a different explanatory model of media attention, which includes five causal forces: the inherent characteristic of the event, such as for instance the magnitude of the earthquake or number of casualties; the cultural, socioeconomic and political homophily between the source (the country in which the event occurred) and the adopter (the country where the event is reported), as well as social network ties between the two, the status and power of the source, and the existence of prior coverage of news from the same source. In contrast to Archetti's model, this framework goes well beyond the familiar focus on the media-politics relationship, and covers a broad range of economic, cultural and political factors, none of which is specific to the media. In fact, the media feature merely as a conveyor belt for messages shaped by external factors. Of course, such a socio-centric model has its drawbacks. While it may be appropriate for explaining the coverage of events such as earthquakes – which, as the authors themselves note, are typically not politicized – a more broadly applicable explanatory framework would need to include also factors internal to media systems, including levels of political parallelism and the political leanings of individual newspapers. Only by using such multi-level explanatory models we can develop a better understanding of the relative role of the media vis-à-vis other factors at work in contemporary societies.

In line with this, we propose a more ambitious theoretical revision of existing typologies and explanatory approaches used in comparative media systems research. In short, we contend that trying to fit CEE media into one of the three media models suggested by Hallin and Mancini, or developing an additional, 'post-communist' media model, does not suffice. What we need instead is to go back to the main premises of comparative frameworks, find ways to improve them, and then test such an enhanced framework using new empirical data.

Expanding the Scope of Comparison: Explanatory Goals, Causal Factors and Methodological Challenges

There are many possible routes for pursuing a revision of existing media typologies and comparative frameworks that go beyond mere geographic expansion. First, we can ask ourselves whether the research goals and questions that dominate existing literature are broad enough to encompass the pressing dilemmas of modern mass communication. If not, we can identify new questions that can be usefully tackled using comparative modes of inquiry. Second, we can interrogate the roster of causal recipes used to explain particular media outcomes, such as tabloidization or the rise and decline of journalistic professionalism. Could the introduction of new causal factors lead to better, more powerful explanations of these phenomena? Third, we can address the methodological challenges faced by comparative media research, and develop new research designs and analytical procedures. In the following paragraphs we briefly outline each of these options, and explain which of the routes are pursued in this book.

New Questions

Like other social scientists drawing on comparative modes of inquiry, and in particular those using comparative historical analysis (Skocpol 1984: 7–12, Mahoney and Rueschmeyer 2003: 7–10), scholars conducting comparative media systems research are typically interested in 'big questions' concerning the development of democratic governance and the consequences of large-scale transformations such as industrialization, urbanization or commercialization. Yet so far, the focus has largely been on the *political outcomes* of these processes, and on the media as *political institutions*. For instance, one of the key questions motivating research in this area has been the impact of commercialization, and of the related processes of globalization, on the quality of public deliberation (e.g., Chalaby 1996, Esser 1999, Benson and Hallin 2007, Aalberg et al. 2010). A related, equally central question concerns the changing practices, structures and contents of political communication, and their causal links with democratization processes and with the global diffusion of Western political practices (e.g., Blumler and Gurevitch 1995, Holtz-Bacha 2004).

While doubtlessly important, such questions leave many other important substantive outcomes of social change, and the role of media in them, unaccounted for. To be able to investigate the full range of these outcomes, we need to acknowledge that the media are not only political, but also *economic* and *cultural* institutions. Apart from filtering, framing and disseminating information about the political processes, the media also play a key role in promoting goods, in shaping and negotiating cultural values and norms, and in fostering particular forms of social cohesion and exclusion. Describing the similarities and differences between media systems with regard to their relationship to political systems is therefore only part of the story. We also need to find ways to account for different relationships between media institutions and economic systems, as well as between the media and socio-cultural structures, including different forms of ethno-cultural diversity, different patterns of gender roles, or for instance class structures. To these we could add the relationships between media systems and *communication technologies*, and, for instance, the relative prominence of newspaper reading, television viewing, or Internet use in media use patterns.

In this volume, we focus on clarifying media's relationships with politics, economy and culture, and with respect to the latter, we pay attention primarily to ethno-cultural diversity and gender relations. Given how central the impact of media commercialization is in existing debates, the relevance of economy as an axis of comparison – addressed in contributions by Sparks and Downey – hardly needs justifying. In relation to CEE, the importance of understanding the media-economy dynamics is perhaps even more pronounced, since the transformation of media systems in the region went hand-in-hand with an accelerated process of economic liberalization. The same is true for media's relationships with ethno-cultural diversity and gender equality, discussed in contributions by Mihelj and Pajnik. On both counts, the countries of CEE have seen wide-ranging transformations – for instance the decline of female participation in the labour force, the disintegration of socialist federations, and the rise of new nation-states – that must have reverberated in the media sector as well. This is not to say that other foci of analysis would not be desirable. Future research might, for instance, look at the growth of new communication technologies, including satellite and cable television and digital media, or examine the shifting relationships between media systems and class structures, exemplified in the growth of the tabloid press and financial dailies.

New Causal Factors, New Explanations

The expansion of research questions inevitably invites a broadening of causal factors that can account for similarities and differences between media systems. Given that the greatest advances in comparative media research have so far been made in the field of political communication, it is hardly a surprise that political factors are at the forefront of existing explanatory efforts. However, understanding the impact of political variables is not enough to explain the variation in media systems – not even when we limit the analysis to the media-politics relationship alone. Developments in post-communist CEE are a case in point. While most countries in the region have adopted a formally democratic political system, implemented new legislation and developed the institutions necessary for a functioning democratic system, the actual operation of political institutions and the media varies significantly from country to county, and in many cases continues to display important continuities with the pre-1989 period. To explain these diverse outcomes, we may need to move beyond political factors, and take into account economic and socio-cultural variables. As Sparks points out in his chapter, the economies of CEE are significantly smaller than those of Western Europe and North America, and this can impose significant limitations on the ability of the region to develop a vibrant, internally diverse media market that is capable of servicing different segments of the population regardless of their income levels. Cultural factors may have played a role as well, argues Jakubowicz in his contribution. It is reasonable to suggest that cultural preferences and patterns of behaviour that survived from the communist period impinged on the autonomy of journalists, and prevented them from acting as detached and critical observers.

Economic and socio-cultural factors are even more important when we try to account for the diversity of media systems in relation to gender roles or ethno-cultural diversity (Mihelj and Pajnik, this volume). It is often suggested that the organizational structures of media systems and the particular visions and divisions of the world they promote play a crucial role in sustaining and reproducing existing forms of social inclusion and exclusion. It is less clear, however, how and why the forms of media segmentation differ from country to country. Why, for instance, are some media systems more open to female journalists, editors and producers, and more inclined to promote them to highest-ranking positions? What helps explain the divergent approaches to ethnic and cultural diversity across different media systems? And also: which of the different approaches to cultural diversity is most likely to foster a truly inclusive democratic culture beyond and above social and cultural differences? These are pressing concerns for communication scholars and practitioners alike, and provide a basis for developing media policies tailored to the needs of contemporary multicultural societies.

Two qualifications are in order at this point. First, although emphasising the importance of contextual factors, we do not want to replace a media-centric approach with an equally one-sided socio-centric approach. While we do maintain that the functioning and shape of media systems are in important ways determined by the political, economic and socio-cultural environment in which they are embedded, we also believe that the media can and do act as a force in their own right. However, the ability of media to function as relatively autonomous agents is largely determined by socio-economic, political, and cultural context. Comparative analysis provides an excellent means of assessing how and under what conditions media independence is likely to increase or decrease. Second, while emphasizing the importance of economic and cultural causes, it was not our intention to suggest that political causes are not worthy of examination, or that they can be subsumed under economic, social or cultural factors. Quite to the contrary – all of the contributions to this volume, including those focusing on economic and socio-cultural aspects of media systems, pay attention to relevant political factors as well. Many also find that these factors still possess substantial explanatory value, albeit within an expanded explanatory framework.

New Methods and Approaches

Unlike sociology, political science, or linguistics, media and communication studies lack a well-established tradition of comparative analysis with a shared set of methodological principles, approaches and procedures (Livingstone 2003, Downey and Stanyer 2010). Several suggestions for improvement have been put forward in recent literature, yet actual applications of these suggestions in empirical research remain few and far between. Let us immediately clarify that it is not our intention to address all of these debates and proposals here – this is a task that deserves a book on its own. Instead, we limit our discussion to two key issues that have the most direct bearing on the aims of this volume. The first concerns the validity and generalizability of findings produced by comparative media systems research. The second relates to the challenges posed by transnational causal factors, and the danger of methodological nationalism.

Hallin and Mancini have never meant their media models to be universally applicable, at least not without significant adaptation (2004: 6). Yet curiously, their typology is repeatedly criticized precisely for its lack of universal representativeness. We believe that this apparent paradox involves more than just plain misunderstanding or careless reading on the part of Hallin and Mancini's critics. Rather, it stems from a failure to acknowledge the distinctive research goals and procedures of comparative media systems analysis vis-à-vis those characteristic of statistical research. To put it differently, the problem lies in the tendency to judge the relevance of comparative media systems research by drawing on criteria derived from quantitative social science. Borrowed from natural sciences, these criteria presuppose the availability of reliable numerical indicators, comparable units of analysis, a large number of cases, and the existence of clear-cut, unidirectional causal patterns. As soon as we move beyond individual communicators and media texts, it is unlikely that any of these conditions will be fulfilled easily. In cross-national media research, the number of variables is typically high, and the number of cases low – a combination that rules out the possibility of statistical testing of competing theories (Lijphart 1971: 686). Causal forces often flow both ways and do not lend themselves easily to a clear delineation between dependent and independent variables. Units of analysis – for instance national media systems or media organizations – are so diverse that direct comparisons between numerical indicators are likely to be misleading, unless accompanied by further explanation. All this appears to cast serious doubts about the validity and representativeness of findings produced by comparative media systems research.

However, such doubts are valid only insofar as we assume that the aims of comparative media systems analysis are the same as the aims of statistical research – namely to produce universally applicable findings. This is misleading. As James Mahoney and P. Larkin Terrie (2008) point out, comparative historical analysis is not aimed at estimating average effects of particular causes for large populations, but seeks to account for particular outcomes in specific cases. Methods of analysis and research designs differ accordingly. For instance, while statistical analysis tests theories by using regression analysis, comparative historical analysis relies on process tracing and comparative set-theoretical thinking. Due to this, it makes little sense to criticize comparative historical research for its inability to provide universally applicable conclusions. The type of knowledge gained by means of comparative historical analysis is of a different kind, and should be evaluated as such. This argument applies also to Hallin and Macini's work, as well as to the contributions in this volume. Each chapter describes and explains the main features of media systems in selected countries, mostly taken from CEE, in a specified historical period, i.e. after 1989. Whether the conclusions reached are applicable to other countries and periods remains to be investigated, though the causal factors and processes identified here can serve as a useful starting point nonetheless – just as the causes and processes discussed by Hallin and Mancini provided a useful point of reference for our own work.

Another methodological challenge of relevance to this volume concerns the relationship between the national and the transnational. The various causal factors affecting the shape and functioning of media systems – whether political, economic or sociocultural – are not limited to the nation-state level, but might operate either at a transnational or at a sub-national level. Much as nation-states themselves, national media systems are increasingly interconnected, and their survival depends not on self-isolation but rather on successful integration into global media structures and flows. This situation has prompted many observers to question the nation-state as the relevant unit of analysis, and seek ways of overcoming the 'methodological nationalism' that purportedly plagues social science research (Beck 2000, McMillin 2007). These debates have certainly helped direct out attention to various important communicative phenomena that would otherwise remain marginal or invisible, including diasporic communication, transnational broadcasting, and city-based media cultures. Yet in many ways, the nation-state remains an indispensable unit of analysis, even when examining transnational forces. Although media systems that are exposed to similar trans-national forces display a degree of similarity, the presence and influence of these transnational structures can vary significantly from country to country. To account for that, we still need comparisons at national level.

To say that globalization and reproduction of national differences are not mutually exclusive is to state the obvious; what is more interesting is to ascertain under what conditions transnational forces will lead to greater global convergence, and how their impact may differ depending on the characteristics of local media cultures, economies and policies. How can we explain the differing levels of foreign media investment in CEE media, or the marked variation in the amount of imported media content? What accounts for differences in receptiveness to competing transnational regulatory pressures coming from the EU, the WTO and the US? It is only by marrying the examination of transnational factors with nation-level comparisons that we will be able to ascertain why and how such variation occurs. This is also the approach pursued in this volume (see chapters by Downey, Harcourt and Štětka, but also Mihelj). The challenge, then, lies not so much in moving beyond nation-level comparisons as such, but in acknowledging that the outcomes we are seeking to explain may have been caused not only by endogenous factors, but also by exogenous ones.

References

Aalberg, T., van Aelst, P., and Curran, J. 2010. Media systems and the political information environment. *International Journal of Press/Politics*, 15(3), 255–71.

Altschull, H.J. 1984. *Agents of Power: The Role of the New Media ain Human Affairs*. New York and London: Longman.

Archetti, C. 2010. *Explaining News: National Politics and Journalistic Cultures in Global Context*. Basingstoke: Palgrave.

Beck, U. 2000. The cosmopolitan perspective: sociology of the second age of modernity. *British Journal of Sociology*, 51(1), 79–106.

Benson, R. and Hallin, D.C. 2007. How states, markets and globalization shape the news: the French and U.S. national press, 1965–1997. *European Journal of Communication*, 22(1), 27–48.

Blumler, J.G. and Gurevitch, M. 1995. *The Crisis of Public Communication*. London: Routledge.

Chalaby, J.K. 1996. Journalism as an Anglo-American invention: a comparison of the development of French and Anglo-American journalism, 1830s–1920s. *European Journal of Communication*, 11(3), 303–26.

Christians, C.G., Glasser, T., McQuail, D. Nordenstreng, K. and White, R.A. 2009. *Normative Theories of the Media: Journalism in Democratic Societies*. Urbana, IL: University of Illinois Press.

Dobek Ostrowska, B. and Głowacki, M., eds. 2008. *Comparing Media Systems in Central Europe: Between Commercialization and Politicization*. Wroclaw: Wroclaw University Press.

Dobek Ostrowska, B., Jakubowicz, K., Głowacki, M. and Sükösd, M. 2010. *Media Systems East and West: How Different, How Similar*. Budapest: Central University Press.

Downey, J. and Stanyer, J. 2010. Comparative media analysis – why some fuzzy thinking might help: applying fuzzy-set qualitative comparative analysis to the personalization of mediated political communication. *European Journal of Communication*, 25(4), 331–47.

Esser, F. 1999. 'Tabloidization' of news: a comparative analysis of Anglo-American and German press journalism. *European Journal of Communication*, 14(3), 291–324.

Gilman, N. 2007. *Mandarins of the Future: Modernization Theory in Cold War America*. Baltimore, MD: Johns Hopkins University Press.

Hachten, W.H. 1981. *The World News Prism: Changing Media, Clashing Ideologies*. Ames: Iowa University Press.

Hallin, D. and Mancini, P. 2004 *Comparing Media Systems: Three Models of Media and Politics*. Cambridge: Cambridge University Press.

Hanitzsch, T. 2011, in press. Populist disseminators, detached watchdogs, critical change agents and opportunist facilitators: professional milieus, the journalistic field and autonomy in 18 countries. *The International Communication Gazette*, 73.

Hanitzsch, T., Hanusch, F., Mellado, C., Anikina, M., Berganza, R., Cangoz, I., Coman, M., Hamada, B., Hernández, M.E., Karadjov, C.D., Moreira, S.V., Mwesige, P.G., Plaisance, P.L., Reich, Z., Seethaler, J., Skewes, E.A., Noor, D.V., and Yuen, E.K.W. 2011. Mapping journalism cultures across nations: a comparative study of 18 countries. *Journalism Studies*, 12(3), 273–93.

Holtz-Bacha, C. 2004. Political campaign communication: conditional convergence of modern media elections, in *Comparing Political Communication: Theories, Cases, and Challenges*, edited by F. Esser and B. Pfetsch. Cambridge: Cambridge University Press, 213–30.

Iyengar, S., Curran, J., Lund, A.B., Salovaara-Moring, I., Hahn, K.S., and Coen, S. 2010. Cross-national versus individual-level differences in political information: a media systems perspective. *Journal of Elections, Public Opinion and Parties*, 20(3), 291–309.

Jakubowicz, K. 2007. *Rude Awakening: Social and Media Change in Central and Eastern Europe*. Cresskill: Hampton Press.

Jakubowicz, K. and Sükösd, M., eds. 2008. *Finding the Right Place on the Map: Central and Eastern European Media Change in a Global Perspective*. Bristol: Intellect Books.

Koopmans, R. and Vliegenthart, R. 2010. Media Attention as the Outcome of a Diffusion Process: A Theoretical Framework and Cross-National Evidence on Earthquake Coverage. *European Sociological Review* – Online First. Available at: http://esr.oxfordjournals.org/content/early/2010/06/25/esr.jcq032.full.pdf [accessed 15 December 2010].

Letham, M.E. 2000. *Modernization as Ideology: American Social Science and 'Nation Building' in the Kennedy Era*. Chapel Hill, NC: University of North Carolina Press.

Lijphart, A. 1971. Political science and the comparative method. *The American Political Science Review*, 65(3), 682–93.

Livingstone, S. 2003. On the challenges of cross-national comparative media research, *European Journal of Communication*, 18(4), 477–500.

Lowenstein, R.L. 1970. Press Freedom as a Political indicator, in International and Intercultural Communication, edited by H.D. Fischer and J.C. Merrill. New York: Hastings House, 129–40.

Mahoney, J. and Larkin Terrie, P. 2008. Comparative-historical analysis in contemporary political science, in *Oxford Handbook of Political Methodology*, edited by J.M. Box-Steffensmeier, H. Brady and D. Collier. Oxford: Oxford University Press, 737–55.

Mahoney, J. and Rueschemeyer, D. 2003. Comparative historical analysis: achievements and agendas, in *Comparative Historical Analysis in the Social Sciences*, edited by J. Mahoney and D. Rueschemeyer. Cambridge: Cambridge University Press, 3–38.

McMillin, D.C. 2007. *International Media Studies*. Malden, MA: Blackwell.

McQuail, D. 1983. *Mass Communication Theory: An Introduction*. London: Sage.

Nerone, J.C. 1995. Revisiting *Four Theories of the Press*, in *Last Rights: Revisiting Four Theories of the Press*, edited by J.C. Nerone. Urbana, IL: University of Illinois Press, 1–30.

Schramm, W. 1964. *Mass Media and National Development: The Role of Information in Developing Countries*. Stanford, CA: Stanford University Press and Paris: UNESCO.

Siebert, F.S., Peterson, T. and Schramm, W. 1956. *Four Theories of the Press: The Authoritarian, Libertarian, Social Responsibility and Soviet Communist Concepts of What the Press Should Be and Do*. Urbana, IL: University of Illinois Press.

Skocpol, T. 1984. Sociology's historical imagination, in *Vision and Method in Historical Sociology*, edited by T. Skocpol, Cambridge: Cambridge University Press, 1–21.

Sükösd, M., and Bajomi-Lázár, P., eds. 2003. *Reinventing Media: Media Policy Reform in East Central Europe*. Budapest: Central University Press.

Chapter 1
Post-communist Political Systems and Media Freedom and Independence

Karol Jakubowicz

Introduction

In view of the stated intention of most post-communist countries to transform into democratic systems, democratic theory and the body of work on the role of the media in democracy would appear to provide the most appropriate framework of comparative analysis of the development of media systems in particular countries of the region, especially as regards freedom and independence of the media. Over the past 20 years – and in many cases, for much longer – the populations of those countries have striven for democracy (Tanase 1999). Despite some caveats (Khakee 2002), the process of democratization and consolidation of media freedom and independence are seen as mutually reinforcing (Coricelli 2007, Faust 2007). Given that democracy is based on the free exchange of ideas, it is clear that the media are necessarily constitutive of any adequate contemporary theory of political democracy (Sparks 1995).

Of course, the relationship is neither obvious nor simple (Jakubowicz 2005, Mughan and Gunther 2000) and media organizations may not share this normative view of their own role in democracy. Nevertheless, it seems feasible to suggest that *the extent of media independence and freedom in the region will be closely related to the extent of democratic consolidation*. In other words, the media are an element of democracy and their freedom and independence will flourish as democracy flourishes. This general approach finds support in the work of Hallin and Mancini (2004), where analysis of the interplay between political systems (especially in the context of the maturation and consolidation of democracy) and media systems forms part of the general framework of analysis. Of course, they originally did not consider post-communist countries, but later stated that the polarized pluralist system might be closest to what is happening in the region (Hallin and Mancini 2009). While there is a clear need to go beyond the general Hallin and Mancini approach in other areas, this does not appear to be the case as far as political determinants of media systems are concerned. However, the intention here is to offer a more in-depth and nuanced analysis of political factors that have played a major, one could even say decisive role in shaping media systems in post-communist countries. It has been said that there are as many processes of post-communist transformation as there are post-communist countries. While shared general trends can be found, the important thing is to abandon the simplistic view of Central and Eastern Europe as a homogeneous grouping of countries and develop tools of identifying the specific circumstances of each country.

The effectiveness of the media's influence on society depends to a large extent on the congruence of their impact with the larger process of political change unfolding in society. The media may and do affect political developments, but at the same time their impact is predicated on the existence of favourable political conditions without which they could not perform that function. To express this differently, the relationship between socio-political factors and media systems is one of non-equivalent or asymmetrical interdependence (cf. Jakubowicz 2007).

Below we will seek to verify this general hypothesis, and use it explain the divergent levels of media freedom and independence in the region. More specifically, our aim is three-fold. *First*, we will demonstrate that the scope of political and administrative control over the media depends on whether a country is democratic, semi-democratic, or autocratic. As we move along this continuum, the policy and legal framework will allow fewer and fewer media sectors and outlets to acquire legal and ownership status putting them outside state and/or political control. *Second*, we will show that specific institutional solutions adopted at the level of the political system are likely to be replicated at the level of the media. This is particularly evident in the broadcasting sector, where the regulatory authorities are a direct extension of the political power structure: their composition is determined by the type of the executive structure and the type of the electoral system. *Third*, we intend to demonstrate that the extent of media freedom and independence depends crucially on the behaviour and normative attitudes among the political elites, specifically on their attitudes to democratic values and behaviour vis-à-vis democratic institutions. As we will show, the threats to media freedom and independence in the region often stem not from a lack of adequate institutions and legislation, but rather from the fact that political elites and civil society actors alike consider it to be their right to use the media to further their goals. Journalists themselves are often no better; they are convinced their role is one of social leaders, called upon to promote the political views or forces they personally support.

This brings us to a key point, namely that the extent of media freedom and independence cannot be explained by reference to political systems alone. Rather, the functioning of both the political and the media system is crucially dependent on cultural factors such as the prevailing attitudes, values and ensuing behavioural patterns. Due to the key role cultural factors play in determining the form and functioning of political systems in post-communist states, we felt it necessary to incorporate this dimension also in our discussion. We should also add that analysts of the Central and Eastern European media scene point often point to the role of proprietors and their business interests, and generally to market forces, as a dominant force in shaping the media system (Jakubowicz and Sükösd 2008). It is undisputable that these economic factors also have the effect of curtailing journalistic and editorial freedom and independence.

The chapter starts by outlining the theoretical and analytical framework for the examination of relationships between democratization and media freedom. The rest of the chapter is divided into three sections, each of which tackles one of the three key propositions outlined above. Each of the sections starts by examining the structure and dynamics of the various political systems across the region, and then goes on to demonstrate how and to what extent these are replicated at the level of media systems.

Democratization and Media Freedom: The Analytical Framework

Some scholars maintain that all that is needed to define democracy is a 'realistic and restricted definition' of a democratic regime, consisting of 'fair and institutionalized elections, jointly with some surrounding ... political freedoms' (O'Donnell 2002: 16). However, in the context of Central and Eastern Europe – and also more generally – it would in our opinion be a mistake to yield 'the fallacy of electoralism' (Diamond 2008). Democracy is not achieved through elections alone[1] (Landman 2008). Munck (1996: 5–6) contends – correctly, in our view – that the institutional systems and procedural rules of democracy structure and shape the conduct of politics only inasmuch as actors accept or comply with these rules. The experience of Central and Eastern Europe suggests that both institutional and cultural approaches are needed to understand, and indeed to plan and implement, systemic transformation.

Successful consolidation of democracy ultimately depends on the institutionalization of new rules and values (see Diamond 1997, Morawski 1998, 2001, Sztompka 1999, 2000) and therefore on cultural factors, which often affect the process of creation of the rules and institutions of democracy and account for their proper use or abuse. Generally, they are subsumed under the term 'civic/political/democratic culture' (Dahlgren 1995, Paletz and Lipinski 1994). Political culture is one of the 'key explanatory factors' in understanding transitions (Wiarda 2001). It largely determines how individuals and the society act and react politically and so whether the society is able to maintain and operate a viable and enduring constitutional democratic system of government, or whether the society must choose between authoritarianism and domestic disorder (see also Linz and Stepan 1996, Offe 1997). It is therefore important to analyse the process of democratic consolidation not only in terms of its institutional dimensions, but also in terms of its behavioural and attitudinal dimensions (see e.g., Bajomi-Lázár 2008).

---

1   Puddington (2009: 12) notes that while elections are a prerequisite to building a democracy, 'more attention must be paid to the suppression of civil society, freedom of association, and freedom of expression. Increasingly, it is nongovernmental organizations and democracy advocates that constitute the most effective societal forces for reform in authoritarian states. Democracies should monitor the state of freedom of association and labor rights ... This also applies to restrictions on the free flow of information, especially on the internet and other new media platforms.'

We propose this approach because we believe that it is precisely the cultural/ attitudinal element of democracy that will determine whether or not democratic institutions will be created and whether they will be designed to be functional or dysfunctional in terms of the operation of democracy (institutional dimension) and how they will be used, or perhaps abused (behavioural dimension).

Democracy and Media Freedom in Post-Communist Countries: Between Democracy and Autocracy

A full examination of democratic development (or otherwise) in post-communist countries would require, in line with the path-dependency approach, an analysis of the process of transition, the outcome of this process of transition, and the process of consolidation (and, indeed, non-consolidation and deconsolidation) of democracy. According to Page (2006: 89), path dependence 'requires a build-up of behavioural routines, social connections, or cognitive structures around an institution'. For reasons of space, however, we will need to leave the process of transition involved in the collapse of the communist system largely out of consideration (however crucially important it is in determining what happened afterwards) and begin with the outcome of transition.

With the jury still out on the final result of transition, any neat and tidy classifications of countries with respect to their level of democratization are bound to be elusive. Nevertheless, it is possible to divide post-communist countries into three broad, partly overlapping groups: democratic, semidemocratic and autocratic (Ekiert et al. 2007). Each of these is of course to be treated as an ideal type: most individual post-communist countries will not conform neatly to one type only, but will constitute hybrid systems.[2] We might also want to think of many of the countries in question as featuring different political sequencing or as being at different stages of a democratization dynamic and thus occupying different locations on a continuum (Bunce 1999), with the possibility of moving 'forward' or 'backsliding'. Indeed, some populist political forces in democratic post-communist countries have expressed impatience with the checks and balances that liberal democracy imposes on the authorities, showing interest in the system of 'electoral democracy' (as giving the majority returned to power a mandate to act without regard for the views of the minority).

According to Ekiert et al. (2007), the first group of *democratic countries* comprises successful countries where the process of democratic consolidation and the progress of economic reforms are well advanced, especially those that have joined the European Union. This group now also includes some of the countries which followed the 'Mediterranean model of transition' (Pusić 2000): Romania, Bulgaria, Croatia, Serbia and Albania. Having failed 'in the first round' to establish

---

2   Cichosz (2006) identifies the following hybrid forms of democracy in post-communist countries: formal democracy, elite democracy, partitocrazia and tyrannical majority.

democracy in 1989 and 1990, they initially ended up with authoritarian or semi-authoritarian systems. The 'second transition' came a few years later and was needed to introduce the missing institutions of democracy and to promote both attitudinal and behavioural dimensions of democracy.

Then, there is a gray 'in between' zone, inhabited by countries oscillating between a *semi-democratic* and *semi-authoritarian system*. This, in turn, encompasses countries which experienced the 'second wave' of transitions in Central and Eastern Europe, sometimes also known as 'colour revolutions' in Georgia, Ukraine and Kyrgyzstan. They were, however, less successful in creating stable democratic systems than in some of the other countries (McFaul 2005, Way 2008). Some countries in this group were, or still are, 'stuck in the stage of inter-regime competition' (Bunce 1999: 242), unable to develop a clearly new political identity. A consequence of this was sometimes violent conflict (as in Tajikistan, Georgia and Bosnia); sometimes it gave rise to regimes that closely resembled their socialist predecessors, as in Belarus or much of Central Asia; and sometimes it produced hybrid regimes that married in haphazard fashion aspects of a liberal order with those of the state socialist past, as in Ukraine. Russia could be seen as another example of this phenomenon (Sestanovich 2004).

Finally, post-communist countries include *authoritarian regimes* that differ from communist dictatorship in some respects but consistently deny their citizens fundamental political freedoms and routinely violate human rights. In such countries (Uzbekistan, Turkmenistan, Belarus) initial political openings have clearly failed and authoritarian regimes have resolidified (Carothers 2002).

It is clear that most of the 'transitional countries', including the relatively successful ones, suffer from serious democratic deficits: poor representation of citizens' interests, low levels of political participation beyond voting, frequent abuse of the law by government officials, elections of uncertain legitimacy, very low levels of public confidence in state institutions, and persistently poor institutional performance by the state. Nevertheless, post-communist countries clearly vary in the extent to which they were able to consolidate elements of democracy and the three-fold typology proposed above corresponds to some of the key features of media freedom and independence in these countries.

The relationship and interdependence between political development and the media is the subject of an extensive body of work (Bajomi-Lázár and Hegedűs 2001, Jakubowicz 2005). Change in the media in post-communist countries was expected to mirror the general process of democratic development and create an 'enabling environment' (Price and Krug 2000) for media freedom and independence. Indeed, media freedom and independence is higher in the democratic countries and progressively lower in semi-democratic and semi-authoritarian and authoritarian countries. Competitive politics and media pluralism prevail in the group of democratic countries; oligarchization and media capture in the semi-democratic/semi-authoritarian countries, and there has been a return to strict censorship (and no media independence) in the outright dictatorships. That this is indeed so, and that backsliding can happen also in this area, is suggested by

Mungiu-Pippidi's (2008: 91) view of the three paths of media evolution in post-communist countries, as shown in Figure 1.1.

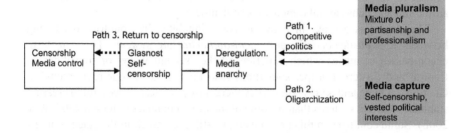

Figure 1.1   Divergent paths from communist media control

Source: Mungiu-Pippidi 2008: 91. Reproduced with permission

We will demonstrate the relationship and interdependence between political development and the media by looking at two aspects: media ownership and general media policy orientations.

Media Ownership

If de-monopolization of the media was the first and fundamental goal of media change, then one criterion for assessing the degree of change is the diversity and pluriformity of media outlets, as well as forms and diversity of ownership. The first indicator is, of course, the existence of privately-owned media. In autocratic regimes, there may be 'privately owned' print media, but – as in Turkmenistan and Uzbekistan – opposition media are banned. In Uzbekistan the state and its ministries and agencies are the founders and financiers of over 70 per cent of the print media. No wonder that they exclude anything that might paint the state and senior officials in an unflattering light. In Belarus 'most non-state periodicals are indirectly controlled by the state through subsidies, participation in equity capital privileges [...] or by other means, so they cannot be regarded independent [...] So, practically the entire system of mass media in Belarus is controlled by the state' (Manaev 2003: 49). In Tajikistan, some nominally independent newspapers are published, yet refrain from carrying 'dissenting' material.

In both autocratic and semi-democratic regimes, private ownership need not mean true de-monopolization, as the owners may be part and parcel of the political elite and use those media outlets to further its goals. Such has been the case in Ukraine (see Kachkaeva and Richter (1992) on the origins of 'non-state' TV in Ukraine, born with heavy involvement of state and local government entities). Another case in point is Russia, where (in addition to continued state ownership of major media and local government ownership of local newspapers), privately owned outlets are often owned by industrial groups either controlled by the State or with close connections to the government (e.g. Gazprom). Rather than 'private,' they are recognized as 'semi-state' (De Smaele 2010).

It is only in the democratic states that private media ownership (often by foreign companies) is structurally separate from the State.

General Media Policy Orientations

In the process of transition and systemic transformation, post-communist countries have engaged in systemic media policy. General media policy orientations evident in post-communist countries after 1989 can be described as follows:

- Idealistic – oriented to the introduction of direct, participatory communicative democracy;
- Idealistic-mimetic – oriented to the introduction of an idealized 'Western media system', involving more elements of citizen participation;
- Mimetic – straight transplantation of the 'Western media system';
- 'Materialist' – promoting outright privatization of all media as a way of eliminating state or political control over them;
- 'Atavistic' – involving continuation or new forms of effective command-and-control systems, allowing political elites to control the media (Jakubowicz 2007).

Idealistic and materialist orientations never gained much support in post-communist countries. As concerns the remaining orientations, we can argue that the 'democratic' post-communist countries have been more predisposed to adopt the mimetic orientation, the semi-democratic and semi-authoritarian ones, a mixture of mimetic and atavistic orientations, and the autocratic ones have adopted primarily the atavistic orientation.

Of course, the match between political system types and the media policy orientations is not perfect. No more than a cursory examination of media policy declarations and measures in post-communist countries is needed to establish that the 'atavistic' orientation has been clearly in evidence also in the first group of democratic countries, including those that are now EU members (Jakubowicz 1995). Partitocratic systems, together with the politicization of all spheres of public life (the post-communist version of the Italian *panpoliticismo*) favoured control of the media by political elites.

While there is no doubt that democratic countries have espoused a mixture of mimetic and atavistic media policy orientations, there are important differences between them and semi-democratic/semi-authoritarian countries. As Bajomi-Lázár (2008: 150–51) explains, Hungarian media policy-makers 'usually did not question the principle of media freedom and plurality, nor did they express any wish to control the whole of the media.' In place of the 'one-party press' of the communist era, some Hungarian post-communist media policy makers aimed to build a 'multi-party press,' content to have newspapers serving as a mouthpiece for a particular political orientation, while accepting the existence of media outlets serving other political orientations. Another approach, as indicated by the Slovak and many other examples, has been to accept that privately-owned print and broadcast media are beyond the control of the political power establishment, but to seek to retain control over 'public service' media. Alternatively, there have been attempts, as in Hungary or Poland, to use public money or public institutions to establish media outlets supportive of a particular political orientation. We may speak in such cases of 'a selective atavistic policy'.

The situation is different in the other two groups of countries. With regard to Russia and other Commonwealth of Independent States countries (encompassing both the intermediate and outright autocratic regimes), Richter (2008: 314) says that their authorities and officials 'use the means at their disposal (by virtue of their status) to exert direct or indirect pressure on media and journalists in order to restrict the gathering, production and distribution of mass information so as to secure their own political interests and ensure lack of monitoring of their political activities. The consequences of political censorship are the debasement of democratic principles, self-censorship by journalists, declining public confidence in both the media and the authorities, and increasing alienation between society and state.' This policy may still be 'selective' to some degree in the semi-democratic/ semi-authoritarian countries, but in Russia, for example, this translates into a high degree of monopolization by the power elite of all the media. Richter calls this 'soft censorship' but this is hardly an appropriate term when the means used to impose it may include the murder of journalists. There is, of course, nothing selective about it in the authoritarian regimes, which seek to control not only traditional media but also the Internet and also access to foreign media (Walker 2007).

Democratic Institutions, Media Regulation, and Media Independence

Institutional settings are a pointer to the shape and health of democracy. Broadly speaking, the institutional structures of political systems in successfully democratized countries will be significantly different from those in semi-democratic, semi-autocratic and autocratic countries. Most important institutional dimensions of democracy include the type of executive, legislature, political parties, constitution and electoral system. In other words, post-communist countries can be divided with regard to their particular choice of executive structure (presidential, semi-presidential or parliamentary), of legislature (single or double chamber), of political parties (adversarial or consociational, and their effective number in parliament) and of electoral system (majoritarian, mixed or proportional). Each of these individually, as well as their combined effects, is crucial to the overall performance and stability of political democracy. The choices of particular institutional solutions result from a number of considerations, including the political power establishment's desire to remain firmly in control.

In formal terms, the institutional settings that emerged from the constitutional change in post-communist countries ranged from parliamentary to presidential democracies (Table 1.1).

Table 1.1   Systems of government

Parliamentary systems			Mixed systems		Presidential systems with cabinet	
Weak president	Medium strong president	Strong president	Parliamentary-presidential systems	Presidential-parliamentary systems	With prime minister	Without prime minister
Yugoslavia	Czech Republic Estonia Hungary Slovakia Slovenia	Albania Bulgaria Macedonia	Lithuania Moldova Montenegro Poland	Armenia Croatia Kyrgyz Republic Romania Russia Serbia Ukraine	Belarus Kazakhstan Tajikistan Uzbekistan	Georgia Turkmenistan

Source: Dauderstädt and Gerrits, 2000. Reproduced with permission

Table 1.2 provides more detailed information about institutional systems introduced in post-communist countries.

Table 1.2   Institutional choices and types of political regime in Eastern Europe

Country	Constitutional type of	Electoral System		
		Type	Distribution of seats in parliament	Electoral threshold
Albania	Semi-presidential	Hybrid/Major.	115/40/-	4%
Armenia	Presidential	Hybrid	75/56/32	5%
Azerbaijan	Presidential	Hybrid/Major.	100/25/-	8%
Bulgaria	Parliamentary	PR	-/240/-	4%
Belarus	Presidential	Majoritarian	110/-/-	-
Croatia	Presidential	Hybrid	151/140/5	5%
Czech Rep.	Parliamentary	PR	-/200/-	5%
Estonia	Parliamentary	PR	-/101/-	-
Georgia	Presidential	Hybrid/PR	85/150/-	7%
Hungary	Parliamentary	Hybrid	176/152+	5%
Lithuania	Semi-presidential	Hybrid	71/70/-	5%
Latvia	Parliamentary	PR	-/100/-	5%

Table 1.2   continued

Macedonia	Semi-presidential	Hybrid/Major.	85/35/-	5%
Moldova	Semi-presidential	PR	-/104/-	4%
Poland	Semi-presidential	PR	-/391+69/-	5%
Romania	Semi-presidential	PR	-/327/19	3%
Slovakia	Parliamentary	PR	-/150/-	5%
Slovenia	Parliamentary	PR	-/88/2	4%
Ukraine	Presidential	Hybrid	224/225/-(114)	5%
Uzbekistan	Presidential	Majoritarian	-/-/250	-

Source: Adapted from Andreev 2003: 9. The situation described is as of the end of 2000
Note: (1) Single seat/ proportional representation/ non-affiliated or reserved seats for minorities.

Parliamentary rule has been the favoured choice of some of the most successful democracies in Eastern Europe (see Fish 2006). The majority of the former Soviet and Yugoslav republics together with Albania opted for a semi- or full-presidential system. As recently created polities with non-established, completely modern national identity, they have tended to choose quite strong, sometimes autocratic, leaders who could guarantee the survival both of the state and the political system. In some cases, though, the powers of parliament and judiciary have been limited to such an extent that these systems hardly qualify as democracies. Poland, Romania and Lithuania also elect strong presidents, meaning that they have variations of French-type semi-presidential regimes.

As for electoral systems, again countries of Central and Eastern Europe have opted for a proportional or hybrid system while most of the ex-Soviet republics, except for the Baltic states and Moldova, have chosen a variety of majoritarian rule. Post-communist countries have confirmed the hypothesis that parliamentarism plus proportional representation in the elections improves considerably the chances that a regime will democratize, though it must be added that the choice of such a system is itself an indicator of a democratic orientation. Thus, the hypothesis advanced by Schneider (2002) that a presidential system is more conducive to consolidation of democracy (see above) has not been confirmed.

Concerning the distribution of seats in the first chamber of parliament between single seat, PR and independents, in the legislatures of some of the former Soviet republics, such as Ukraine, Armenia and Uzbekistan, a relatively large number of independent candidates have been elected. In other countries, such as Hungary, Slovenia, Poland, Romania and Croatia, there are either reserved seats for ethnic minorities or the electoral threshold is artificially lowered in order to facilitate the election of independent and minority candidates – a sign of liberal democracy in action.

The appearance of institutions that limit the discretionary power of political elites is also an important institutional indicator of democratic consolidation. The timeline of introduction of discretion-limiting reforms and institutions shows that this happened earlier in Slovenia, Hungary, and Poland but, as of 2004, remained incomplete and delayed in Bulgaria, Latvia, the Czech Republic and Slovakia (Grzymała-Busse 2004).

The institutional choices discussed above correspond with some of the key characteristics of media systems in post-communist countries, particularly in the broadcasting sector. We will demonstrate this by looking at two main aspects: the introduction of public service broadcasting and the appointment procedures for broadcasting regulatory authorities.

The Introduction of Public Service Broadcasting

On the face of it, the introduction of public broadcasting is very well advanced in all post-communist states. Among European and Central Asian post-communist countries, only some post-Soviet ones (Belarus, Kazakhstan, Russia, Tajikistan, Ukraine, Uzbekistan, Turkmenistan) have so far failed to transform state into public service broadcasting (though Azerbaijan and Kyrgyzstan have both retained state broadcasting and introduced public service stations). As noted by Richter and Golovanov (2006: 1), in some Commonwealth of Independent States countries the introduction of public service broadcasting was due to the 'insistence' of the Council of Europe and 'additional pressure' applied by the office of the Representative on Freedom of the Media of the Organization on Security in Europe.

The weaknesses of public broadcasting in Commonwealth of Independent States countries identified by Richter and Golovanov (2006) (the method of appointment and composition of governing bodies guarantees neither independence nor the widest possible representation of a given society; the system of financing fails to secure their independence; and the ability of society to control the activities of a public broadcasting company is very low) are typical, to different degrees, in all post-communist countries. As can be seen from Table 1.3, political elites play a decisive role in the appointment (and sometimes also dismissal) of the governing bodies of public broadcasters. They do so mostly directly but sometimes also through the intermediary of the broadcasting regulatory authority that is itself an extension of those elites. Therefore, Splichal (2001: 9–10) goes so far as to call the introduction of public broadcasting in post-communist countries a case of 're-nationalization': 'In almost all countries in the region, the new governments – regardless of their specific political orientation – did not hesitate to imitate regulations and strategies of the former regimes to retain control over national broadcasting [..] access to the 'public' broadcasting is ... still severely limited to political elites in most countries of the region'.

Public service broadcasting is thus an interesting case. It has been introduced in all democratic and most semi-democratic countries. In practically all these countries it has been subjected to very similar forms of political control and interference, providing evidence of the determination of political elites to retain as much discretion as possible in this area of mass communication. It also provides telling evidence of another feature of immature democracies, namely government-opposition competition being replaced by government-opposition collusion in preserving a system in which different political forces take turns in exercising control over society and running a patronage system. In such circumstances, public service broadcasting turns into a trophy to be handed over to whomever wins an election, with other political forces waiting to take their turn, once they are returned to power in a successive election. Hence the conclusion: 'In this situation, public service broadcasters in most post-communist countries could be described as 'empty shells,' designed to operate in line with the public broadcasting remit, but largely incapable of doing so' (Jakubowicz 2003: 14, see also Jakubowicz 2004). In both these aspects, therefore, clear distinctions between the two groups of countries pale into insignificance. As in Spain (see Bustamante 1989), this may explain the 'delay' between general democratization and pluralisation and the situation in public broadcasting.

Table 1.3   Governance structures of public service television organizations in selected post-communist countries

Country	Name	Governing bodies	Appointment procedure
Albania	RTSH	Steering Committee	Proposed by: ruling majority (5), opposition (5), NGOs (5), elected by Parliament
		General Director	Nominated and released by the Steering Committee
Bosnia and Herzegovina	BHRT BiH	Board of Governors	Appointed by: Parliament (4), outgoing Board of Governors (3) – upon nominations by civil society + chairmen of the governing bodies of public broadcasters RTV FBiH, RTRS (2)
		Director General	Appointed and dismissed by the Board of Governors
Bulgaria	BNT	Management Board	Council of Electronic Media (CEM), at the proposal of BNT Director General
		Director General	CEM
Croatia	HRT	Programming Council	Parliament at the proposal of NGOs after public contest
		Management Board	Appointed by: HRT Programming Council (4), Worker Unions (1)
		General Director	HRT programming Council (in a public contest)
Czech Republic	ČT	Czech TV Council	Appointed by the Chamber of Deputies at the proposal of civil society organizations
		General Director	Appointed by the Czech TV Council
Estonia	ETV	Management board	Broadcasting Council, in a public contest

Hungary	MTV Duna TV	Boards of Trustees (Executive Committee and ordinary members)	Executive Committee (at least 8 members): delegated by the Government coalition 9half) and opposition (half); chair elected by Parliament; Ordinary members delegated by civil society
Latvia	LTV	Board	Broadcasting council (General Director of the Board); General Director (other 7 members of the Board
Lithuania	LRT	Council of Lithuanian Radio and Television	The President of the Republic (4); Parliament (4); Lithuanian Science Council, Lithuanian Board of Education, Lithuanian Association of Art Creators and Congregation of Bishops (1 by each)
Macedonia	MRT	Board	Parliament (4 are MRT employees proposed by the Council of MRT Employees)
		Financial Supervisory Board	Parliament
		General Director	Parliament
Poland	TVP	Supervisory Council	National Broadcasting Council (KRRiT) (8); Minister of Treasury (1)
		Management Board	Supervisory Board of TVP
		Programme Council	National Broadcasting Council (KRRiT)
Romania	TVR	Council of Administration	Joint parliamentary group (8); President of Romania (1); Government (1); station's personnel (2); national minorities parliamentary groups (1)
		Managing Committee	The Council of Administration
		Director General-President of the Council of Administration	Elected by Parliament
Serbia	RTS	Governing Board	Republican Broadcasting Agency (RBA) Council
		Director General	Governing Board in a public contest
Slovakia	STV	STV Council	Elected by parliament upon nomination by: the Committee for Education, Sciences, Sport and Youth, Culture and Media in Parliament; MPs; or civil society organizations
		Supervisory Commission	Parliament (1); Government (1); President of the Republic (1)
		General Director	Appointed by the STV Council
Slovenia	RTV Slovenia	Council of RTV Slovenia	Civil society and academia (17); Parliament (5); RTV Slovenia staff (3)
		Supervisory Board	Parliament (5); RTV Slovenia Staff (2)

Source: Adapted from EUMAP 2005: 156–62.

National Broadcasting Regulatory Authorities

Similar patterns emerge when we look at national broadcasting regulatory authorities. They have been founded in most post-communist countries, with the exception of Estonia and some Commonwealth of Independent States countries (Belarus, Russia, Kazakhstan, all the Central Asia states; see Richter 2007a) where the role of such authorities is performed by government departments.

As can be seen from Table 1.3, in a great majority of countries, regulatory authorities are appointed by Parliament, sometimes together with the President (Ukraine, Bulgaria, Poland), in some cases together with the President and the Prime Minister (Moldova). In presidential systems (Armenia, Azerbaijan and Georgia), the power of appointment is exclusively in the hands of the president. In two countries (Czech Republic and Moldova), it is in the hands of the government, but in the Czech Republic candidates are nominated by parliament. A special case is Lithuania, where the 13 members of the Radio and Television Commission of Lithuania are appointed as follows: one by the president, three by parliament after nomination by its education, science and culture committee, and one member each is appointed by the Artists', Cinematographers', Composers', Writers', Theatres' and Journalists' Unions, the Society of Journalists, the Bishops' Conference and the Periodical Publishers' Association. This is the only case in post-communist countries of a majority of members of a regulatory authority being appointed directly by civil society organizations.

In short, in all cases (with the exception of Lithuania), broadcasting regulatory authorities are a direct extension of the political power structure. Of the 22 countries listed in Table 1.4, nine (Albania, Bulgaria, Hungary, Latvia, Lithuania, Romania, Serbia, Slovakia, Macedonia) have introduced staggered terms for members of regulatory authorities but elsewhere (given that in only very few countries the law calls for balanced representation of all parliamentary parties) the composition of the regulatory authority directly mirrors the political make-up of the parliament and government of the day. Therefore, although usually the legislation describes them as 'independent', in reality they are 'winner-take-all/most' (if not 'Potemkin') institutions and their independence is open to doubt. This problem is not unique to post-communist countries. It has been noted in relation to all European regulatory authorities that 'a high degree of legal safeguards aiming at preserving the independence of regulatory authorities against political pressure needs to be positively correlated with actual independence in order to fulfil its purpose. On the other hand [...] a strong culture of independence may compensate for a low level of rules' (EPRA 2007: 7). This is as much an institutional issue as an attitudinal and behavioural one, which brings us to the last, and possibly most important, element of our analysis.

Table 1.4   Broadcasting regulatory authorities in post-communist countries

	Nominations					Appointment			
	Civil society	Local government and organizations	Organizations of journalists, publishers, etc.	Other organs of state	Others	Parliament	President	Government/ Prime Minister	Others
Albania[1,2,3]	√			√		√			
Armenia							√		
Azerbaijan							√		
BiH								√	
Bulgaria[3]						√	√		
Croatia				√		√			
Czech Rep.[2]				√				√	
Georgia							√		
Hungary[1,3]				√		√			
Kosovo	√		√	√		√			
Latvia[2,3]						√			
Lithuania[3]						√	√		√
Macedonia[3]						√			
Moldova						√	√	√	
Montenegro	√		√	√	√	√			
Poland						√	√		
Romania[1,2,3]				√		√			
Serbia[3]	√	√	√			√			
Slovakia[3]	√		√	√		√			
Slovenia			√		√	√			
Ukraine				√	√	√	√		

Sources: Media Division 2003, EUMAP 2005, EPRA 2007, Law No. 02/L-15 'On the Independent Media Commission and Broadcasting', adopted by the Assembly of Kosovo in 2005.

Notes:

(1) Formal balance between political parties in the process of appointment

(2) Consultation with civil society, non-political organizations

(3) Staggered terms of office.

Cultural Values and Behavioural Patterns: Do Institutional Changes Suffice?

As indicated in the previous section, the existence of particular institutions such as national broadcasting regulatory authorities or the public broadcasting service does not tell us much about how these institutions will function and indeed whether they will contribute to democratic consolidation. Depending in part on cultural attitudes and behavioural patterns informed by them, formal institutional frameworks can be made ineffective or subservient to the wishes of parts of the political elite.

First, political actors may deliberately fail to design institutions (such as securities and exchange commissions, regional governments, conflict of interest laws, and so on), retaining licence and opportunity to seek rents and minimize effective controls on and opposition to, their rule.

Second, political actors construct winner-take-all or winner-take-most-institutions (e.g. by leaving the power of appointment to these institutions in the hands of the president or prime minister, or by introducing parity with the distribution of seats in Parliament, giving the ruling party/coalition an automatic majority in a collective body). Party funding laws that chiefly favour the incumbents, or award resources according to existing strength, are among the examples of such institutions by explicitly reinforcing initial privilege (which then increases the discretion of ever-more powerful actors to change laws to their benefit). Vague legal provisions on their areas of competence, accountability, etc., may allow those in power to interpret the laws and give them considerable discretion. Deliberate vagueness and premeditated lack of enforcement increase the potential for discretion of such laws.

Third, these may be 'Potemkin institutions', lax or unenforced formal institutions, often characterized by low regulatory standards, ambiguous language, and limited provisions for enforcement (or their informal abandonment). They exist on paper, often to satisfy the requirements of external actors (such as international donors or organizations), but they cannot fulfil their ostensible goals (Grzymała-Busse 2004).

Depending on the balance of forces and the motivations of particular actors, the process of consolidation could lead to the improvement of democratic institutions and their operation and promote democratic attitudes and behaviour patterns or may indeed promote non- or deconsolidation of democracy.

The importance of the cultural/attitudinal dimension is supported by the example of new EU members. Given that preparations for EU membership required the introduction of a legal and institutional framework that meets high EU standards (as listed in the Copenhagen criteria and the entire *acquis*), any deficiencies must largely be ascribed to cultural/attitudinal and behavioural factors: 'The CEE setbacks underline the importance for democratic consolidation of a civic culture – Tocqueville summed it up as the 'habits of the heart' – without which the legitimacy and stability of democratic institutions will always remain doubtful' (Rupnik 2007: 19).

If it is true that most post-communist countries have developed the hybrid forms of democracy, it becomes clear that – in a way typical of young democracies – it is the political class (seeking to extend its power to retain discretionary control and to extract state resources for its own use) that has been most successful in gaining control over both the political regime and society in general. Thanks to this, political society can control the state apparatus, use the rule of law to its own advantage (or subvert it), subordinate economic society and minimize the impact of civil society. In some cases, 'the post-communist state is controlled and discretionarily exploited by political parties, rather than run by apolitical administrators following formalized rules' (Grzymała-Busse 2004: 5). Democratically-elected political parties continue to draw material resources from the public domain of the state and their ad hoc needs drive public policy, public contracts privilege private interests, and nonexistent or poorly specified laws allow resource extraction for private ends (rent-seeking). Such rents can consist of jobs, contracts, or financial transfers. Political loyalty, rather than merit, is a key criterion for their attainment. A clientelist system is the result.

In terms of consolidation of democracy, special importance must be attached to a normative shift involved in elite acceptance of 'fundamental and self-enforcing restraints on the exercise of power', a 'mutual commitment among elites, through the 'coordinating' mechanism of a constitution, related political institutions, and often an elite pact or settlement as well, to enforce limits on state authority, no matter which party or faction may control the state at any given time' (Diamond 1997: 4). However, the elite is hardly likely to accept those restraints if it does not have both positive and negative incentives to do so. Positive – in the sense that acceptance of those restraints will pay off in the long run. Also actors who are out of power must feel that observance of the rules of the game is in their interests. Negative incentives mean that violation will prove costly in terms of public support.

Cultural attitudes also represent a clear obstacle to the implementation of legislation and institutions aimed at securing media freedom and independence. Numerous examples suggest that the political culture of post-Communism favours control of the media by political elites. In Hungary, as Kovats (1994) has noted, two 'incompatible paradigms of the social functions of the media' emerged after the collapse of the communist system, expressive of the views of two major political parties: (i) the liberal paradigm favouring the complete independence and autonomy of the media and therefore complete withdrawal of the state from the media, and (ii) the paradigm of service to national values, reconstruction and reinforcement of national identity, preservation of traditional values, support for the national culture. That paradigm assumed continued state control over the media in order to ensure pursuit of these goals. This is confirmed by Bajomi-Lázár (2008), who adds that in Hungary in the 1990s and early 2000s, the understanding of media policy differed fundamentally from that in advanced democracies. Media policy makers regarded the media as a tool of political agitation and propaganda, a means of political mobilization rather than political information. Media policy was not the outcome of the interplay of a variety of actors but an instrument in the hands of the government of the day. In short, media policy in post-communist Hungary was not a public policy, i.e., one serving the public, but one serving particular interests.

Brečka (1993), using the example of Slovakia, explains that the new post-communist governments which had liberalized the print media were taken aback and stung by what they considered to be completely unjustified critical treatment from the highly politicized press. They felt cut off from public opinion and unable to deliver their message to the population. Accordingly, some sought to delay transforming existing monopolistic government-controlled broadcasting systems into autonomous public service systems and de-monopolising radio and television as this would give their political opponents a chance to start broadcasting to the population. They believed then, and some still believe, that as the new democratically elected governments they have the 'right' to use radio and television to promote the process of reform, although more often than not this has taken the form of manipulation for propaganda and political purposes.

In Bulgaria, the principle, first advanced in Hungary, that there should be 'media controlled by the electoral winners' (Arato 1996: 225) came close to being written into the law in 1996: 'The [broadcasting] law allowed, in effect, the political party in power to have control over the state-owned National Television and National Radio. Soon after, the Constitutional Court repealed the major provisions of this law' (Nikoltchev 1998/99). Also in the Czech Republic (where private media enjoy unrestrained freedom), there was a 'television crisis' at the turn of 2000–2001, triggered by political groups' attempt to gain control over public television. The general public made clear its demand that the political independence of Czech TV be safeguarded but in the end the process led to 'strengthening the influence which the House of Deputies had on it' (Jirák and Köpplová 2008).

The problem does not lie only in the cultural attitudes and behaviour among the political elites but also in the values held by media practitioners and civil society. Media freedom and independence in post-communist countries are not enhanced by the clear political engagement or bias of many journalists who believe their role is one of social leadership, called upon to promote the political views or forces they personally support (see Jakubowicz 2007, for an extensive analysis of this phenomenon). With growing political tension and intensity of political divisions in many countries (e.g. Hungary or Poland), this tendency is on the rise, rather than weakening.

Low journalistic ethics, including a willingness to serve as 'pens for hire,' i.e. to accept *zakazukha* (also known as 'hidden advertising'), to call it by its Russian name, meaning simply bribes for positive coverage of politicians and businesses, is another cultural/attitudinal factor of importance in thwarting efforts to promote media freedom and independence. This is sometimes encouraged by media owners and managers as a way of cutting costs. The practice is best known in Russia (Pankin 1998), but is also well established in other post-communist countries, including for example, Lithuania (Nevinskaite 2009) and in other regions of the world (Lovitt 2004)

Civil society has alternated between active and determined opposition to political constraints on freedom of expression and freedom of the media and cynical and demoralized acceptance of media partisanship under political control. Although genuine support for democratic values is lacking across the region, important differences can be noticed between countries. In line with our general division of post-communist countries into three groups, we may distinguish three broad types of cultural attitudes and behaviour of governments and political elites vis-à-vis the media.

Democratic countries range from far-reaching respect for media freedom and independence (as in Estonia, for example; see Jõesaar 2009), and therefore lack of government or political party interference into their operation, to cases of 'selective atavism', i.e. control over public service media (very widespread in most countries), and either attempts to create private media favouring a particular cause or political force or interference with the work of media opposed to the authorities or a political party.

In the second group of semi-democratic/semi autocratic countries, the situation is different and both the government and political forces are much more active. Originally some of them adopted quite democratic and liberal media legislation and their policy vis-à-vis private broadcast and print media was usually a reactive one: at least officially their freedom was respected but government or public authorities reacted when the media criticized or challenged them. Later pre-emptive strategies to prevent hostile or critical coverage became more common, including (as in Russia or Ukraine) 'systemic' measures to ensure that private media are owned or controlled by individuals or companies selected by the power elite.

Political elites also pursue active day-to-day policies and measures to put pressure on the media and secure favourable coverage. Richter (2008; see also Richter 2007b) has developed a list of methods used for this purpose in CIS countries – some in this, and others in the third, autocratic group:

- State authorities informally circulate guidance to the media (as in the case of the infamous Ukrainian *temniki* before 2004);
- The state or state-controlled media infrastructure refuses to serve independent or opposition outlets (as in Belarus, where the main printing house used by the press is controlled by the President's administration and often engages in such practices);
- Restricting information and advertising for disloyal media;
- Abuse of state subsidies and monopolies to favour loyal media;
- Abuse of regulatory and supervisory functions, for example by using the licensing policy of broadcasting regulatory authorities to reward loyal and punish disloyal media (see also Richter 2007a);
- 'In-house censorship';
- Illegal pressure in response to cases where the journalists or the media challenge the government or public officials (this may include 'censorship by killing' and 'censorship by physical assault and intimidation').

Autocratic countries apply many of these measures but primarily seek to prevent any uncontrolled content to appear in traditional and new Internet media.

Conclusion

On the basis of our analysis, we can now return to our hypothesis and three propositions. Generally speaking, our analysis suggests that the processes in the areas of democracy and media freedom consolidation are certainly interconnected, although the sequencing and intensity may be quite different. In line with the concept of non-equivalent or asymmetrical interdependence of social and media change, liberalization of the media is made possible by the collapse of the old system. Once the old system of media and content control weakens, the opening up of the media is very fast. It both precedes and promotes other processes of inter-systemic transition. For a time, until a new system of control is introduced, the media enjoy extensive freedom from government interference, though not necessarily independence, if they are controlled by political forces. With time, as new power elites introduce new (or revive old) forms of control of the media, consolidation of their freedom may fall behind the general process of democratic consolidation. Because of the importance of the media, political elites will seek to retain as much discretionary power over the media as possible and to accept as few effective restraints on their power as possible. Hence the possibility of 'delay' between general democratization and consolidation of media freedom and independence.

According to our first proposition, the scope of direct political and administrative control over the media depends on whether a country is democratic, semi-democratic, or autocratic. This has partly been confirmed and indeed, the more authoritarian a political system is, the fewer media sectors and outlets can escape state and/or political control. At the level of general media policy orientations, democratic post-communist countries have been more predisposed to adopt the mimetic orientation and 'mimic' media policies characteristic of Western democracies. The idea was to 'test the best of the West', but the enabling socio-political and cultural environment needed for these policies to succeed has largely been absent. In contrast, media policies in semi-democratic and semi-authoritarian ones are characterized by a mixture of mimetic and atavistic orientations, and those in autocratic ones primarily by the atavistic orientation. However, our expectations have not been confirmed fully. We have seen that in the democratic systems there can be cases of 'selective atavism', meaning that some sectors (e.g. public service broadcasting) almost universally remain under political control. Another form of 'selective atavism' is measures to create media, sometimes with the help of public funds, or institutions, serving as a mouthpiece for the government of the day.

Our second proposition, that institutions introduced in the media field are likely to replicate solutions adopted for the institutional dimension of democracy, has largely been confirmed. Whether a system is a parliamentary or presidential one usually determines who has the power of appointment of broadcasting regulatory authorities, or the governing bodies of public service broadcasters and who potentially has the resources and powers of patronage. However, particular solutions may depend on the specificities of the political and public regime in the given country.

Finally, our analysis confirmed that the choice and implementation of particular policy solutions and institutional structures depends to an important extent on cultural attitudes and behavioural patterns. In all types of post-communist countries, attitudinal and behavioral dimensions lead political elites to put pressure on the media, formally or informally, legally or with disregard for the letter of the law, to maintain control and constrain their freedom and independence. This may result in the creation of 'winner-take-all' or 'winner-take-most' institutions in the public sector and in the use of different methods to maintain control over privately-owned media. That alone could introduce an element of hybridity into post-communist political regimes, though certainly there are also many other elements that produce the same effect.

The Open Society Institute report 'Television across Europe' (Dragomir and Thompson 2008) sums up the situation in Central and Eastern Europe as 'more channels, less independence,' noting 'a worrying determination on the part of political elites to reaffirm their influence over broadcasting.' Mark Thompson of the Open Society Foundation Media Programme describes this as 'a sort of 'counter-reformation': Why refrain from exercising political control over these very important institutions when there are no penalties?' (Phillips 2009) This again speaks to the importance of cultural/attitudinal factors – both on the part of the political elite, and the general population which does not appear to care about media freedom and independence enough to punish politicians for limiting them. Consolidation of liberal democracy is far from over and this is telling evidence of this fact.

References

Andreev, S.A. 2003. The role of institutions in the consolidation of democracy in post-communist Eastern Europe. *Centre for the Study of Political Change Occasional Papers*, 13/2003. Available at: http://www.circap.unisi.it/publications/occasional-papers [accessed 30 January 2009].

Arato, A. 1996. The Hungarian Constitutional Court in the media war: Interpretations of separation of powers and models of democracy, in *Rights of Access to the Media*, edited by A. Sajóa and M. Price. The Hague: Kluwer Law International, 225–42.

Bajomi-Lázár, P. 2008. The consolidation of media freedom in post-communist countries, in *Finding the Right Place on the Map: Central and Eastern European Media Change in a Global Perspective*, edited by K. Jakubowicz and M. Sükösd. Bristol: Intellect, 73–84.

Bajomi-Lázár, P. and Hegedűs, I., eds. 2001. *Media and Politics*. Budapest: New Mandate Publishing House.

Brečka, S. 1993. *Transformation of the Slovak Television*. Paper presented to a conference on 'Restructuring TV in Central and Eastern Europe, University of Westminster, London, October 20–23.

Bunce, V. 1999. Lessons of the first postsocialist decade. *East European Politics and Societies*, 13(2), 236–43.

Bustamante, E. 1989. TV and public service in Spain: a difficult encounter. *Media, Culture and Society*, 11(1): 67–88.

Carothers, T. 2002. The End of the Transition Paradigm. *Journal of Democracy*, 13(1), 5–21.

Cichosz, M. 2006. Transformacja demokratyczna – przyczyny, przebieg i efekty procesu, in *Systemy polityczne Europy Środkowej i Wschodniej. Perspektywa porównawcza*, edited by A. Antoszewski. Wrocław: Wydawnictwo Uniwersytetu Wrocławskiego, 35–66.

Coricelli, F. 2007. Democracy in the post-communist world: unfinished business. *East European Politics and Societies*, 21(1), 82–90.

Dahlgren, P. 1995. *Television and the Public Sphere: Citizenship, Democracy and the Media*. London: Sage.

Dauderstädt, M. and Gerrits, A.W.M. 2000. Democratisation after communism: Progress, problems, promotion. *Politik und Gesellschaft Online/ International Politics and Society*, 4. Available at: http:\\orae.fes.de.8081/fes/docs/IPG4_2000/daudiopti2.htm [accessed 30 January 2009].

De Smaele, H. 2010. In search for a label for the Russian media system, in *Comparative Media Systems: European and Global Perspectives*, edited by B. Dobek-Ostrowska, M. Głowacki, K. Jakubowicz and M. Sükösd. Budapest: Central University Press, 41–62.

Diamond, L. 1997. Is the third wave of democratization over? The imperative of consolidation. *The Kellogg Institute Working Papers*, 237. Available at: http://www.nd.edu/~kellogg/WPS/237.pdf [accessed 30 January 2009].

Diamond, L. 2008. The democratic rollback: The resurgence of the predatory state. *Foreign Affairs*, March/April 2008. Available at: http://www.foreignaffairs.org/20080301faessay87204/ larry-diamond/the-democratic-rollback.html [accessed 30 January 2009].

Dragomir, M. and Thompson, M., eds. 2008. *Television across Europe: More Channels, Less Independence*. Budapest: EU Monitoring and Advocacy Program, Open Society Institute.

Ekiert, G., Kubik, J. and Vachudova, M.A. 2007. Democracy in the post-communist world: An unending quest? *East European Politics and Societies*, 21(1), 7–30.

EPRA. 2007. *The Independence of Regulatory Authorities*. 25th EPRA meeting, Prague, 16–18 May 2007.

EUMAP. 2005. *Television Across Europe: Regulation, Policy and Independence. Summary*. Budapest: Open Society Institute.

Faust, J. 2007. Democracy's dividend: Political order and economic productivity. *World Political Science Review*, 3(2), 1–29,

Fish, S.M. 2006. Stronger Legislatures, Stronger Democracies. *Journal of Democracy*, 17(1), 5–20.

Grzymała-Busse, A. 2004. Post-communist competition and state development. *Program on Central & Eastern Europe Working Paper Series*, 59. Available at: http://www.ces.fas.harvard.edu/publications/docs/pdfs/Grzymala.pdf [accessed 30 January 2009].

Hallin, D.C. and Mancini, P. 2004. *Comparing Media Systems: Three Models of Media and Politics*. Cambridge: Cambridge University Press.

Hallin, D.C. and Mancini, P. 2009. Introduction, in *Comparative Media Systems: European and Global Perspectives*, edited by B. Dobek-Ostrowska, M. Głowacki, K. Jakubowicz and M. Sükösd. Budapest: Central University Press.

Jakubowicz, K. 1995. Lovebirds? The media, the state and politics in Central and Eastern Europe. *Javnost/The Public*, 2(1), 75–91.

Jakubowicz, K. 2003. PSB in new member countries: Problems and prospects. *The SIS Briefings*, 56, 12–20.

Jakubowicz, K. 2004. Ideas in our heads: Introduction of PSB as part of media system change in Central and Eastern Europe. *European Journal of Communication*, 19 (1), 53–75.

Jakubowicz, K. 2005. Let the people speak? The (unfinished) evolution of communicative democracy, in *Populism and Media Democracy*, edited by B. Ociepka. Wrocław: Wydawnictwo Uniwersytetu Wrocławskiego, 143–80.

Jakubowicz, K. 2007. *Rude Awakening: Social and Media Change in Central and Eastern Europe*. Cresskill, N.J.: Hampton Press, Inc.

Jakubowicz, K. and Sükösd, M., eds. 2008. *Finding the Right Place on the Map: Central and Eastern European Media Change in a Global Perspective*. Bristol: Intellect Books.

Jirák, J. and Köpplová, B. 2008. The reality show called democratization: Transformation of the Czech media after 1989. *Global Media Journal* [Online], 1(4), 7–23. Available at: http://www.globalmediajournal.collegium.edu.pl/artykuly/wiosna%202008/jirak-kopplova-czech-media.pdf [accessed 30 January 2009].

Jõesaar, A. 2009. Formation of Estonian broadcasting landscape 1992–2007: Experience of the transition state. Impact of the EU legislation on the Estonian television broadcasting since mid-90s. *Central European Journal of Communication*, 1(2), 43–62.

Kachkaeva, A.G. and Richter, A.G. 1992. The emergence of nonstate TV in the Ukraine. *Canadian Journal of Communication*, 17(4). Available at: http://www.cjc-online.ca/index.php/journal/article/view/698/604 [accessed 30 January 2009].

Khakee, A. 2002. Democracy and marketization in Central and Eastern Europe: Case closed? *East European Politics and Societies*, 16(2), 599–615.

Kovats, I. 1994. *Difficulties in the Process of the Democratization of the Media in Hungary.* Paper presented to the 19th IAMCR Scientific Conference, Seoul, Korea, 1994.

Landman, T., ed. 2008. *Assessing the Quality of Democracy. An Overview of the International IDEA Framework.* Stockholm: International Institute for Democracy and Electoral Assistance.

Linz, J.J. and Stepan, A. 1996. *Problems of Democratic Transition and Consolidation: Southern Europe, South America, and Post-Communist Europe.* Baltimore and London: The Johns Hopkins University Press.

Lovitt, J. 2004. *Promotion of Pluralism and Good Governance through Media Development: Summary of Contributions.* Paris: Intergovernmental Council of the International Programme for the Development of Communication, UNESCO. Available at: http://portal.unesco.org/ci/en/files/14887/10812670181jlovitt_TI_UNESCO_IPDS_2april2004.doc/jlovitt_TI_UNESCO_IPDS_2april2004.doc [accessed 30 January 2009].

Manaev, O. 2003 Mass media and social transformations in post-communist Belarus, in *Business as Usual: Continuity and Change in Central and Eastern European Media,* edited by D. Paletz and K. Jakubowicz. Cresskill, N.J.: Hampton Press, pp. 47–74.

McFaul, M. 2005. Transitions from postcommunism. *Journal of Democracy,* 16 (3), 5–19.

Media Division. 2003. *An overview of the rules governing broadcasting regulatory authorities in Europe.* DH-MM(2003)007. Strasbourg: Directorate General of Human Rights, Council of Europe.

Morawski, W. 1998. *Zmiana instytucjonalna. Społeczeństwo. Gospodarka. Polityka.*

Morawski, W. 2001. *Socjologia ekonomiczna.* Warsaw: PWN.

Mughan, A., and Gunther, R. 2000. The media in democratic and nondemocratic regimes, in *Democracy and the Media: A Comparative Perspective,* edited by R. Gunther and A. Mugham. Cambridge: Cambridge University Press, 1–27.

Munck, G.L. 1996. Disaggregating political regime: Conceptual issues in the study of democratization. *The Kellogg Institute Working Papers,* 228. Available at: http://kellogg.nd.edu/publications/workingpapers/WPS/228.pdf [accessed 30 January 2009].

Mungiu-Pippidi, A. 2008. How media and politics shape each other in the New Europe, in *Finding the Right Place on the Map: Central and Eastern European Media Change in Global Perspective,* edited by K. Jakubowicz and M. Sükösd. Bristol: Intellect Books, 87–100.

Nevinskaite, L. 2009 EU structural funds' publicity and the practice of journalism and public relations in Lithuania. *Central European Journal of Communication,* 1(2), 149–66.

Nikoltchev, I. 1998/99. Journalists as lawmakers: Grassroots initiative for media regulation in Bulgaria, 1996–1998. *International Journal of Communications*

Law and Policy, 2. Available at: www.digital-law.net/ijclp [accessed 30 January 2009].

O'Donnell, G.A. 2002. Democracy, law, and comparative politics. *Law, Democracy and Development Series*, IDS Working Paper 1. Available at: http://www.ids. ac.uk/files/Wp118.pdf [accessed 30 January 2009].

Offe, C. 1997. Cultural aspects of consolidation: A note on the peculiarities of postcommunist transformations. *East European Constitutional Review*, 6(4). Available at: http://www.law.nyu.edu/eecr/vol6num4/special/culturalaspects. html [accessed 30 January 2009].

Page, S.E. 2006. Path dependence. *Quarterly Journal of Political Science*, 1(1), 87–115.

Paletz, D. and Lipinski, D.J. 1994. *Political Culture and Political Communication*, Working Paper. Available at: http://www.icps.es/archivos/WorkingPapers/ WP_I_92.pdf [accessed 30 January 2009].

Pankin, A. 1998. *Anatomy of the Russian Media Crisis*. Moscow: Internews.

Phillips, L. 2009. European broadcasters face political 'counter-reformation'. EUObserver. Available at: http://euobserver.com/9/27807 [accessed 30 January 2009].

Price, M.E. and Krug, P. 2000. *The Enabling Environment For Free and Independent Media*. Oxford: Programme in Comparative Media Law & Policy Centre for Socio-Legal Studies, Wolfson College.

Puddington, A. 2009. *Freedom in the World 2009: Setbacks and Resilience*. Available at: http://www.freedomhouse.org/uploads/fiw09/FIW09_Overview Essay_Final.pdf [accessed 30 January 2009].

Pusić, V. 2000. Abandoning the war mentality: Interview with President of the Croatian People's Party, Vesna Pusić. *Central Europe Review*, 2(19). Available at: http://www.ce-review.org/00/19/interview19_pusic.html [accessed 30 January 2009].

Richter, A. 2007a. A post-Soviet perspective on licensing television and radio. *IRIS plus*, 2007–8. Strasbourg: European Audiovisual Observatory.

Richter, A. 2007b. *Post-Soviet Perspective on Censorship and Freedom of the Media*. Moscow: UNESCO Office.

Richter, A. 2008. Post-Soviet perspective on censorship and freedom of the media: An overview. *International Communication Gazette*, 70(5), 307–24.

Richter, A. and Golovanov, D. 2006. *Public Service Broadcasting Regulation in the Commonwealth of Independent States. Special Report on the Legal Framework for Public Service Broadcasting in Azerbaijan, Georgia, Moldova, Russia and Ukraine*. Strasbourg: European Audiovisual Observatory.

Rupnik, J. 2007. From democracy fatigue to populist backlash. *Journal of Democracy*, 18(4), 17–25.

Schneider, C.Q. 2002. *The Consolidation of Democracy in Different Contexts: Complex Causation and Preliminary Data on 28 Third-wave Democracies*. Paper presented at the Advanced Research Workshop of 'The European

Political Economy Infrastructure Consortium', 16–22 May, 2002, Florence/ Italy.

Sestanovich, S. 2004. Force, money, and pluralism. *Journal of Democracy*, 15(3), 32–42.

Sparks, C. 1995. The media as a power for democracy. *Javnost /The Public*, 2(1), 45–61.

Splichal, S. 2001. Imitative revolutions: Changes in the media and journalism in East-Central Europe. *Javnost/The Public*, 8(4), 31–58.

Sztompka, P., ed. 1999. *Imponderabilia wielkiej zmiany. Mentalność, wartości i więzi społeczne czasów transformacji.* Warsawa and Krakow: Wydawnictwo Naukowe PWN.

Sztompka, P. 2000. *Trauma wielkiej zmiany. Społeczne koszty transformacji.* Warsaw: Instytut Nauk Politycznych PAN.

Tanase, S. 1999. Changing societies and elite transformation. *East European Politics and Societies*, 13(2), 358–63.

Walker, C. 2007. *Muzzling the Media: The Return of Censorship in the Commonwealth of Independent States.* Freedom Mouse. Available at: http:// www.freedomhouse.org/uploads/press_release/muzzlingthemedia_15june07. pdf [accessed 30 January 2009].

Way, L.A. 2008b. The real causes of the color revolutions. *Journal of Democracy*, 19(3), 55–69.

Wiarda, H.J. 2001. Southern Europe, Eastern Europe, and comparative politics: 'Transitology' and the need for new theory. *East European Politics and Societies*, 15(3), 485–501.

Chapter 2

The Interplay of Politics and Economics in Transitional Societies

Colin Sparks

Introduction

Political economy is a tradition of social analysis that dates at least from the eighteenth century and, in the works of Smith and others was concerned to understand the dynamics of what was then the new economic order of nascent industrial capitalism. Up until the middle of the nineteenth century, it was more or less synonymous with what is today called 'economics'. Always a field of contention, in the hands of Marx and Engels it became, famously and perhaps indelibly, linked with the critique of capitalism and working class efforts to establish a socialist society.

Applying this tradition of analysis to Eastern Europe inevitably faces the problem that, for nearly half a century before 1989, the region was ruled by parties that proclaimed their allegiance to Marxism. What had been born as a revolutionary current on the radical wing of the democratic movement of 1848 became, in effect, the state religion of monstrous dictatorships. Recovering and developing this radically democratic version of Marxism is a major intellectual project. Winning an audience for this recovered version anywhere is a difficult task, particularly in countries which have experienced the effects of communist rule. Both of these endeavours are extremely important, but lie well beyond the scope of this chapter, which has a much more modest goal. Here, it is assumed that such a recovery is both possible and desirable, and the focus of attention is upon the ways in which political economy might be helpful in understanding what has occurred in the media of the former communist countries.

Accordingly, this chapter begins with a brief discussion of the political economy of the media, clarifying some of the issues and confusions that have surrounded it. It then moves on to begin the application of this method to the analysis of the mass media since the fall of communism. Despite the theoretical commitment to the study of the social totality that is implicit in the project of political economy, the two dimensions are initially separated: the political is considered first, followed by the economic. In the final two sections, the interaction between the political and the economic is discussed revealing why the political economic approach provides a superior explanation of the historical trajectory of the media in Central and Eastern Europe than the main alternative that concentrates on political factors.

What is Political Economy?

The first problem in discussing how far the political economy of the media provides a useful guide to the changes that have taken place in the former Communist countries of Central and Eastern Europe is determining exactly what one means by the term 'political economy'. There is a very wide range of practices that have been subsumed under this category, many of them from quite opposite intellectual and political positions. After all, a tradition that can count both Adam Smith and Karl Marx in its lineage is bound to contain a variety of different views.

One answer to this question is that the political economy of the media is simply another term for Marxist analyses. Certainly, a number of the most prominent writers on the political economy of media and communications have been, at least at some points in their career, heavily influenced by one or other current of Marxism: Smythe, Schiller, Mattelart, Garnham, Murdock and Golding, Mosco, Wasko, McChesney, and many others, all demonstrate clear, and often explicit, debts to that intellectual tradition. It would be wrong, however, simply to subsume all works of political economy into the Marxist camp. Some of the most famous radical work in contemporary political economy, that of Herman and Chomsky, most certainly cannot be simply 'labelled "Marxist"', despite many obvious convergences in critical perspective (Herman and Chomsky 2008). There are other, far less radical, voices that can also be incorporated into political economy without straining the concept unduly (McChesney 2007: 80–81). Indeed, some prominent contemporary political economists have moved from an early engagement with Marxist critiques of the market to an emphatic defence of it role in ensuring allocative efficiency in the distribution of scarce resources. The researcher's normative attitude towards the market is not a defining characteristic of political economy as an intellectual pursuit, and there are, in fact, a variety of different political positions within the broad category of contemporary political economy (Mosco 2009: 50–61).

Despite these reservations, however, Marxism is one of the main reference points, positive or negative, for almost all work in this field. Political economists of all stripes share with Marxism a stress upon the primacy of economic factors in determining the history and contemporary forms of the media. As Murdock and Golding put it in one of the founding texts: 'The obvious starting point for a political economy of mass communications is the recognition that the mass media are first and foremost industrial and commercial organizations which produce and distribute commodities' (1974: 205–6). This stress upon the extent to which all cultural production is grounded in the social relations of a capitalist society is one of the first marks of distinction of political economy, in that it sets it off from the other major critical current in the field of media and communication, namely cultural studies, which has tended to concentrate on the analysis of the internal organization of media artefacts abstracted from the conditions of their production (Garnham 1990: 1–2)

This heritage also gives political economy its strongly historical bent, as evidenced in the term 'historical materialism'. Murdock and Golding identify historical work as the second defining feature of the tradition (Golding and Murdock 1991: 17). Similarly, in discussing what he terms 'the historical turn', McChesney makes the point that 'media systems...are not 'natural' in any society' (2007: 118). This historical dimension is central to the tradition since it is concerned to understand the dynamics of development of the media, both in the general sense of the rise, dominance and decline of different forms of media and in the more narrowly technical sense of understanding the processes of change within and between media over shorter time periods.

Such emphases, however, would hardly distinguish political economy proper from media economics, pure and simple. While they include the aim of economics to understand 'how the economy allocates scarce resources, with alternative uses, between unlimited competing wants,' the ambitions of political economists are rather grander than this (Hoskins et al. 2004: 3). As Mosco writes, political economy is concerned with the overall shape and direction of society and: 'First and foremost, a commitment to the social totality means understanding the connection between the political and the economic' (1996: 31, 2009: 29). The concept of 'totality' is one of the more distinctively Marxist elements in political economy, derived as it is from the writings of George Lukács, where it is attributed a central role: 'the category of totality, the all-pervasive supremacy of the whole over the parts is the essence of the method which Marx took over from Hegel' (1971: 27). This approach, while it certainly accepts both the centrality of economic life in explaining the nature of human experience, and the importance of the technical analysis of economic processes, emphatically rejects the notion that 'the economy allocates scarce resources' as a classical instance of reification and commodity fetishism (Lukács 1971: 83ff). The allocation of resources within society, political economy insists, is the result of human actions and decisions, and thus subject to conscious direction and redirection.

This stress upon the ways in which political and economic factors are mutually entwined in the production of media artefacts is differentiated from the similar concerns of regulatory economics. The latter is concerned with analysing the consequences for particular industries resulting from different regulatory arrangements whereas political economy has more general social concerns. It follows Adam Smith in investigating: 'The causes of this improvement, in the productive powers of labour, and the order, according to which its produce is naturally distributed among the different ranks and conditions of men in the society.' More narrowly, the political economy of media and communication is concerned with 'how the making and taking of meaning is shaped at every level by the structured asymmetries in social relations' (Golding and Murdock 1991: 18). In practice, as Golding and Murdock go on to argue, this has led political economists to the rather narrower project of considering the interactions between the market and the state, most obviously in the discussion of public broadcasting (Golding and Murdock 1991: 24–6). These poles are, of course, extremely important in understanding what has occurred in the former communist countries, but in principle this concern with differential social power could be much broader, and more radical. The scope of possible debate about the organization of the mass media is not exhausted by a spectrum opinion ranging from anarchic free marketers to statist authoritarian command economists.

Political Economy and Post-communism

Given its strong Marxist heritage, political economy would not, one would anticipate, receive a warm welcome in the post-communist world. Some of the most prominent practitioners of the political economy of the media had been more or less enthusiastic supporters of 'actually existing socialism' at one point or other in their careers, and at the very least the collapse of European communism required a certain reassessment of one's intellectual universe on the part of self-proclaimed Marxists. Welcome or not, however, there is no doubt that political economy is a particularly useful way to approach the analysis of post-communist societies. These are, after all, societies undergoing what appears to be a total transformation. One system, encompassing economics, politics, social life, leisure and entertainment, even psychology, was replaced by another which, for most of a century, had been portrayed as its polar opposite, and which for forty years had been its armed antagonist. A method which proclaims the category of totality as the centre of its concerns, and which is especially concerned with the dynamics of historical development, is obviously well placed to test such claims.

In the area of the mass media, a political economic analysis is concerned with understanding the ways in which the general crisis of these societies impacted upon the mass media and how the spectacular transformations of the political world were reflected in them. Whatever may have been the long term origins of the final crisis of European Communism, and whatever may subsequently have occurred in terms of their development, the transformation of the media during and immediately after 1989 was the result of political choices. The nature of these choices varied from place to place – for example, the toleration of the effective theft of newspapers by their employees in Hungary was different from the controlled sale of titles in Poland – but none of these paths can be explained in purely economic terms. In the Hungarian case political, and eventually legal, sanction was given to the de facto seizure of titles, while in Poland the Solidarity government both decided upon an orderly sale and intervened to ensure that, in the first instance at least, the 'right' owners gained control of the titles.

Similar considerations clearly also apply to subsequent developments. In many, if not all, cases it is possible to demonstrate that, in significant ways, the trajectory of the mass media was not determined by the operation of a market economy. On the contrary, the allocation of resources was very often directly the product of political factors. The protracted wrangling over the legal position of television, and in particular the bitter struggles over the award of commercial franchises is an obvious case in point. To take the most egregious example, the award of the initial commercial franchise in the Czech Republic was widely recognized as a political act, was challenged almost immediately on political grounds, and was then defended politically when the franchisees fell out with each other and began a bitter struggle between themselves for the revenues generated by TV Nova.

If it is true that the academic study of the mass media has generally been most developed in relatively stable and slow-changing societies like the USA and the UK, then the marginalization of the political economic approach is easy to understand: the basic decision about the shape of the mass media were settled for most of the last half-century. So, as a result of a political struggle, the USA enjoyed commercial broadcasting while, as a result of a different political conjuncture, the UK enjoyed public service broadcasting. While there remained scope for serious investigation about ownership and about the shape of the regulatory regimes, challenges to these basic settlements were more or less marginal and where they occurred, as in the introduction of commercial television to the UK in the 1950s, they were quickly contained within the existing set of relations. As Mosco correctly points out, one powerful reason for the re-emergence of an interest in political economy is because the concatenation of globalization, neo-liberalism and technological change has thrown the whole of this settlement into turmoil, and opened a broad arena for the discussion of the relationship between political and economic forces (Mosco 2009: 14–16).

The former communist countries of Central and Eastern Europe have been anything but relatively stable and slow-changing societies. On the contrary, they have been marked by rapid economic change, both at the quantitative and qualitative level, and by rapid political transformations, both from communist dictatorships into what we might term 'Schumpeterian democracies', and to an alternation of governing groups. If political economy in general, and the political economy of the media in particular, was ever going to find a fertile field for the analysis of the ways in which the political and the economic interact, then it is here that it will be found.

It is the contention of this chapter that no purely political account of the media in Eastern Europe, for example one which talks purely in terms of 'democratization' can explain the real pattern of events over the last 20 years. But neither can a purely economic account, which talks simply of the workings of the market, offer an adequate basis for analysis. On the contrary, while both of these dimensions are clearly powerful factors in determining media outcomes, the complete picture is available only by considering the ways in which they are inter-related and acted upon each other.

Two Dimensions of Political Power

In any society in which social power, including access to material and symbolic goods, is unevenly distributed, as was the case in the Central and Eastern Europe both before 1989 and since, there are two dimensions upon which we can consider this distribution. One is the way in which power is distributed within the group to whom it disproportionately accrues, which we may term the elite, or ruling class, should we wish to follow the Marxist tradition more closely. This, concerning the relations of power within the elite, we may term the horizontal dimension of power. The other, which concerns the relations between the elite and those who are relatively disadvantaged in the distribution of social power, we may term the vertical dimension of power. A political economic analysis would be concerned to determine what changes there had been on each of these axes.

In terms of the mass media, these considerations would concern, in their horizontal dimension, the distribution of allocative control over media outlets, the nature and extent of competition between media outlets, and the degree to which they can be identified with particular sections of the elite. With regard to the vertical dimension, the key issue is the extent to which there is popular control over the mass media, expressed through mandatory seats on boards, forms of collective ownership, or other forms of 'empowerment of civil society'.

The media in the old order were closely integrated into the state machine and subordinated to the control of the ruling party which was, at least on the surface, a single unified grouping. Whatever internal disputes might rack the party, and historically they had been very intense indeed, the ruling class, roughly equivalent to the *nomenklatura*, exercised its control over society, and thus over the media, collectively. No individual, family, or limited company owned a media outlet and the editorial line was determined by reference to the appropriate party bodies. It is possible to overstate the degree of uniformity that this produced in the mass media, but there is no doubt that over major issues the entire media system spoke with one voice: the collective voice of the party leadership. There was, in other words, a very high degree of horizontal power integration in this kind of system.

The new order is characterized everywhere by at least a limited plurality of parties, and in many of the countries in question there are more or less free and fair elections to decide which one of them shall form the government. Whether these all constitute 'democracies' is much disputed, and we can leave it to one side in this context. What political economy would predict as a result of such a situation is that the ruling elite is today much more fragmented and it owes its elite position to a range of different social forces. Some are members of the economic elite and enjoy their social position as a result of their current economic position. Others, the political elite, owe it to the fact that they lead a significant political force, usually a party represented in the legislature. There are some marginal cases, entertainers and cultural figures for instance, whose position rests on other factors, but these are not significantly different from their status in the old order. The extent to which the media tend to reflect this relative disintegration is the measure of the distance between the new societies and the old.

From the point of view of the cohesion of the elite, it is obvious that there has been, almost everywhere, a significant move towards what we may term 'disintegration'. The bonds binding the different members of the elite together with each other have been dramatically altered: they now owe their position to individual or family factors and they are free to express their views, and pursue their interests, in any way they so choose.

To the extent that they have diverging interests, we would expect the mass media to reflect rather faithfully the groups who control them. This is because of the second, vertical, dimension of power. Before the revolutions of 1989 (very nearly) all power was concentrated in the hands of the elite. The mass media were a mechanism of transmission for the views of the elite. The population enjoyed no effective institutional mechanism for influencing the direction of society. Before the revolution, the price of sausages was a political question, and if it seemed unreasonable then the obvious recourse was also political: you rioted, as Polish workers did on frequent occasions. The theoretical result of the transition was to remove a great deal of social power from the political arena. After the revolution, the price of sausages is a market question, and if it seems unreasonable, then what on earth can one do about it? Certainly, there is no obvious political recourse. The dramatic reduction in the scope of 'the political' is a common characteristic of many societies in the years following the elections of Thatcher and Reagan, who pioneered this approach, but it was particularly rapid in the former communist countries.

'Democratization' was thus a paradox in terms of the distribution of social power. The fall of the dictatorships empowered the mass of the population to vote for who was to control the political dimension of power, but at the same time it radically reduced the areas of social life that were subject to political control. So far as the elite was concerned, however, political power mattered enormously because it was the main mechanism whereby economic power was transferred from the state to corporate owners, so control of this process was essential. The distribution of the various elements of the mass media is a clear indication of the importance of political power in the transfer of what was previously 'state' property into private hands: the hands in which newspapers, and later television stations, settled in were in the main selected on the basis of political connections and political power.

The Economic Dimension

The impact of economic factors requires lengthier treatment because it can be considered at a number of levels, from the general and systemic down to the micro-level of the particular media firm. This chapter will consider a number of these levels across a number of cases. We begin at the most general level, where the cases under consideration have the extremely unusual feature of what might be termed the highly accelerated acquisition of a market system. The overall economic landscape within which the media operate is first surveyed, then the patterns of advertising are examined in more detail. In both cases, comparisons are made with the patterns observable in the more developed market economies.

The mass media today, in almost all of the former communist countries, correspond to the general features of the European media model. This is distinguished on the one hand by a broadcasting industry with a relatively strong state owned component and a complementary private sector. On the other hand, there is a privately owned, although often state-subsidized, press sector. There are, within this general model, a wide range of different versions with important consequence for media performance. The extent to which the state broadcaster competes for advertising revenues is one obvious variable and the degree to which the newspaper market is dominated by large national titles is another. It is, however, clearly a model that is quite distinct from the USA, in which the broadcasting sector is overwhelmingly dominated by commercial broadcasters.

The introduction of commercial models for the press and broadcasting was an abrupt process, and very often took the form of the import of established methods from abroad. The eventual predominance of the European model is hardly surprising, since the EU, to membership of which many post-communist countries ardently aspired, exerted considerable influence over the formal media policies of its candidates and this attraction was sufficient to outweigh any sentimental desire for a US model based on free market principles.

The issue of press ownership was resolved almost everywhere more or less spontaneously, and the advertising supported model of press finance was adopted more or less unanimously. The political impetus towards 'empowering civil society' nowhere found institutional expression in the press: there was no mandatory representation of readers on editorial boards; no mandatory allocation of titles to collectives of citizens organized around common concerns; no attempt to create conditions in which minority voices were encouraged to find expression and enabled to survive in the market. Within a decade, experienced foreign companies had entered the press market, and forms of journalism – from pornographic magazines to tabloid newspapers – that were established in the Western part of the continent but new to the east – had been introduced.

The regulation of broadcasting was seldom so simple, with decisions about the precise models of governance often proving extremely contentious to different political currents, but almost everywhere what might be termed a politicized (French) model of governance was the one adopted. Here there were distinct efforts to 'empower civil society' through specifying the composition of various governing and regulatory bodies, but they were invariably transformed, consciously or unconsciously, into the empowerment of sections of the political elite. The introduction of commercial broadcasting, although in most cases a more orderly process, took place within the first decade of change and was often predicated upon reliance on outside forces for the regulatory framework, capital investment, business model and programme content. Gaining a franchise very often involved an alliance between foreign expertise in commercial broadcasting, a significant section of 'national' capital, and local political connections legitimized through a role in the former opposition.

In common with the aftermath of repressive regimes elsewhere, these countries experienced an explosion of new media outlets: as in Spain and Portugal 15 years before, the end of the censorious restrictions of the old dictatorship led to the publication of hundreds, or perhaps thousands, of new papers, magazines and books that explored areas that had previously been strictly forbidden. In this case, the shift from a command economy to the beginnings of a market economy also mean that alongside material containing content previously forbidden, there were many new publications seeking to fill market niches that were either unpopulated in the old regime or very inadequately served by the existing titles.

The general characteristics of economic change were thus its extreme speed and what many commentators have considered its imitative, and frequently dependent, character, and in this it differed from developments elsewhere on the continent. The general outlines of the new media environment were determined by political forces, but the pace and direction of development was heavily influenced by the specific characteristics of the newly-emerging market in the post-communist countries.

The media experienced their rapid marketization in societies undergoing partial social and economic collapse. For many hundreds of years, the east of Europe has been much poorer than the west, and the existence of command economies for fifty years had done little or nothing to alter that material gap. The change of political and economic systems that took place very rapidly after 1989 could not be expected to eliminate these historic inequalities overnight. As the comparison of gross domestic products (GDPs) in Figure 2.1[1] shows, the economies of even some of the larger and more successful countries remained very small by European standards. Indeed, there is not a great deal of evidence that these countries were in fact 'catching up' with their western neighbours, despite various competitive advantages like much lower wage rates. The German economy, by far the biggest in Europe, grew by 30 per cent between 1990 and 2009, despite the difficulties of absorbing the former East Germany, while the Netherlands grew by 53 per cent and Greece by 65 per cent. Poland grew faster than all these, by 104 per cent, but Hungary grew by 27 per cent and the economy of the Russian Federation by a mere 2.4 per cent.

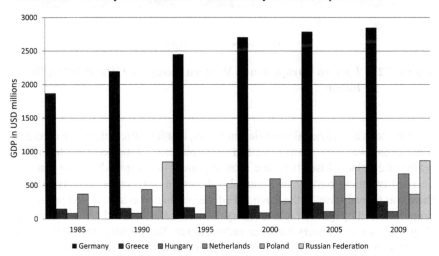

Figure 2.1   Comparative GDPs of selected countries at 1995 USD billion

---

1   The source for Figures 2.1, 2.2 and 2.3, and Table 2.1, is the UN Statistics Division's National Accounts Main Aggregate Database (2011).

One of the foundations of the command economy model is the drive for autarchic economic development, which meant that, at least within the area of Comecon, these countries were insulated from the direct workings of the world market. They had thus developed industries that, whatever their other virtues, were unlikely to prove internationally competitive in a genuinely open market. The ending of the autarchic model thus meant that there was everywhere the closure of many uncompetitive industries, and for the survivors an attempt to reduce employment in order to render them more efficient and enable them to survive. Everywhere, there were sharp falls in Gross Domestic Product and a sharp rise in economic inactivity. Overall, the decline was quite sharp, and the recovery has been long and slow, as Figure 2.2 shows.

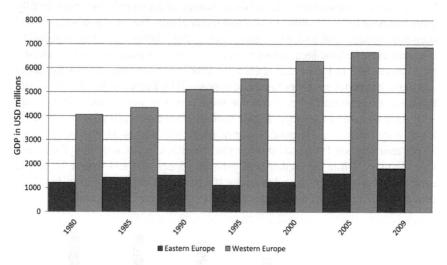

Figure 2.2   Eastern European and Western European GDP at 1995 USD billion

If we look at individual countries, however, a rather different picture emerges. The decline was very sharp indeed in some places, and the recovery has never really taken place. Elsewhere, the economy grew rather quickly in the last few years of twentieth century, as Figure 2.3 shows. In some cases, notably Poland, there was a steady rise. In the Russian Federation, there was a sharp and protracted drop, followed by quite a rapid recovery. In other cases, while there was an initial drop, the pace of recovery has been rather slower. The statistics for 2009 are not available at the time of writing, so it is impossible to give an accurate picture of the likely impact of the world crisis, but anecdotal evidence suggests that it has been more severe in most post-communist countries than in the west, with the possible exception of Poland. Despite these differences, however, it is clear that the first twenty years of market economy have not transformed the former communist countries overnight into states enjoying the same levels of prosperity as those in the west.

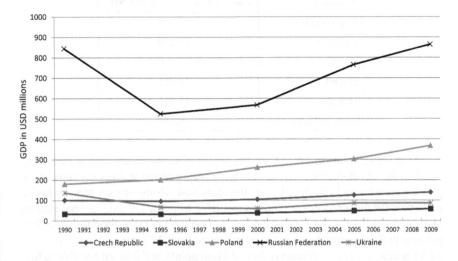

Figure 2.3   GDP of selected countries at 1995 USD billion

The climate within which the media operated in all of these cases was, therefore, a rather unstable one, and one that is likely to be even more unstable in the present economic crisis. All of the media were operating in economies which were, by the standards of the developed world, small and poor, and all of them experienced a decline in real living standards during at least the first part of the period, while for some there was a recovery after the middle of the 1990s. In such circumstances, the overall resources available to the media would thus not be generous, and foreign capital investment would be bound to be attractive as a way of modernising plant and equipment, not to mention management skills. From the point of view of foreign media companies, on the other hand, the small size and poverty of the markets would mean that they were less likely to be attractive to first tier global media players. Of the economies under review, only that of the Russian Federation in any way compares in size even with the Netherlands, and even today (well, at the time of writing, but maybe not on the date of publication) Greece remains a richer market than Poland or Hungary. From the point of view of media consumption, too, the general level of poverty in the region would mean that consumption of media goods would be likely to be at a much lower level, and canted more towards 'free' offering like advertising supported TV, than in the western part of the continent. Even in 2009, as Table 2.1 shows, the per capita income in Poland was still less than 25 per cent of that in the Netherlands. The decline in living standards, too, would be likely to reduce the overall consumption of paid for media products like newspapers and magazines.

Table 2.1   Gross national income per capita, 2009

Country	2009 GNI per capita in USD
Netherlands	46,595
Germany	41,100
Greece	28,209
Poland	10,911
Hungary	12,241
Russian Federation	8,454

On the other hand, however, the rapid degree of social polarization would likely result in the development of niche consumer media aimed at those sections of the population who had benefitted from the transition. Using our six representative countries, the most recent Gini indices available from the United National Human Development Report show a range from 26.9 per cent in Hungary through to 39.9 per cent in Russia, which compares with a range from 28.3 per cent in Germany to 34.3 per cent in Greece. Whatever their starting points, and it is not possible to find equivalent figures for the pre-1999 period, the fact is that today these countries display the same kinds of income inequality as do those of Western Europe, and might be expected to display at least some of the niche publications present there. High-quality magazines catering for the wealthy reader, for example, would likely proliferate, and be well-supported by advertising, whereas general interest newspapers would find it harder to stay solvent.

The old system of media finance depended largely on the political allocation of resources. In almost all cases after 1989 there was a move towards the familiar western system, based on the combination of direct payments and advertising support. While there appears to be no direct relationship between the amount of advertising expenditure and the size or wealth of an economy, it is approximately the case that a richer economy will spend a higher proportion of it national income on advertising, and even more clearly have a higher per capita expenditure. If we compare the 2007 advertising spend, and advertising spend per capita, for our selected group of countries, we can see very clearly that the level of advertising spending is much lower than that prevailing in Western Europe.

The numbers in Table 2.2[2] give us two slightly different pictures, but they are clearly illuminating the same situation. The dollar expenditure figures are at contemporary (January 2009) exchange rates. These give a picture of the absolute magnitude of the advertising expenditure in each country. A better guide to the magnitude of advertising expenditure inside the country is given by the dollar figures adjusted for Purchasing Power Parities. Both sets of figures clearly

---

2   The source for Table 2.2 and Figures 2.4, 2.5, 2.6, 2.7 and 2.8 is the World Advertising Research Centre (2011).

demonstrate that expenditure in the region is much lower than in Western Europe. Even adjusted for local conditions, therefore, the media of the region are operating with much smaller budgets than those of the West.

Table 2.2   Comparative advertising expenditure in USD

Country	2007 expenditure in USD millions	Per capita in USD 2009	Per capita at PPP 2007
Germany	23,074	276	251
Netherlands	5,215	319	278
Greece	2,555	230	247
Poland	2,095	54	96
Hungary	881	87	144
Russian Federation	6,753	47	N/A

The distribution of advertising expenditure is also rather different from that in the larger economies of the West. Figures 2.4 and 2.5 compare the proportions of expenditure by different categories for Germany, Poland, Greece and Hungary. It is clear that Germany (which is closer to the Western European norm) differs from the other three in that newspaper advertising is the largest single category of expenditure. In the other three cases, it is television that is the largest, and in two of the three cases, Greece and Hungary, magazine publishing accounts for a greater proportion of advertising revenue than do newspapers, while in the third, Poland, it is of a comparable size. In Germany, newspapers account for more than twice as much advertising expenditure than do magazines. Interestingly, Poland and Hungary both have a slightly greater proportion of Internet advertising than does Germany, with Greece lagging a long way behind.

Table 2.3 gives a more detailed breakdown for the distribution of Polish advertising expenditure over the last decade. As one would expect, given the steady growth of the whole economy during the period, there is a steady growth in advertising expenditure, both in total and in all areas. In point of fact, in money terms, advertising expenditure grew by 226 per cent during the period up to 2007, while the whole economy grew by 93 per cent. Over the shorter period of 2006–2007 the growth of the gross domestic product was 9.7 per cent (6.5 per cent in real terms), while that of advertising was slightly larger in money terms, at 10.5 per cent.

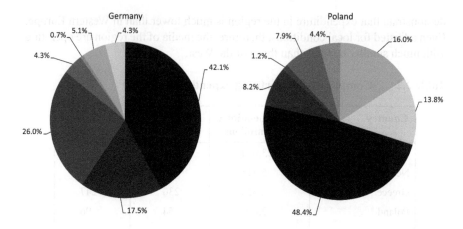

Figure 2.4   Comparison of advertising expenditure: Germany and Poland, 2007

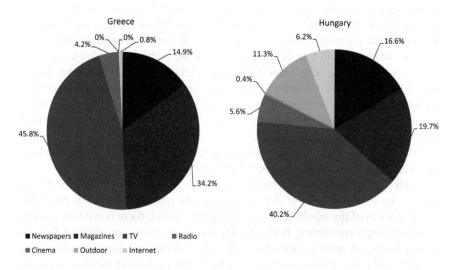

Figure 2.5   Comparison of advertising expenditure: Greece and Hungary, 2007

Table 2.3   Polish advertising expenditure in Polish Zlotys

Year	Total	Newspapers	Magazine	Television	Radio	Cinema	Outdoor	Internet
1998	2,174	294	304	1,438	134	3	-	-
1999	3,120	333	459	1,862	172	4	290	-
2000	3,502	435	521	1,992	190	8	340	16
2001	4,340	462	581	2,701	216	14	342	24
2002	4,533	467	580	2,837	264	13	340	33
2003	4,696	497	643	2,852	319	29	306	50
2004	5,216	627	766	2,904	378	38	415	87
2005	5,901	876	892	3,031	432	53	470	148
2006	6,417	961	973	3,153	510	65	541	215
2007	7,375	1,135	978	3,435	582	86	559	599
2008	8,092	1,148	991	3,678	633	125	624	893
% change 07/08	9.7%	1.1%	1.3%	7.1%	8.7%	44.5%	11.6%	48.9%

In this relatively short historical perspective, it appears that the balance between newspaper and television advertising is shifting in the favour of the former. In 1998, newspaper advertising expenditure was 13.5 per cent of the total, and 25 per cent of that of television, but by 2007 it had reached 16 per cent of the total and stood at 33 per cent of television expenditure. The rise in Internet advertising is another obvious feature of this time series, although does not as yet appear to be at the expense of newspapers.

Overall, we can say that advertising expenditure in the region is rising rapidly, although from a very low base, and it still remains extremely small by Western European standards. The current economic crisis may alter this pattern, at least in the short term, since advertising expenditure is normally cyclical, but the trend is unlikely to be altered. The pattern of expenditure is heavily skewed towards television and away from the press. In this, the countries examined display a closer relationship to the patterns observed in Greece, and perhaps more generally in Southern Europe, than to the large economies of the Northwest of the continent. In all of these cases, magazines receive a surprisingly large share of the market, and in at least some cases the Internet is winning a rapidly increasing proportion.

Causes and Consequences

As indicated above, the heavy concentration on television advertising can be explained by the novelty of the market economy and the relative poverty of the region. In a developed market economy, newspaper advertising has as its staples in real estate, jobs and automobiles. These all depend upon a mature and highly fragmented advertising market. They stand in contrast to the mass advertising that dominates television, and which depends upon the actions of few large companies and agencies. In the former communist countries, the market for classified advertisements remained in the early stages of development, while mass advertising was much more easily promoted.[3]

The same factors, and notably that of relatively low average incomes, explains the importance of television in the ways in which people interact with the media since free to air television is one of the most cost-effective leisure activities. As Figure 2.6 demonstrates, we once again find the pattern of a difference between the richer North Western countries and the poorer ones in the South and East.

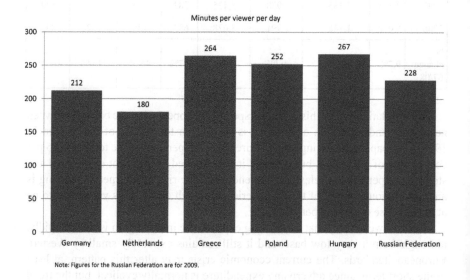

Minutes per viewer per day

Note: Figures for the Russian Federation are for 2009.

Figure 2.6   Television viewing in selected countries, 2010

Note: Figures for the Russian Federation are for 2009

---

3   We should also note that the rise in internet advertising expenditure suggests that newspapers in the region will never experience the golden age that their cousins in Europe and the USA enjoyed for more than half a century. As the classified advertising market develops, so it will also flow increasingly to the internet.

The figures for daily newspaper consumption are more fragmentary, and tend to vary erratically from year to year. They are thus of more dubious reliability, but those that are available are presented in Figure 2.7. As is evident, they tend to support the relative balance with television that we have noted above. The average circulation density is again fragmentary but it, too, gives a picture of a large gap between North Western Europe and the South and East. In this case, however, it is clear from Figure 2.8 that the evidence to support the bipolar model seems very much weaker, since circulation in Greece is proportionately far lower relative to Poland and Hungary than they are to Germany and the Netherlands. It is clear that this distinction cannot be easily accommodated within any model that is based on high level economic factors alone. The daily reach of newspapers, on the other hand, fits the model rather better: 75 per cent of Germans and 74 per cent of Netherlanders see a daily paper, while for Greece the figure is 60 per cent, for Hungary 51 per cent and for Poland 35 per cent.

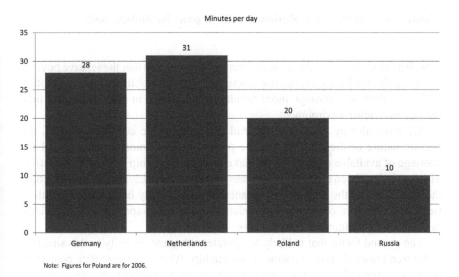

Note: Figures for Poland are for 2006.

Figure 2.7   Daily newspaper consumption, 2008

Note: Figures for Poland are for 2006

These overall constraints form the framework within which the micro-economics of the media industries work themselves out. Although these have been most fully developed in the study of western media systems, there should be few differences of principle between them and the former communist countries, since in both cases we are considering what are today more or less market economies. True, there are important legacies from the communist past at the economic level

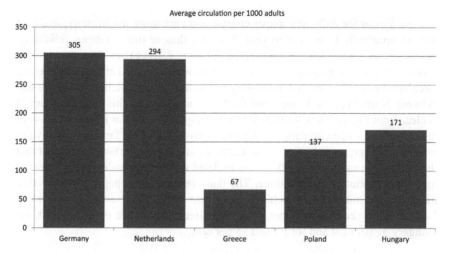

Figure 2.8   Average circulation density of paid-for dailies, 2005

as well as elsewhere, but the main difference is likely to be that the relative poverty of the media landscape means that some of the well-established laws of motion will work their way through more rapidly and intensely in such a scenario than they do in a richer environment.

We have already noted that the end of the autarchic economic system, the chaotic nature of the transition in the printed press in most countries, and the shortage of available capital, would make foreign ownership extremely attractive. This has indeed been the case, in all areas of the mass media, although as we noted the small sizes of the markets has meant that it has mostly been second and third tier media organizations that have purchased or set up newspapers and magazines, or established commercial broadcasters.

The second factor that is likely to operate with great intensity in this situation is the trend towards concentration of ownership. While the immediate post-1989 period was marked by an enormous flourishing of print publications, the small size of the market meant that most of them were doomed from the start, irrespective of their orientation. In fact, the survivors appear in general to be the larger and better funded titles inherited from the old regime, with only one or two of the oppositional titles which were either founded or emerged from illegality in the period after 1989. The new entrants into the market that have been successful have tended to be launched by larger and more established companies, very often foreign owned and introducing new editorial policies designed to fill empty market niches. The most obviously successful of these have been the new 'tabloid' titles which have won a considerable market share in the countries in which they have been launched. While the established 'political' press appears to be experiencing some decline in circulation, in common with titles across the continent and in the USA, the 'tabloids' are growing in circulation.

The result of these different developments is that in a number of countries the situation in the press market corresponds to what is technically known as oligopolistic competition, although it appears to be evolving towards monopolistic competition. In the former situation, a small number of firms dominate the market and compete on the basis of product differentiation. In the latter case, they have fully differentiated their products so as to be the sole occupants of a particular niche sub-market. One would expect the former situation to be sustainable in conditions of an expanding market, but the pressures would remain strong given the relative poverty of the countries in question. Certainly, any contraction in the market would be extremely likely to lead to one firm coming to dominate a particular niche, whether defined geographically, socially or in terms of editorial orientation.

Towards Some Conclusions

If we try to bring these political and economic factors together, we obtain a picture of media operating in small and poor markets, where there is intense competition for resources. In addition, the 'titles' to media properties are almost all very recent and are the result primarily of political, rather than economic, factors. In situations of intense competition, it is commonplace for enterprises to seek political support of one kind or another in order to improve their relative competitive position: this is a general form of what some economists term 'rent seeking.' On the other hand, the manifest political element in the distribution of ownership means that this dimension is transparently contestable. If one government gives property rights to one set of people, then why should not another government take them away and grant them to another set?

The interaction of politics and economics thus means that, whatever the intentions of owners or employees, the mass media in post-communist countries are likely both to be highly politicized and highly partisan. Their current owners can only defend their property through political means, and they can improve their survival chances in the market by seeking political protection. It is therefore entirely understandable that the mass media would seek to align themselves with political factions, that they would develop forms of journalism that seek to discredit their opponents, that they would put the interests of their faction far above any notional 'public interest' and so on. In those cases, like state broadcasting, it is entirely understandable that a change of government would most often mean a change in the personnel who run the company: again, party interest trumps public interest.

There is a strong temptation to bewail these realities. This note is frequently struck by the adherents of the 'democratization' thesis, who regard the widespread examples of party politicization as pathological symptoms of a disease that needs to be cured, through re-educating journalists in western practices, through enjoining politicians to behave themselves, through enforcing legal changes that enshrine EU principles in statutes regulating broadcasting, and so on. The fact that these remedies have been applied in a host of countries over the last two decades without producing the desired result should give their supporters pause for thought. Perhaps these are not pathological symptoms of a disease but evidence of a 'normal' response to specific conditions?

To say that these obvious features of post-communist media systems are 'normal' is not say that they are desirable. On the contrary, they are very bad indeed judged from the standpoint of the narrowest Schumpeterian concepts of democracy, and very much worse from the far broader concept that this author would much prefer to see institutionalized. From any perspective, the original desire to have newspapers like the *New York Times* and broadcasters like the BBC, was a preferable outcome to any that has transpired in the region. But while normative judgements have their place, they are not a substitute for understanding why and how the conditions that exist in the media of the former communist countries take the form that they do. The question that requires an answer concerns what conditions actually do exist, not what kinds of media ideally should exist.

In order to answer those questions, it is the argument of this chapter, we need to move away from the narrowly political concentration upon democratization. In order for the kinds of media that so many commentators believe would be desirable to flourish, certain political and economic conditions are necessary, and these either do not pertain, or are only present in embryo, in the region. Looked at from a political economic perspective, we can say that the central realities of the countries in question concern a struggle between different sections of the elite, both generally and in the media, over extremely scarce resources. This elite is divided amongst itself, and in general enjoys fragile and uncertain legitimacy. The media are both a weapon in the 'horizontal' struggle within the elite, used to promote allies and discredit opponents, and a weapon in the 'vertical' struggle to convince the mass of the population that political power can no longer be expected resolve many of the most pressing questions of daily life and, to the extent that the people have a say in the composition of the political elite, to promote support for this or that faction.

References

Garnham, N. 1990. *Capitalism and Communication: Global Culture and the Economics of Information*. London: Sage Publications.

Golding, P. and Murdock, G. 1991. Culture, communications and political economy, in *Mass Media and Society*, edited by James Curran and Michael Gurevitch. London: Edward Arnold, 15–32.

Herman, E. and Chomsky, N. 2008. *Manufacturing Consent: The Political Economy of the Mass Media*, anniversary edition. London: The Bodley Head

Hoskins, C., McFadyen, S. and Finn, A. 2004. *Media Economics: Applying Economics to New and Traditional Media*. London: Sage Publications.

Lukács, G. 1971. *History and Class Consciousness*. London: Merlin.

McChesney, R. 2007. *Communication Revolution: Critical Junctures and the Future of the Media*. New York: The New Press.

Mosco, V. 1996. *The Political Economy of Communication*. London: Sage.

Mosco, V. 2009. *The Political Economy of Communication*. 2nd Edition. London: Sage.

Murdock, G. and Golding, P. 1974. For a political economy of mass communications. *Socialist Register*, 10, 205–34.

UN Statistics Division. 2011. *National Accounts Main Aggregate Database*. Available at: http://unstats.un.org/unsd/snaama/introduction.asp [accessed 13 June 2011].

World Advertising Research Centre. 2011. Available at: http://www.warc.com.ezproxy.westminster.ac.uk/LandingPages/Data/Default.asp [accessed 13 June 2011].

Chapter 3

Between Segmentation and Integration: Media Systems and Ethno-cultural Diversity in Central and Eastern Europe

Sabina Mihelj

It does not take much to show that the contemporary media landscapes in Eastern and Western Europe alike are not congruent with the physical geography of nation-states. The media systems of individual countries are typically segmented along cultural lines, and are often characterized by significant regional variation. In many cases, two or more distinct, sometimes territorially circumscribed and even linguistically diverse media systems coexist within the same state. Europe's 'stateless nations' – the Catalans, the Welsh, the Scots – are tuned into a 'dual' communicative sphere, one limited to the nation itself, the other encompassing the whole state population (Schlesinger 2009). In countries such as Switzerland, Belgium or Bosnia and Herzegovina the internal segmentation is so pronounced that it seems difficult to see what, if anything, ties the different sub-state spheres of communication together (Bašić Hrvatin et al. 2008). Even in culturally most homogeneous states, the unity of communication, culture and polity is continuously disrupted by satellite television and the Internet, as well as by the flows of transnational migration and diasporic media (e.g. Kosnick 2007).

In comparative media research, these diverse patterns of cultures, states and media spheres remain largely invisible. For most authors, the only unit of analysis is the nation-state, and even if they do acknowledge that such an approach has its drawbacks, they abstain from addressing the relationship between media systems and cultural diversity in a sustained manner (e.g. Hallin and Mancini 2004: 71–2). However, the problem does not lie simply in using the nation-state as the main unit of analysis. Much more decisive is the neglect of culture and social structure as autonomous factors involved in the shaping of mass communication systems. There is of course no denying that recent research made considerable progress in clarifying the relationships between the modern media and their broader economic, political and social environments and abandoned the narrowly normative focus of early theorizing in this area (see in particular Esser and Pfetsch 2004, Hallin and Mancini 2004, Christians et al. 2009). Still, the vast majority of this recent wave of comparative media research remained limited to the dynamics of either media-politics or media-economy, examining issues such as the level of politicization or political parallelism in the media sector (e.g. Pfetsch 2001), regulation of media content and ownership (e.g. Harcourt 2006), or the impact of commercialization on the nature of news coverage (e.g. Benson and Hallin 2007). In contrast, issues pertaining to cultural and social factors and their impact on the functioning of media systems receive scant attention.

In short, existing comparative studies of media systems treat the media primarily as political and economic actors involved in the formation and circulation of political ideas and economic capital. Yet modern media are far more than that. As James Carey (1989) reminds us, mass communication is aimed not only at the transmission of messages in space, but also at the maintenance of community in time. While imparting information about the political process or promoting goods, the media also shape and consolidate a particular view of the world and a specific form of belonging and exclusion. News, as Michael Schudson argues, should not be seen only 'as the raw material for rational public discourse, but as the public construction of particular images of self, community, and nation' (2003: 69). It follows from this that media systems can be analysed and compared not only with regard to their relationships with the political and economic systems but also with respect to how they engage in community-formation.

One of the key issues to address when examining the involvement of the media in community-building is its relationship to cultural diversity. How do different media systems respond to ethnic and cultural diversity within modern states? What consequences do different approaches to diversity have, particularly for majority-minority relationships and minority participation in democratic processes? These questions cut to the core of contemporary political debates across the West, and are often stimulated by concerns over the alleged failure of integration policies and the alienation of minority populations. For obvious reasons, much of the public and scholarly debate on these issues is normative in character and aimed at evaluating existing policies. Often, solutions that seem to work in one context are assumed to be universally applicable everywhere and are exported as part of democratization packages to social and political environments that may have entirely different needs.

This chapter initially steps back from the normative debate by providing a comparative analysis of available approaches to cultural diversity within the media and the forces that shape them. Instead of looking for a universally valid solution, the chapter sheds light on the historical processes and the demographic, political and economic factors that have contributed to the development of contrasting ways of dealing with diversity, in particular contexts. Once we appreciate these multiple and diverse causes, we may be in a better position to understand why certain policy solutions fare better in some contexts rather than others. Only then might we be able to start asking questions about the steps needed to ensure that the media can make a positive contribution to culturally diverse societies.

The first section of the chapter examines the key historical processes that have necessitated the congruence of polity and culture, and thereby stimulated the rise of nation-states and national public spheres. Despite these processes, cultural diversity is not incompatible with modern states. As historical evidence demonstrates, states have developed a variety of different strategies for dealing with cultural diversity within their borders; while some of these involved the eradication of difference, others were premised on its accommodation. A similar diversity of approaches can be found in the realm of media policy, and the second section of the chapter proposes to distinguish between two main approaches: one involving the development of a segmented media system, the other aimed at establishing an integrated media system. The third and main section of the chapter turns to examining the key domestic and international factors that influence the way a particular state deals with the mediation of cultural difference. While the analysis focuses on selected Central Eastern European states, the analytical framework used has wider applicability.

Responses to Cultural Diversity: Eliminate or Accommodate?

At first sight, the systemic requirements of modern political and economic systems seem to militate against cultural diversity within states. A modern economy requires a mobile population – mobile both socially, in the sense that its members can move across different social occupations and strata, as well as geographically, meaning that they are capable of migrating, should the needs of the occupation so require, from one end of the state to the other. The basic prerequisite for such mobility is a common mass culture, shared both territorially, across all regions and locales of the state, and socially, across different social strata – in short, a national culture that coincides with the limits of the polity (Gellner 1983). It is this shared culture that allows the members of industrialized societies to understand the requirements of their occupation wherever they go, and perform their duties regardless of the region or social environment they find themselves in. Furthermore, shared mass culture also facilitates the growth of commerce, providing the pool of common cultural references to be drawn upon when selling products on a large scale.

The union of polity and culture seems necessary also for the functioning of modern political systems. While earlier forms of political power followed hereditary lines of succession and derived their legitimacy from divine sources, the rule of the modern state was perceived as legitimate only in so far as it was based on the will of 'the people' (Bendix 1964). Although the definitions of 'the people' could differ, they invariably involved a degree of shared culture, at least in the sense of a common commitment to the democratic political process. This common cultural 'glue' proved necessary also for the functioning of modern, functionally differentiated state bureaucracies (Breuilly 1994). It is only such complex, internally differentiated yet unified state apparatuses that could appropriately service the needs of modern societies. Due to profound shifts in the nature of social organization, these needs could no longer be satisfied by poly-functional corporate institutions acting on behalf of religious congregations, guilds or local communities but demanded large-scale, function-specific organizations such as schools, political parties, retail industries and media systems, all of which needed a cohesive bureaucratic framework to operate in a concerted manner.

In short, it is not difficult to see why it makes sense to assume that modern states are internally homogeneous and treat them as nation-states. Yet this would mean mistaking what is essentially a political ideal for an accomplished fact. While many modern states have indeed embraced the nation-state ideal as the sole legitimate model of socio-political organization, the persistence of cultural heterogeneity, fuelled by migration flows, have prevented this ideal from being translated fully into reality. We should also keep in mind that the homogenizing processes unleashed by the rise of modern economy and politics often encounter resistance, sometimes provoking disintegration rather than integration. From the centre, the introduction of a common culture and language may well be seen as 'unification', yet when observed from the periphery, the same process can be interpreted as 'cultural invasion' and 'linguistic assimilation' of non-dominant groups and languages, and may lead to the strengthening rather than weakening of cultural differences (Burke 2004: 167; Hroch 2006: 28).

It is instructive to look at the ethnocultural composition of modern states to appreciate just how far most of them are from the nation-state ideal. In 1971, when the term 'nation-state' was already well-entrenched in everyday talk, political debate and scholarly discussion, only about a third of all the states in the world contained a nation that accounted for more than 90 percent of the total population (Connor 1978). Four decades later, little has changed. As a result of the break-up of multinational socialist federations, the total number of would-be nation-states increased, and most of the newly formed states are nationally far more homogeneous than their socialist predecessors. Yet the vast majority still contain at least one significant minority, and only few have a core nation that exceeds 90 per cent of the total population. This is not to say that the nation-state is not a powerful political ideal or that it did not exert influence in its own right. Still, it is important to keep in mind that the nation-state is only one of the available modern responses to cultural diversity, and that even when adopted, it remains an unfinished project (Chernilo 2007).

In other words, cultural diversity is here to stay and modern states have no other choice but to cope with it. Historically, states have responded to the challenge of diversity in a variety of ways. It is worth pausing for a moment to consider the full range of these different strategies before looking specifically at those that are most common in contemporary Europe. John McGarry and Brendan O'Leary (1993) proposed to distinguish between two broad categories of ethnic conflict regulation. The first includes policy options aimed at eradicating or at least minimising difference, ranging from genocide and mass population transfer to secession or partition and different forms of assimilation or integration. The other comprises strategies for 'managing' difference, such as various forms of territorial autonomy including federalism, different types of non-territorial (or cultural) autonomy including consociationalism, and the establishment of hegemonic control or 'majority rule', whereby one ethno-cultural group assumes control over others and makes any challenge to its authority unthinkable.

Many of these strategies are of course considered illegitimate and indefensible, and the vast majority of contemporary observers and policymakers tend to advocate one of the following options: federalism or territorial autonomy; consociationalism or cultural autonomy; integration or assimilation. Most of the countries in Western Europe have adopted either a federal structure (Belgium, Austria, Germany) or granted selected minorities regional autonomy (Italy, Spain, United Kingdom, Finland, Portugal, Denmark), while Eastern European countries have largely opted for a form of integration or assimilation, or a limited level of cultural autonomy, though cases of consociational power-sharing exist as well, for instance in Bosnia and Herzegovina and Macedonia (cf. Liebich 2007: 36; Bieber 2004).

Mediating Cultural Diversity: Between Integration and Segmentation

A compatible range of responses to cultural diversity can be found also in the realm of mass communication. Much as in the case of state building, the ideal of cultural homogeneity was a goal pursued by media policies in many countries, but this proved impossible to achieve and sustain over the long term. The construction of internally homogeneous communicative spheres, congruent with state boundaries, had to give way to more complex configurations of culture, state and communication. Looking at the media landscape of contemporary Europe, we can distinguish between two main types of responses to cultural diversity: one involves the establishment of a segmented media system, divided along ethno-cultural lines, while the other aims at integrating provisions for different cultural groups into the mainstream media system (Table 3.1).

Table 3.1   Media systems and cultural diversity

Segmented media system	Integrated media system
• Fully fledged parallel media systems, complete with periodical press, radio, television and internet websites catering for different cultural groups. • Quantity and range of minority content comparatively large. • Audience preferences follow ethno-cultural lines. • Public and commercial minority media.	• Minority content provided mostly within the framework of mainstream media (esp. radio, television). Separate minority publications. • Quantity and range of minority content comparatively small. • Little evidence of audience segmentation along ethno-cultural lines. • Mostly publicly funded minority content.

A segmented media system typically comprises one or more parallel, fully-fledged media systems, complete with the periodic press, radio, and television as well as internet websites, each catering for a particular ethno-cultural group. Consequently, the quantity and range of minority content tends to be relatively large.

Audience preferences vary significantly with ethnicity, which creates commercial incentives for ethnically-specific media content even if its production is not directly encouraged by the state. Typical examples of such media systems can be found in long-established multinational and multilingual media systems such as those of Switzerland and Belgium, but also in more recently 'devolved' Western democracies such as the United Kingdom and Spain. For instance, the Swiss Broadcasting Corporation established its three national transmitters – French, German and Italian – in the early 1930s, later adding regular programmes in Romansch, with an analogous development taking place in the realm of television from the late 1950s (Erk 2003). Belgian broadcasting history is similarly linguistically diversified, and resulted in separate radio and television services for the three main language communities: Flemish, French and German (Jongen et al. 2005).

Examples of segmented media systems are found also in Eastern Europe. For example, the broadcasting landscape of Bosnia and Herzegovina is clearly along ethnocultural lines. Audience preferences largely follow the ethnic key as well (Jusić and Džihana 2008). Media systems in Estonia and Macedonia fit the same pattern. Each includes a range of public and commercial broadcast media aimed respectively at Estonians and Russians, and Macedonians and Albanians. In both countries, audience research confirms that ethnicity remains a key factor affecting media use (Vihalemm 2006; Šopar 2008: 128–32).

Integrated media systems differ significantly from the ones just surveyed. Here, minority content is provided primarily within the framework of mainstream or majority media, for example in the form of daily or weekly broadcasts of special programmes, often in minority languages, aimed at members of individual ethnic or cultural minorities. Separate minority media do exist, but are mostly limited to print publications and websites, or to very narrow, local audiences. The range and quantity of minority content is comparatively small and mostly publicly funded. A typical example of such a media system can be found in Sweden, where broadcast minority content is produced mostly within the framework of the Swedish public broadcaster, the public access 'open channels', the non-commercial community radio stations, and to some extent also within commercial local television (Camauër 2002: 15–21). Although the latter two technically constitute separate minority media, their reach is far too limited to generate anything resembling a segmented media system. On the whole, minority media rely primarily on state subsidies and the degree of commercialization is low (Camauër 2003).

The broad contours of the German media system are similar, although the provision of media programming for its largest, Turkish, minority has been growing steadily over time. In particular, the media landscape in Berlin has become increasingly segmented, with not only a host of Turkish-language minority publications but also separate commercial radio and TV channels broadcasting in Turkish twenty-four hours a day. However, survey data suggest that German Turkish audiences, especially younger and middle-aged ones, prefer a mixed diet of both German and Turkish media, which indicates that the ethnic segmentation of media markets remains limited (Mushaben 2008: 75). Also, apart from Turkish media, minority media produced in Germany are limited primarily to print publications and to weekly or daily programmes produced by publicly funded multicultural broadcasters (Raiser 2002).

A few qualifications are in order before we proceed. First, most media systems include elements of both the segmented and the integrated system. This is due to the fact that minority media provisions usually differ significantly from group to group. As the case of German Turks in Berlin attests, it is possible for a semi-segmented media system to exist at local level, despite the fact that the state-wide media system is predominantly integrated. Vice versa, segmented media systems will typically also include a layer of 'integrated' minority programming within mainstream media, directed at more recently formed immigrant communities. For instance, different branches of the Belgian public broadcasting system sporadically produce weekly or monthly ethnic minority programming aimed at Moroccan, Turkish, Italian and other minority audiences, and some programming of similar kind is occasionally offered also by commercial broadcasters (Ormond 2002: 103–6).

Towards an Explanation: Factors Affecting the Mediation of Cultural Diversity in Central and Eastern Europe

How can we explain these diverse approaches to the mediation of cultural diversity in Europe? What are the key factors that can help understand why a segmented media model is adopted in one case, while an integrated model prevails in another? A useful starting point is provided in Bernd Rechel's (2009: 5) overview of domestic and international factors influencing domestic minority policies in Eastern Europe. Domestic factors include ethnic composition, minority representation, historical legacies, nation-building and use of nationalism by political elites, state capacity, party constellations and popular attitudes toward minorities. Among international factors Rechel lists kin states, the EU and various other international inter-governmental bodies, including the Council of Europe, NATO and the UN, as well as international nongovernmental organizations and bilateral actors.

Since media systems form integral parts of every society, many of the factors influencing the shaping of domestic minority policies will also have an effect on the structure and functioning of media systems. Often, this influence will be exerted through minority policies themselves, for instance in cases where a state amends its minority provisions as a consequence of foreign intervention or mediation, and these new provisions include e.g. minority media subsidies, quotas for minority participation in media governance, or a certain level and type of support for particular minorities. At other times, the influence will not be dependent solely on policy changes. For instance, the size and structure of the minority population is likely to be an autonomous factor regardless of legal provisions.

Comparative research on political communication suggests that larger media markets are more likely to be compatible with external pluralism, i.e. with a range of different media outlets reflecting different opinions (Hallin and Mancini 2004: 47–8). In contrast, smaller media markets tend to be characterized by internal pluralism, i.e. by different points of view being represented within each individual media institution, or suffer from a lack of pluralism. We can therefore expect that larger minorities will be capable of sustaining a greater range of minority media, and thus potentially give voice to a wider array of minority opinions, even without support from the state. In contrast, smaller minorities will be more dependent on state funding and unless that is substantial, will probably have access to a limited range of minority media, which in turn will be more likely to provide a rather homogeneous portrayal of the minority and its views.

In addition to factors listed by Rechel we should include a number of those that are of particular importance to the media sector. Especially in cases where the minority population is large, the presence of kin-state media is likely to play an important role in the shaping of the media system. If the popularity of satellite television among minority audiences is provoking anxieties over integration, as for instance in the case of Turks in Germany (Aksoy and Robins 2000), its presence may stimulate greater levels of state support for domestically produced minority media. At the same time, however, the presence of satellite channels can also make it harder for domestically produced media to attract audiences and generate sufficient advertising revenue. Other important international factors include international civil society organizations interested in promoting freedom of expression and information, such as the International Federation of Journalists, Reporters Sans Frontiers or the Open Society Institute with its Media Program. Finally, we should also take into account factors internal to the media system, such as the availability of appropriate distribution networks for minority media, technical equipment, and trained minority journalists and media producers. Figure 3.1 provides a schematic overview of these various factors.

To examine the relative influence of each of these factors, we will look at seven Central and East European countries: Bulgaria, Bosnia and Herzegovina, Estonia, Hungary, Macedonia, Poland and Slovenia. While Bosnia and Herzegovina, Estonia and Macedonia all have a segmented media system, the media systems of Poland and Hungary, Slovenia and Bulgaria are predominantly integrated. However, in the latter three, there is some evidence of a segmented system developing for particular communities at local level. In the case of Slovenia, a fairly wide range of Italian language media exists, including a TV and radio channel as well as several print publications, all limited to the coastal region, and sustained and funded in collaboration with neighbouring Croatia (Petković 2006: 676–8). In Bulgaria, some evidence of local segmentation is evident in the province of Vidin, where a Roma TV station was established in 1998 (Zlatev 2006: 250). In Hungary, a separate Roma news agency has operated since 1995, and a local radio station targeting the Roma population was established in Budapest in 2001 (Bauer, T.A. and Vujović 2006: 352–5).

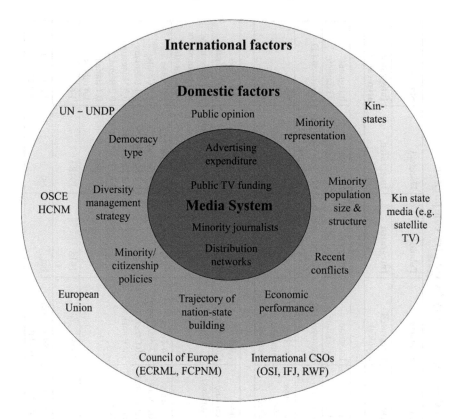

Figure 3.1   Factors affecting the mediation of cultural diversity in Central and Eastern Europe

Source: Adapted from Rechel 2009: 5

The selected countries vary significantly with respect to many of the factors that are thought to affect the mediation of cultural diversity (Table 3.2). The remainder of this section examines each of the factors to assess how important its influence is in determining the responses to cultural diversity within the media system.

Table 3.2   Factors affecting the mediation of cultural diversity – country by country comparison

	Macedonia	Bosnia and Herzegovina	Estonia	Bulgaria	Poland	Hungary	Slovenia
Prevailing media system type	Segmented	Segmented	Segmented	Integrated - atypical	Integrated	Integrated	Integrated - atypical
Domestic factors – politics							
Diversity management strategy	Accommodate	Accommodate	Integrate/Assimilate	Integrate/Assimilate	Integrate/Assimilate	Integrate/Assimilate	Integrate/Assimilate
Type of democracy[1]	CD	CD	Improved ED	Improved ED	LD with elements of ED and CD	LD with elements of ED and CD	Improved ED
Minority legislation: 'traditional' minorities privileged	Yes	Yes	No: all groups over 3000 recognised	No: linguistic minorities recognised only	Yes	Yes	Yes
Domestic factors – demography and history							
Total population	2,022.540 (2002 census)	4,590.310 (2008 estimate)	1,360.000 (2001 census)	7,928.901 (2001 census)	38,230.080 (2002 census)	10,198.315 total (2001 census)	1,964.036 (2002 census)
Ethnic majority (or constituent groups), % of total population	64.2 Macedonian	48.0 Bosniaks, 37.1 Serbs, 14.3 Croats	68.1 Estonians	83.9 Bulgarians	96.7 Poles	92.3 Hungarians	83.1 Slovenians (8.9 unknown or undeclared)
Minority population size and structure, % of total population	25.2 Albanians 3.9 Turks 2.7 Roma 1.8 Serbs 0.8 Bosnians 0.3 Vlachs 1.7 others	1.0 Roma	25.7 Russians 2.1 Ukrainians 1.3 Byelorussian 0.8 Finns 1.7 others	9.4 Turks 4.7 /9.0 Roma[1] 1.0 Other 3.0 Pomaks[1]	1.2 Others	1.9–5.5 Roma 0.6 Germans 0.2 Slovaks 0.2 Romanian 0.2 Croats 0.2 others	2.0 Serbs 1.8 Croats 1.1 Bosnians 0.3 Hungarians 0.2 Roma 0.1 Italians 1.4 others
Continuous independent statehood from	1991	1991	1991	1908	1918	1918	1991
Recent inter-ethnic conflict or tensions	2001 tensions, Ohrid Agreement	1992–95 Yugoslav Wars	1989 Singing Revolution	1989 Turkish exodus	No	No	1991 Short armed conflict

	Macedonia	Bosnia and Herzegovina	Estonia	Bulgaria	Poland	Hungary	Slovenia
Domestic factors – economy and popular attitudes							
% uncomfortable with Roma neighbours[2]	-	-	28%	36%	12%	20%	24%
% uncomfortable with diff. ethnicity elected[3]	-	-	21%	32%	12%	28%	21%
GDP (PPP) per capita in USD, 1999–2008[4]	6,855	7,325	8,174	12,859	16,626	14,435	20,748
Funding of public TV per capita in EUR[5]	7.8 (2004)	-	9.9 (2004)	3.2 (2004)	10.9 (2004)	15 (2003/04)	56.6 (2003)
Advertising expenditure per capita in EUR, 2003[6]	21.8	3.9	74.3	24.3	36.8	138.5	139.5
International factors							
Kin-state neighbour perceived as a threat	Yes: Albania	Yes: Serbia, Croatia	Yes: Russia	No	No	No – Hungary itself a kin state	No
Kin-state media	Yes: Albanian/ Kosovar	Yes: Serbian and Croatia	Yes: Russian	Not significant	Not significant	Not significant	Not significant
International mediation in ethnic conflicts	Yes: Ohrid Agreement 2001	Yes: Dayton Accords 1995	No	No	No	No	No
EU membership	Candidate	-	Member 2004	Member 2007	Member 2004	Member 2004	Member 2004
CE ECRML – signing/ entry into force[7]	1996/ -	2005/ expected	-	-	2003/ expected	1992/ 1998	1997/ 2001
CE FCPNM– signing/ entry into force[8]	1996/ 1998	2000/ 2000	1995/ 1998	1997/ 1999	1995/ 2001	1995/ 1998	1995/ 1998

Notes and sources: 1. CD – consociational democracy, ED – ethnic democracy, LD – liberal democracy; 2. and 3. Eurobarometer (2008), data from 2007; 4. 10-year average (1999–2008) based on International Monetary Fund data; 5. and 6. Based on absolute figures provided in EUMAP 2005: 169–70 and 174 respectively; 7. Council of Europe – European Charter for Regional or Minority Languages (ECRML), status as of January 2009; 8. Council of Europe – Framework Convention for the Protection of National Minorities (FCPNM), status as of January 2009

Political Factors

The characteristics of the political system – the type of democracy, the prevailing approach to cultural diversity, and the specificities of minority legislation – seem an obvious place to start. As we have discussed the different approaches to cultural diversity earlier, for the purpose of this analysis we will retain only the most basic distinction between: (a) strategies aimed at integration or assimilation; and (b) strategies based on accommodation, which include either consociationalism or some form of territorial autonomy. Some analysts find it important to distinguish between integration and assimilation, arguing that the former involves recognition and accommodation of cultural differences within common institutions, while the latter is intent on developing a culture-blind state infrastructure (e.g. Kymlicka and Norman 2000: 14). It is indeed true that important differences exist between the two strategies. However, for the purpose of this chapter, this distinction is of marginal importance, and we will therefore treat the two strategies under a common heading.

A closely related aspect of the political system to consider is the type of democracy, or more precisely, the relative balance of individual and collective rights within the democratic system, as evident from citizenship legislation. Literature on the topic distinguishes between four types of democracy: (a) liberal democracy, which recognizes only individual rights, (b) multicultural democracy, which recognizes collective rights but avoids their political institutionalization at sub-state level; (c) consociational democracy, which recognizes collective rights as well as institutionalises them, and does so equally for all groups involved; and (d) ethnic democracy, which also recognizes as well as institutionalizes collective rights yet gives only one of the groups – the majority – full collective rights, while other groups are not recognized at all or are guaranteed a more limited range of collective rights (Smooha 2004). In terms of approaches to cultural diversity, liberal, multicultural and ethnic democracy are likely to be compatible with a strategy of integration or assimilation, while consociational democracy by definition involves a strategy of accommodation.

In the early 1990s, all of the seven countries in our sample shared at least some features of ethnic democracies. The privileging of one ethnic group was not immediately visible from the key citizenship laws or constitutional documents themselves but typically surfaced in constitutional preambles, requirements for naturalization, special provisions for co-ethnics living abroad, etc. (cf. Hayden 1992, Liebich 2007: 24–31). Two of the countries also opted for solutions that effectively deprived many minority members of citizenship: Russians in Estonia and former Yugoslav immigrants in Slovenia (Järve 2004; Zorn 2009). Still, none of the countries was able to consolidate fully its ethnic democracy. In the case of Bosnia and Herzegovina and Macedonia, internal conflict and ethnic cleansing provoked international intervention, ultimately leading to the adoption of consociational democracy (cf. Bieber 2004). Estonia, Slovenia and Bulgaria all gradually improved the level of minority protection and offered an extended range of cultural rights to minorities that were initially excluded from such provisions. As a consequence, they all approach what Smooha describes as the 'improved ethnic democracy', i.e. an ethnic democracy within which minorities are accorded a higher level of collective rights, including a degree of political representation (Smooha 2004: 34)

In Poland and Hungary, the features of ethnic democracy were relatively weak already in the early 1990s, and largely limited to special provisions for co-ethnics in neighbouring countries. Hungary also introduced a comprehensive system of minority protection in 1993, which offers its traditional minorities both self-government and cultural autonomy (Vizi 2009), while Poland introduced a similar system in 2005. It should, of course, be noted that both countries limit minority rights to groups specifically defined in legislation, and that the discrimination against the Roma in Hungary continues. Apart from that, however, both countries come close to the ideal type of liberal democracy, and it is therefore appropriate to treat them as liberal democracies with elements of ethnic and consociational democracy.

It certainly appears that there are some clear parallels between media systems and political systems: a segmented media system seems more likely to appear in consociational democracies and countries that have opted for a strategy of accommodation, i.e. Bosnia and Herzegovina and Macedonia. However, this does not apply in the case of Estonia, where a segmented media system is in place within the context of a unitary state. Also, on closer inspection, it becomes clear that institutionalized forms of autonomy or power sharing in both Bosnia and Herzegovina and Macedonia came only *after* a segmented media system was already in place. We can thus conclude that segmented media systems are indeed more likely to be found in countries that adopted consociationalism, federalism or territorial autonomy, yet that these particular forms of diversity management do not constitute a necessary condition for the development of a segmented media system.

While political factors cannot explain the variation *between* the two types of media systems, they can be useful when accounting for variation *within* each of them and, in particular, when explaining the unequal support provided for different minority groups within the same state. Particularly important in this respect are minority policies and especially the official definitions and categorizations of minorities in a particular country. Most countries in the sample grant minority rights only to a limited number of minorities, which tend to be categorized as 'traditional' or 'autochthonous'. Most of these minorities were created by the shifting of borders and incorporation of ethnically mixed territories rather than by immigration and are seen as being entitled to a greater range of minority provisions.

For instance, Poland's Minority Law, adopted in 2005, recognizes 13 minorities, distinguishing between those who have an external homeland – Germans, Belarussians, Ukrainians, Russians, Lithuanians, Slovaks, Jews, Armenians, Czechs, Tatars – and those who do not – Roma, Karaites, Lemkos (Vermeersch 2003: 177n). While ethnic minorities are granted linguistic and cultural rights, national minorities also enjoy special electoral rights, including a lower electoral threshold (Dembinska 2008: 921). Most importantly, the law does not recognize the country's largest minority, the Silesians, since its language is considered insufficiently distinct (ibid.: 922). Also left without recognition are the more recently established immigrant minorities, such as the Chinese and the Vietnamese.

The situation in Poland is far from unique. Slovenia, Hungary, Bosnia and Herzegovina and Macedonia also provide more support for designated 'traditional' minorities than the more recently established immigrant communities (Zorn 2009, Vize 2009, Čićak and Hamzić 2006, Bieber 2004). Bulgaria does not recognize ethnic minorities per se, but only 'citizens whose mother tongue is not Bulgarian', which effectively prevents the recognition of those groups – such as Pomaks – who may regard themselves as a separate ethnic group yet do not share a separate language (Rechel 2007: 355–6). Among the seven countries, only Estonia grants cultural autonomy equally to all minorities larger than 3000, though even in this case, this right is extended also to specified historical minorities that were fairly large in the past but whose numbers have subsequently fallen below the specified threshold (Lagerspetz 2007: 92–3).

Demographic and Historical Factors

Among demographic factors, the size and structure of minority population is particularly important. As evident from Table 3.2, states with largest minority populations, composed of one or more proportionally large ethnic groups (Macedonia, Bosnia and Herzegovina and Estonia), have segmented media systems, while those with ethnic minority populations smaller than 20 per cent of the total population (Hungary, Poland, Slovenia, Bulgaria), have integrated systems. Countries whose media systems come closest to the ideal-type integrated media system (Hungary and Poland) are also the ones with smallest minority population. We can provide two explanations for such patterns. First, a larger minority population is more likely to constitute a sizeable enough media market to sustain commercially viable media. Second, a large minority group can provide an electoral base for parties seeking to promote an ethnic or multicultural agenda, and seek the institutionalization of minority rights, including provisions for minority media.

Of course, minority size alone cannot always explain why specific minority groups are served by a greater range of media outlets than others. For instance, in Slovenia, one of the smallest minorities (Italians) has access to the greatest range of media outlets, including a TV and radio channel, while the three largest minorities (Croats, Serbs, Bosnians) only have a handful of designated print and on-line outlets (cf. Petković 2006). Similarly, Bulgaria's large Turkish minority, numbering over 740,000 members, has a rather limited array of media resources, and no separate domestically produced broadcast media (cf. Zlatev 2006: 245–53). As indicated earlier, an important factor that helps explain such instances are the countries' minority policies, and in particular their established ways of categorizing minorities and granting official recognition. In addition, however, we need to take into account historical factors and legacies, in particular, the trajectories of nation-building and the treatment of minorities during the socialist period, the presence of recent inter-ethnic conflicts, and the persistence of ethnic prejudice engendered by them. These are often at the root of both demographic characteristics and minority policies as well as media systems' characteristics. Let me briefly demonstrate this for the cases of Bulgaria and Slovenia.

Bulgaria has maintained independent statehood since 1908, yet remained ethnically highly diverse well into the second half of the twentieth century. While initially encouraging cultural diversity, communist Bulgaria later adopted an increasingly assimilationist policy that involved forced adoption of Bulgarian-sounding names and the outlawing of public expressions of Muslim faith. The assimilationist campaign escalated in the 1980s, and provoked a mass exodus of Bulgarian Turks in 1989 (Rechel 2008: 333–4). These extreme forms of ethnic assimilation were later condemned, yet the Bulgarian political mainstream was reluctant to institute any form of protection for minority cultures, and the post-communist constitution even expressly prohibited the formation of ethnic parties. In this context, the Movement for Rights and Freedoms, whose main electoral base was the Turkish minority, was forced to keep its minority demands at a minimum (Rechel 2008: 334). The idea of introducing radio and TV broadcasts in ethnic minority languages as part of mainstream media programming also encountered strong public opposition, and was realized only in 2000 (Nancheva 2007: 381). In sum, although the size of the Turkish population suggests favourable conditions for the establishment of a domestic minority media market, recent ethnic tensions, popular prejudices, and the continued exclusion of ethnic minorities qua minorities from the political process, have prevented its establishment.

A similar conclusion can be reached for the case of Croat, Serb and Bosnian minorities in Slovenia. While they are numerically considerably larger than the Italian and Hungarian minorities, the prejudices formed during the 1980s and exacerbated by the armed conflict in 1991 presented an important obstacle to improvements in the area of minority protection and integration (cf. Komac 2005: 215–28). In contrast, the provisions for the Hungarian and Italian minority, introduced during the socialist period, remained virtually unchanged despite the small size of both populations. One of the reasons for that was the desire to secure protection for co-ethnics abroad, which originally emerged in the Cold War context, but persisted also after 1989. For instance, support for Italians in Yugoslavia was expected to be matched by similar measures for Slovenians in Italy (cf. Troha 2003). Another important factor was Slovenia's accession to the EU, and in particular Italy's initial attempts to block accession negotiations (Repe 2005). In this context, Slovenia was very keen to prove its commitment to minority protection, and thus demonstrate its compliance with 'European standards' (e.g. Polzer et al. 2002).

As is evident from the cases of Bulgaria and Slovenia, the trajectory of nation-building and the presence of recent conflicts can exert an important influence on the shaping of minority provisions, and through that on the development of minority media. Intensive nation-building, aggressive assimilation policies and armed conflicts are likely to create a lasting legacy of negative attitudes and prejudice. These can be easily exploited by political elites long after conflicts have ceased, and forced assimilation measures have been abandoned. The importance of the trajectory of nation-state building is confirmed when we look at the cases of Hungary and Poland. Both have enjoyed independent statehood considerably longer than most other countries in the sample, and underwent a comprehensive process of ethnic simplification and 'unmixing' already in the first half of the twentieth century (Brubaker 1996: 84–103, 156–60). In contrast, Macedonia, Slovenia, Bosnia and Herzegovina and Estonia all achieved independent statehood only in the early 1990s. While Bulgaria also achieved independence relatively early, the last wave of ethnic simplification occurred only in the 1980s, and its consequences are still felt today. In such a context, quick changes seem unlikely, unless they are accompanied by a strong steer from international actors or neighbouring countries. This is likely to occur only in cases of prolonged ethnic conflicts that threaten to destabilize the wider region, as in the case of the 2001 tensions in Macedonia and the 1992–95 war in Bosnia and Herzegovina.

Economic Factors and Popular Attitudes

As mentioned earlier, popular attitudes can act as a major impediment to changes in minority provisions. For example, although the new EU member states in Central and Eastern Europe have adopted anti-discrimination measures to secure equal opportunities for minority groups and thereby contribute to their social inclusion, implementation is lagging behind due to ethnic prejudices and lack of public awareness of anti-discrimination policies (Schwellnus 2009). These circumstances have an effect also on the implementation of policy measures aimed at introducing or enhancing support for minority media. In Bulgaria, for instance, public pressures delayed the introduction of minority language programming on mainstream broadcast channels (Nancheva 2007: 381). Judging from opinion polls in five of the seven countries included in the sample, shared stereotypes are most likely to affect the mediation of cultural diversity in Bulgaria and to a somewhat lesser extent in Slovenia, Estonia and Hungary, where substantial proportions of the populations feel uncomfortable with Roma neighbours and members of a different ethnicity being elected to the highest political positions (Table 3.2).

Popular attitudes are believed to be decisive especially in the case of provisions for recently established immigrant minorities. According to some authors, xenophobic attitudes towards immigrants are among the key factors responsible for the lack of public discussion on immigration and weakly developed integration policies in Central and Eastern Europe (Wallace 2002: 618–21). A good case in point is Slovenia, where a public opinion survey revealed that over 60 per cent of the interviewees were opposed to recent immigrants having their own newspapers, radio or TV channels, while at the same time over 68 per cent believed this was entirely appropriate for the 'autochthonous' Italian and Hungarian minorities (Komac 2005: 228).

Similarly, public opposition and resistance from local officials and populations have proved to be a major obstacle to effective implementation of Roma policies across the region (Guglielmo 2004: 45–6). Although Roma media in the region have quickly proliferated, and there is evidence of enhanced public awareness and acceptance of Roma populations, stereotypes persist. The rise of Roma stars in mainstream popular culture, including song contests and TV reality shows (Imre 2009), provides a case in point. The new image of the Roma promoted by these cultural forms is fairly positive, yet it also continues to perpetuate the long-held stereotype of the Roma as exotic, colourful and innately musical beings, completely unsuited for participation in the serious matters of a nation's politics and economy.

Finally, the mediation of cultural diversity is influenced also by economic factors, which can easily obstruct the production and distribution of minority content even in cases where adequate legislation is in place and popular attitudes are favourable. It is probably not a coincidence that Bulgaria, where minority media are dependent primarily on private donors rather than advertising or public funding, is also among the countries with the lowest per capita gross domestic product, advertising expenditure, and public TV funding (Table 3.2). All other countries with integrated media systems – Slovenia, Poland and Hungary – have considerably greater per capita rates of both public TV funding and advertising expenditure, as well as gross domestic product. It is these economic factors that make it possible for their minority media to rely primarily on public funding, and for minority content to appear predominantly within publicly funded broadcast programmes rather than commercial ones. Furthermore, lack of advertising revenue can also help explain some of the characteristics of Roma media across the region, in particular their reliance on private donors and public funding. In this case, however, the lack of advertising revenues is not a consequence of low advertising expenditure at national level but rather derives from the low purchasing power among the Roma, which means advertisers are reluctant to advertise in Roma media (Gross 2006: 485).

International Factors

As other chapters in this volume demonstrate, media systems are increasingly organized on a transnational level, and affected by transnational regulatory pressures, ownership structures and cross-border media flows (see Downey, Harcourt and Štětka, this volume). These factors have an impact also on the mediation of cultural diversity. As with domestic factors, demography and history play a key role also at international level, and are particularly visible in the influence exerted by kin-states and their media. The triadic relationship between kin-states or 'national homelands', nationalizing states and national minorities is of crucial importance for the dynamics of ethnic politics in the region (Brubaker 1996) and it is reasonable to expect that it will have its counterpart also at the level of mass communication. Indeed, all countries with segmented media systems in our sample are also those in which the presence of kin-states and kin-state media is, or at least recently was, seen as a threat to national integration (e.g. Kolar-Panov 1997, Vihalemm 1999: 46).

Arguably, concerns over kin-states and their media were among the factors that prompted the development of more comprehensive national integration policies, and fuelled support for domestically produced minority media that would counteract the allegedly harming effect of kin-state media. In Estonia, anxieties over the possibility of a conflict with Russia or the Russian-speaking inhabitants of the country were an important issue in parliamentary debates after 1997, when ethnocentric concerns slowly gave way to the formation of an official integration policy (Langerspetz 2005: 21–22). The shift from fear and exclusion to acceptance and integration occurred also within the realm of the media. The new integration programme, adopted in 2000, gave rise to several media-related activities, including integration-related training of journalists and editors, professional training for Russian-speaking journalists and media producers, the promotion of integration-related media coverage, and media monitoring (Langerspetz 2005: 30–31).

It is often argued that international political actors played a key role in stimulating changes in minority provisions in postcommunist Central and Eastern Europe. Yet, similarly as with domestic political factors, the influence of international political actors alone cannot explain why a particular country is likely to develop a segmented rather than an integrated media system. Two of the three countries with segmented media systems (Bosnia and Herzegovina, Macedonia) have recent experience with international mediation in inter-ethnic conflicts, which led to the adoption of the Ohrid Agreement in Macedonia in 2001, and the signing of Dayton Accords for Bosnia and Herzegovina in 1995. In both cases, the agreements reached also laid the foundations of the new media policies. However, as argued earlier, segmented media systems were in place already before the agreements were reached and in fact prior to the escalation of conflicts. Rather than being an outcome of political factors alone, be it domestic or international, the segmented character of media landscapes arose gradually out of an interaction between political, demographic and historical factors. The same can be said for Estonia, where a segmented media system exists in spite of the lack of explicit international intervention.

One can of course argue that other, indirect international political pressures were more decisive in the shaping of the region's media systems. The European Union is particularly often mentioned in this context, along with the Organization for Security and Cooperation (OSCE) and the Council of Europe (CE). The requirements for minority protection, set out in the European Commission's *Agenda 2000*, triggered domestic policy changes in several countries: most new policy initiatives related to minorities were introduced after 2000 (Vermeersch 2003: 21–2). The EU has also been successful in raising awareness of the plight of the Roma: the repeated requests for improvements appearing in the official reports on candidate countries prompted the formulation of a range of new policy solutions (ibid.: 22–3).

In a similar vein, the OSCE's High Commissioner on National Minorities was instrumental in issuing early warnings and prompting diplomatic activities aimed at resolving majority-minority tensions before they escalate. In Estonia, for instance, HCMN advice played an important role in initiating the shift from exclusion to integration in the 1990s (Langerspetz 2005: 22). The Council of Europe, on the other hand, contributed to the standardization of minority policies through its European Charter for Regional or Minority Languages (ECRML) and the Framework Convention for the Protection of National Minorities (FCPNM). In Bulgaria, the adoption of the FCMN in 1999 led to the introduction of the term 'minority' into the country's postcommunist legislation (Rechel 2008: 338). For a country that long denied the existence of national minorities, and granted rights only to 'citizens whose mother tongue is not Bulgarian', this was certainly an important symbolic change.

On the whole, the involvement of these intergovernmental bodies in the accession process has certainly contributed to important shifts in public discourse, to greater public awareness of cultural diversity, and to a noticeable standardization of minority legislation across the region. However, we should be wary of overstating the impact of these changes. The basic shape of minority policies and media systems in Central and Eastern Europe was formed already in the early to mid-1990s, before the EU accession process started in earnest. While the EU did insist on some changes to minority legislation, none of the countries was denied entry due to minority discrimination. This happened even in cases where the European Commission had been well informed of the situation, as in the case of Slovenia's reluctance to confer citizenship rights to long-term inhabitants – immigrants from former Yugoslav republics – who were deleted from the register of permanent residents in 1992 (Zorn 2009: 221).

Also worth noting is the rather patchy implementation of international minority provisions. For instance, although Slovenia has signed and ratified the ECRML and the FCPNM, the remit of both is limited to traditional minorities and to some extent to the Roma community, and does not extend to recently established immigrant groups (Zorn 2009: 214). An important reason for this lies in the lack of enforcement mechanisms. Even in cases where the adoption of international acts is legally binding, the lack of effective monitoring and enforcement measures meant that policy changes make little difference on the ground (Sasse 2009). Furthermore, the guidelines provided by intergovernmental bodies are often rather vague, and allow for significant variation in interpretation and implementation (cf. Vermeersch 2003: 9).

If intergovernmental bodies such as the EU, OSCE and CE were contributing primarily to public awareness and policy shifts, international civil society organizations seem to have been instrumental chiefly in prompting changes at the level of the day-to-day functioning of media systems. This is visible in the case of the Open Society Institute, the Soros Foundations Network and similar organizations that provide assistance to minority outlets, support journalism and media management training in areas of cultural diversity and human rights, and conduct monitoring of media legislation and content. Such support appears to be of particular importance in countries with weakest economies, where the availability of public funding for minority media is scarce, as is the case in Bulgaria, Macedonia and BiH (Bauer and Vujović 2006). The situation is especially acute in countries where low advertising expenditure and low economic productivity are coupled with highly fragmented media markets and a plethora of minority media, which suffer not only from a lack of funding but also from a low level of independence and professionalism. A good case in point is Macedonia (Spasovska 2006: 367–9).

On the whole, we can conclude that with the exception of kin-states and their media, international factors played an important though largely secondary role in shaping the mediation of cultural diversity in the region. The fundamental shape of media systems – namely the development of segmented as opposed to integrated systems – was largely decided by domestic factors. Intergovernmental bodies and international civil society organizations were influential mostly in sensitizing the public to issues of cultural diversity, prompting policy changes at micro-level, and providing financial, technical and training support to minority outlets.

Conclusions

To sum up, the analysis of the chosen seven cases suggests that the choice between the integrated and the segmented media model is affected primarily by the ethnic composition of the domestic population, historical factors such as the trajectory of nation-state building, the presence of recent inter-ethnic conflicts, and the presence of a kin-state and kin-state media that are perceived as a threat. A segmented media system is most likely to develop in states with large minority populations that have not made much headway in nation-state building, have recently experienced high-intensity inter-ethnic conflicts, and border kin-states with cross-border media that are perceived as a threat. Political factors – be it domestic (e.g. democracy type) or international (eg accession to the EU) – do play a role, but their influence is limited and secondary, and always operates in conjunction with historical and demographic factors. In other words, political factors do not affect the overall structure of the media system as a whole (integrated vs. segmented), but rather contribute to gradual changes to existing arrangements, be they based on integration or on segmentation.

These results have important implications for some of the vexing normative dilemmas of cultural diversity and mass communication, especially those concerning the relative advantages and disadvantages of segmented and integrated media systems. To many observers, the fragmentation of national media landscapes, fostered by the growth of minority media outlets, poses a threat to the quality of public deliberation. In their view, the centrifugal forces of 'public sphericules' prevent us from engaging in a sustained discussion of shared interests beyond cultural, social and ideological differences, and from debating competing solutions to common problems (Gitlin 1998). Culturally segmented communication is seen as particularly harmful in the context of societies already riven by deep-seated suspicions and hostilities between culturally distinct groups. In such cases, separate minority outlets are believed to exacerbate rather than alleviate existing fissures, and threaten civic bonds and solidarities (e.g. Snyder 2000: 180). Instead of addressing the communicative needs and interests of culturally diverse audiences via segmented spaces of communication, we therefore ought to seek ways to integrate these audiences into the same, nation- and state-wide communicative sphere.

Other commentators argue that the social impact of a culturally segmented mass communication is not necessarily so grim, and that the particularism of minority media does not automatically involve a rejection of universalism or a retreat from the wider public sphere (Siapera 2010: 106–10). Sometimes, minority media provide a safe space inside which a marginalized minority can search for ways to improve its present situation – as was the case with some of the historical African-American newspapers (Herbst 1994: 71–9). Rather than being an obstacle to public deliberation, a segmented media landscape can therefore contribute to the formation of more integrative and inclusive public spheres. Also, the integrative, cross-cultural media programmes are not always the panacea they are believed to be. Successful multicultural programmes are often driven by commercial imperatives, and as such, they are compelled to downplay cultural differences and controversial issues and focus instead on lifestyle choices and individual experiences (cf. Leurdijk 2006). As a consequence, the programmes they produce will probably make only a limited contribution to the development of civic virtues and sensibilities that are essential to the functioning of a multicultural democracy (cf. Jaggar 1999: 323–6).

Yet if the choice between segmentation and integration is affected primarily by demographic and historical factors rather than political will alone, then such normative debates appear somewhat futile – unless we are prepared to resort to political measures designed to eradicate cultural diversity. Rather than contemplating the pros and cons of an integrated as opposed to a segmented media system, we should therefore look for ways to assess and improve the quality of public deliberation in each of the two systems separately.

References

Aksoy, A. and Robins, K. 2000. Thinking across spaces: Transnational television from Turkey. *European Journal of Cultural Studies*, 3(3), 343–65.

Bašić Hrvatin, S., Thompson, M. and Jusić, T. eds. 2008. *Divided They Fall: Public Service Broadcasting in Multiethnic Societies*. Sarajevo: Mediacentar.

Bauer, T.A. and Vujović, O., eds. 2006. *Media and Minorities in South East Europe*, Vienna: SEEMO.

Bendix, R. 1964. *Nation-building and Citizenship: Studies of Our Changing Social Order*. New York: Wiley.

Benson, R. and Hallin, D. 2007. How states, markets and globalization shape the news: The French and US national press, 1965–97. *European Journal of Communication*, 22(1), 27–48.

Bieber, F. 2004. Power sharing and ethnic representation in post-conflict societies: The cases of Bosnia, Macedonia, and Kosovo, in *Nationalism after Communism: Lessons Learned*, edited by A. Mungiu, A. Mungiu-Pippidi and I. Krastev. Budapest: Central European University Press, 231–49.

Breuilly, J. 1994. *Nationalism and the State*. 2nd Edition. Chicago: Chicago University Press.

Brubaker, R. 1996. *Nationalism Reframed: Nationhood and the National Question in the New Europe*. Cambridge: Cambridge University Press.

Burke, P. 2004. *Languages and Communities in Early Modern Europe*. Cambridge: Cambridge University Press.

Camauër, L. 2002. *Mapping Minorities and their Media: The National Context – Sweden*. Available at: http://www.lse.ac.uk/collections/EMTEL/Minorities/papers/swedenreport.doc [accessed 04 October 2009].

Camauër, L. 2003. Ethnic minorities and their media in Sweden: An overview of the media landscape and state minority media policy. *Nordicom Review*, 24(2), 69–88.

Carey, J. 1989. *Communication as Culture: Essays on Media and Society*. Boston: Unwin Hyman.

Chernilo, D. 2007. *A Social Theory of the Nation-State: The Political Forms of Modernity beyond Methodological Nationalism*. London and New York: Routledge.

Christians, C.G., Glasser, T., McQuail, D., Nordenstreng, K. and White, R.A. 2009. *Normative Theories of the Media: Journalism in Democratic Societies*. Urbana, IL: University of Illinois Press.

Connor, W. 1978. A nation is a nation, is a state, is an ethnic group, is a ... *Ethnic and Racial Studies*, 1, 377–400.

Čićak, G and Hamzić, D. 2006. *Bosnia and Herzegovina: National Minorities and the Right to Education*. Minority Rights Group International. Available at: http://www.minorityrights.org/963/micro-studies/bosnia-and-herzegovina-national-minorities-and-the-right-to-education.html [accessed 07 August 2008].

Dembinska, M. 2008. Adapting to changing contexts of choice: The nation-building strategies of unrecognized Silesians and Rusyns. *Canadian Journal of Political Science*, 41(4), 915–34.

Erk, J. 2003. Swiss federalism and congruence. *Nationalism and Ethnic Politics*, 9(2), 50–74.

Esser, F. and Pfetsch, B. 2004. *Comparative Political Communication: Theories, Cases, and Challenges*. Cambridge: Cambridge University Press.

EUMAP. 2005. *Television across Europe: Regulation, Policy and Independence* – Summary, Budapest: Open Society Institute.

Gellner, E. 1983. *Nations and Nationalism*. Ithaca, NY: Cornell University Press.

Gitlin, T. 1998. Public sphere or public sphericules? in *Media, Ritual and Identity*, edited by T. Liebes and J. Curran. London: Routledge.

Gross, P. 2006. A prolegomena to the study of the Romani media in Eastern Europe. *European Journal of Communication*, 21(4), 477–97.

Guglielmo, R. 2004. Human rights in the accession process: Roma and Muslims in an enlarging EU, in *Minority Protection and the Enlarged European Union: The Way Forward*, edited by G.N. Toggenburg. Budapest: Open Society Institute, 37–58.

Hallin, D. and Mancini, P. 2004. *Comparing Media Systems: Three Models of Media and Politics*. Cambridge: Cambridge University Press.

Harcourt, A. 2006. *European Union Institutions and the Regulation of Media Markets*. London: Manchester University Press

Hayden, R. M. 1992. Constitutional nationalism in the formerly Yugoslav republics. *Slavic Review*, 51(4), 654–73.

Herbst, S. 1994. *Politics at the Margins: Historical Studies of Public Expression outside the Mainstream*. Cambridge: Cambridge University Press.

Hroch, M. 2006. Modernization and communication as factors of nation-formation, in *The SAGE Handbook of Nations and Nationalism*, edited by G. Delanty and K. Kumar. London: Sage, 21–32.

Imre, A. 2009. *Identity Games: Globalization and the Transformation of Media Cultures in the New Europe*. Cambridge, MA: MIT Press.

Jaggar, A.M. 1999. Multicultural Democracy. *The Journal of Political Philosophy*, 7(3), 308–29.

Järve, P. 2004. Re-independent Estonia, in *The Fate of Ethnic Democracy in Post-Communist Europe*, edited by S. Smooha and P. Järve. Budapest: Local Government and Public Service Reform Initiative and Open Society Institute, 61–79.

Jongen, F., Voorhoof, D. and Braeckman, A. 2005. Media System of Belgium. Project Report for the *Study on Co-regulation Measures in the Media Sector*. Available at: http://www.hans-bredow-institut.de/forschung/recht/co-reg/reports/1/Belgium.pdf [accessed 27 May 2009].

Jusić, T. and Džihana, A. 2008. Bosnia and Herzegovina, in *Divided They Fall: Public Service Broadcasting in Multiethnic Societies*, edited by S. Bašić Hrvatin, M. Thompson and T. Jusić. Sarajevo: Mediacentar, 81–119.

Kolar-Panov, D. 1997. Crowded airwaves: Ethnic, national and transnational identities in Macedonian television, in *Programming for People: From Cultural Rights to Cultural Responsibilities*, edited by K. Robins. Rome: Radiotelevisione Italiana in association with the European Broadcasting Union, 76–87.

Komac, M. 2005. Varstvo 'novih' narodnih skupnosti v Sloveniji, in *Percepcije slovenske integracijske politike*, edited by M. Komac and M. Medvešek. Ljubljana: Inštitut za narodnostna vprašanja, 207–36.

Kosnick, K. 2007. *Migrant Media: Turkish Broadcasting and Multicultural Politics in Berlin*. Bloomington & Indianapolis: Indiana University Press.

Kymlicka, W. and Norman, W. 2000. Citizenship in culturally diverse societies: Issues, contexts, concepts, in *Citizenship in Diverse Societies*, edited by W. Kymlicka and W. Norman. Oxford: Oxford University Press, 1–41.

Lagerspetz, M. 2007. Estonia, in *European Immigration: A Sourcebook*, edited by A. Triandafyllidou and R. Gropas. Aldershot: Ashgate, 87–98.

Leurdijk, A. 2006. In search of common ground: Strategies of multicultural television producers in Europe. *European Journal of Cultural Studies*, 9(1), 25–46.

Liebich, A. 2007. Introduction: Altneuländer of the vicissitudes of citizenship in the new EU states, in *Citizenship Policies in the New Europe*, edited by R. Bauböck, B. Perchinig and W. Sievers. Amsterdam: Amsterdam University Press, 17–40.

McGarry, J. and O'Leary, B. 1993. Introduction: The macro-political regulation of ethnic conflict, in *The Politics of Ethnic Conflict Regulation: Case Studies of Protracted Ethnic Conflicts*, edited by J. McGarry and B. O'Leary. London: Routledge, 1–47.

Mushaben, J.M. 2008. *The Changing Faces of Citizenship: Integration and Mobilization among Ethnic Minorities in Germany*. Oxford: Berghahn.

Nancheva, N. 2007. What are norms good for? Ethnic minorities on Bulgaria's way to Europe. *Journal of Communist Studies and Transition Politics*, 23(3), 371–95.

Ormond, M. 2002. *Mapping Minorities and Their Media: The National Context* – Belgium. Available at: http://www.lse.ac.uk/collections/EMTEL/Minorities/reports.html [accessed 05 October 2009].

Petković, B. 2006. Media and minorities in Slovenia, in *Media and Minorities in South East Europe*, edited by T.A. Bauer and O. Vujović. Vienna: SEEMO, 676–81.

Pfetsch, B. 2001. Political communication culture in the United States and Germany. *The Harvard International Journal of Press/Politics*, 6(1), 46–67.

Polzer, M., Kalčina, L. and Žagar, M., eds. 2002. *Slovenija in evropski standardi varstva narodnih manjšin*. Ljubljana: Informacijsko dokumentacijski center Sveta Evrope pri NUK, Inštitut za narodnostna vprašanja and Avstrijski inštitut za vzhodno in jugovzhodno Evropo.

Raiser, U. 2002. *Mapping Minorities and their Media: The National Context – Germany*. Available at: http://www.lse.ac.uk/collections/EMTEL/Minorities/reports.html [accessed 05 October 2009].

Rechel, B. 2007. State control of minorities in Bulgaria. *Journal of Communist Studies and Transition Politics*, 23(3), 352–70.

Rechel, B. 2008. Ethnic diversity in Bulgaria: Institutional arrangements and domestic discourse. *Nationalities Papers*, 36(2), 331–50.

Rechel, B. 2009. Introduction, in *Minority Rights in Central and Eastern Europe*, edited by B. Rechel. London: Routledge, 3–16.

Repe, B. 2005. Slovensko-italijanski odnosi od Londonskega memoranduma do osamosvojitve Slovenije, in *Vojna in mir na Primorskem*, edited by J. Pirjevec,

G. Bajc and B. Klabjan. Koper: Univerza na Primorskem, Založba Annales, Znanstveno-raziskovalno središče Koper and Zgodovinsko društvo za Južno Primorsko, 323–38.

Sasse, G. 2009. Tracing the construction and effects of EU conditionality, in *Minority Rights in Central and Eastern Europe*, edited by B. Rechel. London: Routledge, 17–31.

Schlesinger, P. 2009. Cultural and communications policy in the stateless nation. *Catalan Journal of Communication and Cultural Studies*, 1(1), 9–14.

Schudson, M. 2003. *The Sociology of News*. New York: W.W. Norton.

Schwellnus, G. 2009. Anti-discrimination legislation, in *Minority Rights in Central and Eastern Europe*, edited by B. Rechel. London: Routledge, 32–45.

Siapera, E. 2010. *Cultural Diversity and Global Media: The Mediation of Difference*. Oxford: Wiley-Blackwell.

Smooha, S. 2004. The model of ethnic democracy, in *The Fate of Ethnic Democracy in Post-Communist Europe*, edited by S. Smooha and P. Järve. Budapest: Local Government and Public Service Reform Initiative and Open Society Institute, 5–60.

Snyder, J. 2000. *From Voting to Violence: Democratization and Nationalist Conflict*. New York: WW Norton.

Spasovska, K. 2006. Minority media landscape. In *Media and Minorities in South East Europe*, edited by T.A. Bauer and O. Vujović. Vienna: SEEMO, 360–70.

Šopar, V. 2008. Macedonia, in *Divided They Fall: Public Service Broadcasting in Multiethnic Societies*, edited by S. Bašić Hrvatin, M. Thompson and T. Jusić. Sarajevo: Mediacentar, 119–58.

Troha, N. 2003. Slovenska manjšina v Italiji in Italijanska v Jugoslaviji med letom 1945 in 1990 – primerjava položaja. *Acta Histriae*, 11(2), 151–80.

Vermeersch, P. 2003. EU enlargement and minority rights policies in Central Europe: Explaining policy shifts in the Czech Republic, Hungary and Poland. *Journal of Ethnopolitics and Minority Issues in Europe*, 4(1), 1–32.

Vihalemm, T. 1999. Local and global orientations of media consumption in Estonia, 1993–1998. In *Estonian Human Development Report 1999*. Tallinn: UNDP.

Vihalemm, P. 2006. Media use in Estonia: Trends and patterns. *Nordicom Review*, 27(1), 17–29.

Vizi, B. 2009. Hungary: a model with lasting problems, in *Minority Rights in Central and Eastern Europe*, edited by B. Rechel. London: Routledge, 119–34.

Wallace, C. 2002. Opening and closing borders: Migration and mobility in East-Central Europe. *Journal of Ethnic and Migration Studies*, 28(4), 603–25.

Zlatev, O. 2006. Media and Minorities in Bulgaria. In *Media and Minorities in South East Europe*, edited by T.A. Bauer and O. Vujović. Vienna: SEEMO, 241–58.

Zorn, J. 2009. Slovenia: Ethnic exclusion in a model accession state, in *Minority Rights in Central and Eastern Europe*, edited by B. Rechel. London: Routledge 210–24.

Chapter 4

Gender (In)equity in Post-socialist Media

Mojca Pajnik

Media can be seen as one of the actors that bind women to particular social and economic structures at a specific point in time. As such, their practices and outcomes appear as both a source and a confirmation of the structural gender inequalities. Media industries act as agents that engage and employ women where job types and arrangements reflect the bias of gender roles. They also appear as image producers and presenters where several patterns of representations are developed that reproduce gender inequality. In a manner comparable to other institutions, the media appears as an actor that largely reinforces rather than challenges gender divides in Central and Eastern European media systems.

Feminist scholarship has shown strong gender divides across the globe and the dominance of stereotypes in mass media persist despite some advances in employment of female media workers. Practices and policies of engaging female media workers point to ways of directing women into jobs traditionally occupied by women and to more precarious jobs. Most media workers are still male; women have difficulties to access managerial positions; they are less present in the media overall; less credible as sources, less newsworthy and less quoted. An analysis of gender inequality requires both consideration of structures of media organization, specific to a place and time, and analysis of media images of women. Here questions are relevant such as: how much space are women given in the media and what kind of space it is, when are women speaking, how are they represented when they speak, i.e. are they allowed to speak with dignity and authority, to what extent are traditional gender roles, for example in relation to family and home reinforced, what is the portrayal of women in photographs, in what genres are women present or absent and so on.

This chapter debates gender and the media in Central and Eastern Europe, taking into account historical developments and the specific roles women were subjected to. Post-socialist / post-communist countries share a common history (and thus several similarities) while there are important differences as well as far as their political, economic, social and cultural life is concerned. Development in the area of gender equality is very different in Russia compared to Poland; Slovenia has approached gender imbalances significantly differently from Bulgaria. Media systems vary as well. Despite differences, these countries have some common experiences in the process of media democratization, i.e. the differentiation, pluralization and professionalization of journalism. Comparison between countries in the region would scarcely be possible unless they had a common background; they all experienced systemic and social changes compared to previous regimes. Taking this into consideration, this chapter aims to develop a framework for analysing gender and the ways it relates to the media in the Central and Eastern European region. The analysis enables both comparison and contrast with Western and Northern European countries and aims at identifying some patterns of change and their impact on relations and differences between gender-related spaces of communication. The discussion is based on data that describes gender-media relations in specific countries focusing on the situation in Central and Eastern Europe but also taking into account experiences of Western European countries. The chapter examines gender by ways of reflecting on various structurally conditioned issues of gender inequity and by moving the analysis beyond simple comparison of various national units.

The chapter starts by discussing the legacy of gender equality in the region as implemented before 1989 and explores its development and transformation during transition. Here we see how the legacy helps to explain differences in gender equality between Central and Eastern Europe and Western Europe. Levels of subordination of women vary across Europe. Differences in women's positions in political and economic systems affect the gender divide in the media system. The chapter looks into systemic differences and explores the argument that the decline of gender equality in the region in general and in media in particular in post 1989 owes much to the growing impact of market forces and the spread and proliferation of commercial media.

Women in Transition: Between Gains and Losses

Post-communist states' emphasis on high rates of labour participation created regimes that can be seen as supportive of women, both as paid employees and as mothers. Since the planned economy required a large workforce, social services provision addressed the consequences of the need for women's labour. In general, legislation was adopted to minimize tensions between work and family, such as paid maternity leave, family allowances, free health care etc. – women's high participation in the labour market was possible due to extensive social policy. Family law provided an apparent equality in marriage and divorce, supports for motherhood and care through family benefits and parental leave required for care, and enabled women to combine paid employment with motherhood. However, we must question what kind of an achievement greater gender equality is in an oppressive state, and, if state services support women at work, how beneficial actually these services are? (Pascall and Manning 2000: 244–45).

The *Women in Transition* report (Monee project 1999: 6) that evaluates the situation in 27 countries in Central and Eastern Europe and the former Soviet Union points to the fact that women in the transition region had high rates of participation in the labour force compared to women in Western countries. Women made up 50 per cent of the labour force in the 1970s and 1980s, significantly more than the around 30 per cent in Western Europe. In the Baltic states or in Russia, Belarus and Ukraine the gender gap in labour force participation was just a few percentage points, comparable to Sweden. Moreover, in contrast to Western economies, women in these countries usually had full-time jobs throughout their working lives.

In contrast to Western European countries that often assumed men were the sole breadwinners, countries of Central and Eastern Europe have had dual earner households since the end of World War II. The gender regimes in in the region appeared to be similar to the Scandinavian model with high female labour market participation and gender pay gaps at around 20 per cent. The main difference however was that women were pressed to enter the labour market while men were not brought into domestic and care work. This resulted in high levels of domestic inequality. The demands of industrialization and production meant that governments wanted women to be workers, but they also wanted them to be mothers. Policies primarily sustained and naturalized women's roles in households (Pascal and Kwak 2005: 4–5, 11). In this respect the Central and Eastern European countries adopted 'state-supported mothering' (Ibid.: 46) by sustaining traditional gender divisions in households. Women had to put in long hours of work at home as well – a 'double burden' averaging close to 70 hours per week, about 15 hours per week more than the working burden of women in Western Europe (Monee project 1999: 6).

Working conditions prior 1989 were also far from unproblematic: state socialism made little attempt to ameliorate working conditions for women. Instead, policies promoted protective legislation and emphasized women's reproductive roles rather than their productive capacities. Also, state socialist regimes put significant pressure on women to engage in all spheres of life, from local participation, union engagement to neighbourhood committees, schools. 'The resulting triple burden caused severe stress, overburdening women to the point that it is understandable if many perceived – or perceive, in retrospect – the right to work as yet another obligation, rather than a right on which they might pride themselves' (Pascal and Kwak 2005: 117). The rhetoric of motherland and the esteemed value of family contributed to the fact that women workers had to become 'superwomen.' Gender equality in Central and Eastern Europe was thus primarily about equality in the labour market, and as stated by Corrin (1992: 18), the rhetoric of women's equality hardly matched up the reality of women's lives.

Despite laws and policies aiming at equality, gender relations were therefore marked by difference rather than equality (Pascall and Manning 2000: 245). Although more women participated in the labour market compared with Western European countries, labour markets were highly segregated. Data shows that job disparity was not alien to socialist practice: women were concentrated in lower status occupations, had lower salaries, and were employed in low-paid sectors of economy. Although they were present in all industries, they remained clustered in female-dominated light industrial production, such as the textile, health and education sectors, and in clerical and administrative branches. Disparities existed between the preferred industrial occupations dominated by men and the non-preferred jobs in the feminized sectors that were poorly paid (Einhorn 1993: 122, Corrin 1992: 16). In addition, women were not treated as equal citizens in the sense of promoting their dissent and political action. They had little defence against domestic violence, there is little evidence that marriage and divorce laws actually brought the choice to live outside families, and single parenthood was not a choice for those who wanted to keep out of poverty. Women played a minor role in political life, senior positions in the labour market were occupied by men, and, also, the women's movement was far from strong (Pascall and Manning 2000: 262, True 1999: 364).

Despite substantial regional and cultural diversity, socialism imposed remarkably uniform family laws and policies across the region. These policies aimed at achieving the state's goal of high levels of female education and employment, while maintaining fertility levels which would assure a strong workforce in the future. Indeed, female labour force participation was high, while total fertility rates were close to or higher than those in Western countries. However, in contrast to women in Western industrialized countries, women in the planned economies married young and had their first children at a young age. Similar regimes brought comparable policies, although some differences existed: Hungary and Slovenia, for example, developed different social and family policies that supported women's labour market positions to a greater extent than in Poland. However, the long experience with the communist and socialist era left similar consequences across the region of the move from a welfare state system to free markets and individualism (Pascal and Kwak 2005: 7). During transition gross domestic product in Central and Eastern Europe dropped if compared to the 1989 level and governments reduced spending in education, health, pensions and child benefits (Ibid.: 11). In addition, some of the states in the region saw a collapse of activities for gender equality that existed during the previous regime, due to conservative governments taking power in post 1989. Under a conservative government, for example, Poland replaced the Office for Women's Issues with the Office for Family Issues. This move was underpinned by a conservative religious perspective that reduced all women's issues to family issues.

The transition has changed the labour landscape in the region enormously and weakened job security for both women and men. This resulted in the decline of female labour force participation since 1989. While male participation in the labour force has generally fallen, women have tended to lose more than men in almost every dimension of labour market activity (Monee project 1999: 6). With the introduction of market economies dual earner households became 're-traditionalized' with women's employment becoming more fragile and women have also begun to lose previous levels of social and economic welfare. Women's employment has fallen across the new European Union (hereafter EU) member states, particularly in Poland, less in Estonia. Still, the majority of countries in the region, apart from Czech Republic, have gender employment gaps below the figures in the EU15, but well above Sweden (Pascal and Kwak 2005: 40–41). The proportion of women in work across the new member states is a bit higher than in the EU15 despite job losses. Women's unemployment is growing, especially in Poland, but is only slightly higher than men's, suggesting that economic problems predominate over gender issues. While occupational segregation was high during socialism, Central and Eastern European countries still have a less-segregated labour market than the EU15. In addition, in these countries more women occupy higher job positions and are more commonly employed in technical occupations and as skilled workers (Ibid.: 43, 65).

Accounts for the Baltic states (Novikova 2004: 8–9) suggest that during the Soviet period women were employed in industries fully integrated into the Soviet economic system and have consequently experienced downward social mobility after the break-up. Especially for women over 30, employment opportunities are poor and discrimination is particularly pronounced in the private sector where employers offer short-term contracts and casual work to younger women to avoid having to pay maternity benefits. In particular, women from Russian-speaking minorities faced the most severe deterioration of their situation, leaving many forced to accept work in informal labour markets. A similar trend of women accepting low paid, insecure work in informal economies (even more pronounced if they do not belong to the major ethnic community) can be observed throughout the Central and Eastern European region. It is also common for women from the region, faced with a lack of opportunities, to accept work in Western European countries where, regardless of their qualifications, they end up performing domestic and care work. Many migrant women are left with no choice but to work in the sex industry (Pajnik 2008).

The end of the 1990s has shown that women's economic futures are more closely tied to the shrinking rather than to the growing economic sectors. Data shows that women are strongly represented in fields that are likely to remain in the public sector – health care, education, social services, and public administration. Despite opportunities for private enterprise, studies indicate that women have been slower to take up private-sector jobs. In most countries self-employment is more common among men than among women, and women are also less likely than men to be entrepreneurs (Monee project 1999: 7).

A gender gap in wages is evident across Europe. Women earn less on average than men in the former communist countries, but the gap is slightly larger in Western Europe. Data shows that women earn less than men in every post-communist country: the wages of women ranging from 70 to 90 per cent of men's wages. The gender gap has remained relatively stable during transition, despite the significant growth in overall wage inequality and the massive changes in the labour market. The gender balance in education tends to reduce the pay gap, while the fact that women seem to be clustered in lower paying occupations tends to widen the gap (Monee project 1999: 7–8).

Western Europe remains at a 'one-and-a-half earner norm at best', while Central and Eastern European countries have had a dual income system for about half a century. Despite the traditional division of labour in the private sphere and the lack of active civil society, the dual system has left strong social policies that are still seen today, despite rising unemployment. Pascall and Kwak (2005: 65) argue that gender equality in Central and Eastern European countries might be interpreted as a strength of these environments in comparison to the EU15. Patterns are changing but, according to the authors, claims of increasing gender inequality and retraditionalization for these countries have been overstated.

The childcare environment has also changed during the transition. The population of infants and young children is greatly reduced; public childcare facilities are less available; childcare fees have increased, and stay-at-home parenting is being promoted. Maternity entitlements have remained relatively untouched and, along with parental leaves, have even been extended in some countries. However, the good intentions behind maternity and parental leave measures often go unfulfilled in the new labour markets. It is typically women who must adapt and take on more responsibilities in order to cope with the new circumstances. There is evidence that employers are unwilling and parents unable to take full advantage of the leave. In the Czech Republic, 23 per cent of legally available maternity leave went unused in 1993, compared to 5 per cent in 1989. In Poland, more than two thirds of women with higher education returned to work early from parental leave. Male participation in parental leave remains negligible. Enrolment rates in nurseries have fallen throughout the region during the transition. Also, in the Czech Republic and Slovakia, for example, nurseries have practically ceased to exist (Monee project 1999: 9, 11–12). All this implies that changing patterns of gender equality in Central and Eastern Europe after 1989 did not have so much to do with an inadequate democratization process but rather with the growing impact of market forces that has substantially weakened welfare states.

Realities of Gender Mainstreaming

With respect to the media and gender relations, we will use the concept of gender mainstreaming to gain insight into media policies and practices, stratified by gender. The European Commission defines gender mainstreaming as 'efforts mobilising all general policies and measures specifically for the purpose of achieving equality by actively and openly taking into account at the planning stage their possible effects on the respective situation of men and women (gender perspective)' (EC 1996). Furthermore, 'gender mainstreaming may be described as the (re)organization, improvement, development and evaluation of policy processes, so that a gender equality perspective is incorporated ...' (Council of Europe 1998: 12).

Gender mainstreaming points to the gendered character of systems, procedures and organizations, and aims at the incorporation of women's concerns in regular policymaking (Verloo 2007). There is still a lot of confusion about the meaning of the concept, since some tend to equate it with equal opportunities, equal participation or affirmative action. Research shows that this lack of general understanding results in EU member states adopting policies that are simply a continuation of the previous ones. Some also argue that gender mainstreaming has a counter-effect, i.e. it is largely used as an alibi for eroding positive action (Stratigaki 2005: 180) since it only provides slight modifications to highly uneven systems. The concept has also been criticized for its ethnocentrism. Kašić (2004), who claims that much of the diversity in culture and history within the East is neglected by the gender mainstreaming concept, proposes a theoretical alternative, called 'feminist cross-mainstreaming' that tries to 'decolonize' the representational matrix of the West.

The assessment of the current state of affairs in thirty European countries (EC 2008b) indicates that there are large differences in the organization and implementation of gender mainstreaming. The assessment of active labour market policies, of employment policies, of pay and career policies and of reconciliation policies (supporting the combination of professional and private life) in European countries indicates that gender mainstreaming remains uneven and rather narrow in focus. With the exception of the Nordic countries, a systematic and comprehensive approach is generally lacking in all counties (EC 2008b: 5–9).

Still, there are some examples of both good and bad practices: Lithuania has seen an increase in the level of pay in low-paid jobs; Ireland, UK and the Netherlands reported a lengthening of leave provisions, and the UK and the Netherlands are also moving toward higher coverage of childcare facilities. Central and Eastern European countries reported little changes in length of leave but have seen an increase in the flexibility and the change in entitlements. Some countries in the region also experienced a clear downward trend, and all reported an uneven involvement of men (EC 2008b: 5–9). Gender mainstreaming of reconciliation policies has entered the public agenda in most countries in the region, but it is still mainly seen as a women's problem, especially in Latvia, Estonia and Poland. An exception is Lithuania, where the reconciliation of private and professional life has been identified as an issue for both women and men. Childcare facilities are lacking in most of these countries if compared to the previous period, men are excluded from reconciliation policies, meaning that parenthood is still mainly seen as the mother's responsibility (Ibid.: 55, 65, 71–72).

There is no evidence of gender mainstreaming in labour market policies in the Czech Republic, and only little evidence in Estonia, Cyprus, Hungary, Slovakia and Romania. Latvia, Lithuania and Poland show a slightly more favourable situation (EC 2008b, 47). Tackling the gender pay gap is not on the policy agenda in the Czech Republic, Romania and Bulgaria, and despite the higher awareness, Estonia, Latvia, Poland, Slovakia lack concrete programmes. Wage policy is not sufficiently addressed in Hungary but is more present in policy documents in Slovenia. As far as Western European countries are concerned, gender mainstreaming is high on the political agenda in some countries, but little has been done in practice. Several Western European countries have shown a greater level of awareness but, with some exceptions from the Nordic countries (for instance, Denmark with high unemployment benefits), there is hardly any progress that would change the gender division of labour.

Quality of Women's Work: Trends across Europe

A recent European Commission report (EC 2008a) has noted the steady growth of employment of women in EU27 and consequently the narrowing of the employment rate gap between women and men. Still, several aspects of the quality of women's work through Europe remain problematic: the indicators for pay, labour market segregation and the number of women in managerial positions have not shown an increase for several years. The pay gap persists, sectoral and occupational segregation by gender is not diminishing and is even increasing in some countries. Reconciling professional and private life continues to be a problem as well. Women generally predominate among part time workers while temporary employment contracts are also more common for women. The gap in all areas grows wider with age. Long-term unemployment is still more common among women and they are exposed to a greater extent to the risk of poverty (Ibid.: 8).

Data on women's employment in the media should be seen in the context of other general statistical trends in a specific country or region and not in isolation from these. While there are several data sets that track the general gender division trends in the labour market, there is little research that would consider specific sectors, such as the media. There is little recent data for employment in the media, while more data is available that describes the situation in the 1990s. Women's employment status in the media in the mid-1990s tends to be much more precarious than that of men: women in general form a much higher proportion of part-time, temporary, freelance staff than men. These are the kinds of jobs that rarely enable career advancement and research shows that women tend to accept these jobs due to lack of an alternative and not out of choice (Gallagher 1995: 15–17). In European countries it is clearly still Western Europe (particularly Belgium, Italy, Portugal and Spain) which fall behind in terms of equal opportunities in employment for women in the media.

Employability and Job (In)security

In general in the EU, a female worker with the same educational level, the same number of years of work experience and job tenure as a male worker has an employability level that is 0.128 points lower than that of the male worker (Eurofound 2008b: 15–16). While the employment rate of women has risen on average since 2006, significant differences exist across the EU. For instance, the employment rate of women in 2006 in Malta (34.9 per cent) was less than half that reported in Denmark (73.4 per cent) or Sweden (70.7 per cent).

Some countries, particularly the Czech Republic, Romania and Sweden saw a decrease in employability of women in 2006 compared to the situation in 2001, and a growing gender gap (EC 2008a: 13, 24). Female employment rates are above 70 per cent in Denmark and Sweden, and above 65 per cent in Estonia, Finland, the Netherlands and the UK. Nonetheless, female employment rates remain below 50 per cent in Malta, Italy, Greece and Poland. For the EU27 average, the increase in female employment is 0.3 per cent points over the five-year period 2001–2006 (Eurostat 2008: 36). Women accounted for only 44 per cent of all persons employed across the Union in 2006. The five EU countries with the highest share of female workers (between 47 per cent and 50 per cent) all border the Baltic sea – Estonia, Lithuania, Latvia, Finland and Sweden. At the other end of the scale, women account for the lowest shares of employment in some of the countries bordering the Mediterranean – Spain, Italy, Greece and Malta (EC 2008c: 35). We can see that frequently former communist states are not grouped together despite common historical experiences and similar transition processes. In general a shortfall in Central and Eastern Europe can be explained by the economic recession and restructuring of the transition to market economies during which women's employment rates declined dramatically, and recovery has only been partial.

The unemployment rate of women is higher than the rate for men in most of the EU27, except for Estonia, Ireland, Germany, Latvia and Romania (Eurofound 2008a: 34). Eurostat detects three country groups for 2007: differences between the female and male employment rates are the lowest in the Scandinavian and Baltic countries, Bulgaria and France, and highest in the Mediterranean states, Greece, Spain, Italy and especially Malta. The remaining countries, post-socialist states among them, are placed in-between (Eurostat 2008: 2).

In many new EU member states, such as Bulgaria, Latvia, Lithuania, Slovakia and especially Romania fixed-term employment is not widespread. The gender gap has increased in 8 member states in 2007 compared to the situation in 2000, among them in Cyprus, Czech Republic and Slovenia as new member states (Eurostat 2008: 4). According to data for 2006 women in the EU27 are more likely to hold a temporary employment contract than men, while the general number of people employed on such a contract has increased compared to the year 2001 (Eurofound 2008a: 39).

The Eurofound (2008b: 23) analysis detects a clustering of countries into three groups when the issue of job (in)security is at stake. The first group comprises mainly Central and Northern European countries, where levels of both subjective and objective job insecurity are low. In Mediterranean countries subjective insecurity is low but its objectively measured counterpart is high. Eastern European countries form a cluster with an objectively low but a perceived (subjectively) high job insecurity. This latter remark underlines the widespread feelings of insecurity among workers in Eastern European countries where perceptions are often compared with experiences in the previous regime. In addition, Mediterranean countries show low employability and high objective job insecurity, while Nordic countries appear to be in a better position, showing high employability and low job insecurity. Eastern European countries lie between these two groups. Average subjective job insecurity and vulnerability are clearly positively correlated across countries – with the presence of three outliers, the Czech Republic, Lithuania and Poland – that display a disproportionally high degree of vulnerability, both in terms of the share of vulnerable people and the degree of vulnerability (Ibid.: 23–25).

Areas of Gender Bias: Part-time Work, Sectoral Segregation and Wage Discrimination

Women's participation in the labour market is still largely characterized by a high and increasing share of part-time work. In 2007, the share of women employees working part-time was 31.4 per cent in the EU27 while the corresponding figure for men was 7.8 per cent. The share of female part-timers exceeded 30 per cent in France, Ireland, Denmark and Luxembourg, 40 per cent in Sweden, Austria, Belgium, United Kingdom and Germany and even reached 74.9 per cent in the Netherlands. Conversely, the share of part-timers among female workers was very low in 2007 in most new Eastern European member states, especially in Bulgaria, Slovakia, Hungary, the Czech Republic and Latvia, where it was below 10 per cent. Women predominate among the employees with temporary contracts in Spain, Portugal, Finland, Sweden, Cyprus, Netherlands, Italy, France, Belgium, and also Slovenia, while men prevail in most Central and Eastern European member states, especially Estonia, Romania, Latvia, Lithuania, Poland, Hungary, Bulgaria, but also in Germany and Austria (EC 2008a: 13–14, 17, 22, 23).

Data from the European Labour Force Survey for 2006 (Eurofound 2007: 10) show that part-time employment is rare for women in nine of the EU27 countries, where it accounts for no more than 10 per cent of their employment; these countries are Greece plus eight post-communist member states that have known widespread full-time inclusion of women in the labour market – Bulgaria, the Czech Republic, Estonia, Hungary, Latvia, Romania, Slovakia and Slovenia. The Eurofound (2007: 5–6) analysis on working conditions reports the changed gender gap in the eight member states from Central and Eastern Europe (Czech Republic, Estonia, Hungary, Latvia, Lithuania, Poland, Slovakia, Slovenia) in 2001 and 2005 – three years before membership and one year after they joined the EU. The changes tend to have been towards increased inequalities in working conditions between male and female workers: for instance, the proportion of women working part time in these eight countries has increased slightly, while the proportion of men working part time has declined slightly.

For these countries the proportion of women working more than 48 hours a week declined from 19 per cent to 14 per cent over the five-year period. This decrease was entirely among blue-collar women, who reported a reduction in long working hours in their main job from 30 per cent to 19 per cent. As the Eurofund report notes, these changes indicate that the gender gap is widening, and that the labour markets of these new member states 'come to resemble patterns typical for western European labour markets, where women typically work shorter full-time or part-time hours' (ibid.: 6).

As a consequence of segregated labour markets women are under-represented in sectors crucial for economic development: for example, only 29 per cent of scientists and engineers in the EU are women (EC 2008a: 14). Generally speaking, women work in jobs that involve caring, nurturing and providing services for people. Men tend to monopolize senior management and manual jobs which involve using machinery or production processes considered to be physically onerous. Women hold the majority of jobs in clerical (69 per cent), service and sales (58 per cent), and technical or associate professional positions (56 per cent). They constitute the majority of the workforce in domestic services in private households (82 per cent), health (79 per cent), education (72 per cent) and other community, social and personal services (59 per cent), and half of the workforce in hotels and restaurants (Eurofound 2007: 11, 14).

Studies in EU27 (Eurofound 2008b: 39) show that gender wage discrimination is also apparent in all countries: women are mainly concentrated in the lower part of the wage distribution, while their male counterparts are mainly concentrated in the upper part. It emerges that women still earn lower wages than men with equal characteristics. Women employed full time are much less likely to have earnings in the highest income bracket. Women employed part time are even more likely to be less well paid than men employed part time. Gender segregation is a major factor in the gender pay gap, as women are disproportionately concentrated in lower paid jobs and the lower ranks of the better-paid managerial and professional occupations. Furthermore, women still earn less than men even when they have similar jobs, qualifications and experience, due to sex discrimination and unequal treatment (Eurofound 2007: 17).

Women in Decision-making: Underrepresented across Europe

Data shows an overall low share of women in decision-making across Europe with significant country and regional differences, including between the Central and Eastern European countries. The average proportion of female members of national parliaments (single/lower houses) was 23 per cent in 2007, unchanged since 2004. This share was exceeded in Belgium, Spain, Denmark and the Netherlands (35 per cent) and in Finland and Sweden (40 per cent). However, it was below 15 per cent in Greece, Cyprus, France, Slovenia, Ireland, Romania and Hungary and below 10 per cent in Malta (EC 2008c: 25–27). The share of women amongst members of national parliaments of the EU27 countries has increased by almost half in the last decade, from 16 per cent in 1997 to 23 per cent in 2007, but this is still well below the generally accepted minimum target of 30 per cent (EC 2008c: 11). Women are still under-represented as parliamentary leaders. In 2007 there were ten EU countries that had 30 per cent or more women ministers, among which there are no Central and Eastern European countries apart from Bulgaria. Women ministers are rarely promoted to the top position in government, and are most often responsible for socio-cultural portfolios (EC 2008c: 25–27).

Women are under-represented in all managerial positions across Europe; women working full- time and part-time are less likely to be in senior management than their male counterparts. However, women are not under-represented in senior management in six countries (from EU27) – the Czech Republic, Estonia, Latvia, Malta, the Netherlands and Portugal – and appear to be over-represented in this regard in Bulgaria (Eurofound 2007: 13–14). Regarding decision-making in the economic sphere, women's share among managers in enterprises and administrations was 32.6 per cent in 2006, up from 30.1 per cent in 2001. This share exceeded 35 per cent in Hungary, France, Latvia and Lithuania, but was lower than 20 per cent in Malta and Cyprus (EC 2008a: 14).

Data for 2007 indicates that less than 3 per cent of the blue-chip companies in each of the 27 EU states have a woman leader of the highest decision-making body. Moreover, even this low figure is significantly affected by higher numbers of female business leaders in the new member states, which account for more than three quarters of the total. In the twelve new member states just over 7 per cent of the leading companies are led by women compared to 1 per cent for the EU-15 countries (EC 2008c: 36). In the judiciary, the groups of judges presiding over each of the national supreme courts comprise an average of 70 per cent men and 30 per cent women but this balance is significantly influenced by high numbers of women in the courts of some of the countries that joined the EU in the last two accessions – in particular Bulgaria (76 per cent women) and Romania (74 per cent) (EC 2008c: 53). Still, among lawyers, for example, women typically specialize in family law and men in corporate law, while in the teaching profession, women are under-represented as head teachers and in other leadership positions (Eurofound 2007: 13).

Gender Segregation in Media Employment

Social circumstances in the post-socialist period with distinct gender disparities shape specific gender relations, among them those in the media field. In the 1990s, the European media sector, and journalism in particular, has become increasingly feminized. This trend was expected to continue in the first decade of the 2000 and is reflected in high proportions of females enrolled in journalism study programs. A closer look, however, reveals some of the old patterns of gender imbalance; women typically occupy lower rank jobs while the upper editorial and managerial positions still remain a predominately male domain throughout Europe. In sections that follow we examine the gendered character of media systems taking as a starting point the assumption that both historical legacies and the placement of women within the specific economic and political context affects the position of women in the media (Figure 4.1).

Gallagher points to the gulf between perception and reality that lies in the fact that women while present in all of the media are still confronted with barriers when striving for a career in the media (Gallagher 1995: 2). Women are discriminated against at the stage of recruitment, they occupy jobs such as assistants, administrators, secretaries, writers, announcers, while decision-making power in the media is still mostly a male domain (Ibid.: 5, 7, 10). These are, despite some differences, characteristics of both Western and Central and Eastern European countries.

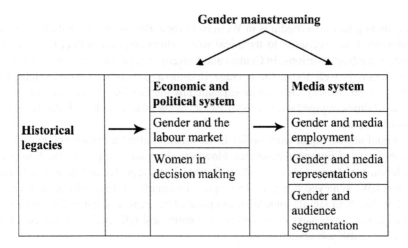

Figure 4.1   Gender and media systems

Data for the mid-1990s shows sub-regional patterns for Europe. Women's share of media employment in television and radio is highest in the Baltic states (Estonia, Lithuania – 47 per cent), followed by other Central and Eastern European countries (Bulgaria, Hungary, Romania, Russian Federation – and average of 45 per cent), the Nordic states (Denmark, Finland, Norway, Sweden – 41 per cent), and Western Europe (Belgium, France, Germany) with other states (Greece, Ireland, Italy, Luxembourg, Netherlands, Portugal, Spain, UK – 35 per cent) at the bottom (Gallagher 1995). The recent European Federation of Journalists study, however, revealed somewhat different patterns. Portugal reported 80 per cent of women among journalists, Serbia 57 per cent, Finland 55 per cent and Latvia 50 per cent. Cyprus, Croatia, Estonia, Slovakia, Denmark, Norway and Sweden all reported 40 per cent or more female journalists, while Germany, Italy and UK and Ireland had a rate of above 30 per cent (Witt-Barthel 2006).

Data also confirms that many women working in the media end up in assistant rather than leading positions. Female announcers and presenters are more likely to be found in television than radio, which can be explained by the fact that the media values women's presence on the screen to attract audiences. Producers and directors are mostly male, and senior production jobs are also a male domain – 11 per cent is the average for women in Europe. However, some Central and Eastern European countries prove an exception: in Estonia, Romania, Bulgaria and Lithuania women's share in production executives is more than 25 per cent, although gender disparity is evident also in these countries. The overall European average of 16.6 per cent women in senior broadcast management is inflated by the high proportions of women in these positions in the Baltic states, in Bulgaria and in Romania. Women's share in this occupational group is also above average in Nordic states, while it is lower than 5 per cent in Germany, Italy and Luxembourg.

Technical area in the media is in Western Europe almost entirely a male domain; few women are recruited to technical work which does not reflect the share of women's job applications. In Central and Eastern Europe the proportion of female technicians is well above the average if compared to other regions (Gallagher 1995: 25, 30, 38, 47). This can be explained by the fact that planned economies in socialist times engaged women in all sectors of the labour market, skilled technical work included.

Equal pay for equal work policy in the media is also far from being realized in the majority of European countries. However, there are exceptions: the European Federation of Journalists study (Witt-Barthel 2006) reports that Croatia, Italy and Serbia have achieved this goal. In Cyprus, Denmark, Finland, Slovakia, Sweden and Switzerland female journalists are paid 10 per cent less that male journalists, while their counterparts in in Norway, Germany and UK receive 20 per cent less for comparable job assignments.

Gender based segregation is also noted in the allocation of work assignments where women are directed towards 'soft' topics of human interest, social affairs, culture, rather than 'hard' areas such as business, finance and/or economics. Research also shows that when restricted to 'soft' topics, promotion prospects for women may be limited (Gallagher 1995: 54–55). These patterns apply to media environments across Europe, with Southern countries being the worse off and the Central and Eastern European region with a slightly better situation, a fact that can be attributed to the socialist heritage.

Bias in Content Production, Representation and Media Readership

There is a lack of research in recent decades that systematically analyses gender in relation to media content in post-socialist countries. Research on women and the media remains highly fragmented and mostly focused on portrayals of women in national television or press content. The *Report on Existing Research in the European Union* finds out that quantitative studies are more or less limited to relatively straightforward counts of the number of women and men who appear in the media, and of attributes such as their occupation or family status (EC 1999: 6). Trends point to an increase in qualitative studies where the emphasis has shifted from figures, job and task description to more complex gendered substructures that include symbols, values, meanings and significations (Bruin 2000: 225). Still, research remains limited to case study analysis placed in national environments and there is a lack of cross-country comparison. These national case studies tend to examine the broader social meanings of gender images, but lack a comparative dimension that would address the European media sphere in wider terms.

Consequently, a characteristic of the field is a strong focus on micro-level analysis, e.g. content analysis of specific media genres, rather than broader research approaches that would take into account also media ownership patterns, regulation, or economic and political indicators that shape gender representation.

Also notable is a strong focus on popular culture and entertainment. Genres such as women's magazines, soap operas, melodrama, which had been neglected in male-dominated research, are the focus of feminist media analysis, while genres of news, current affairs and other factual media content is neglected (EC 1999: 6–7).

Women Underrepresented as News-makers and News-subjects

The Global Media Monitoring Project, which periodically examines the representation of men and women in the media (television, radio and newspapers and also the internet), demonstrates that women are dramatically under-represented in the news across the globe (Gallagher 2010). Only 24 per cent of news subjects – i.e. the people who are interviewed, or whom the news is about – internationally are female. Women's points of view are rarely heard in the topics that dominate the news agenda. There is not a single major news topic in which women outnumber men as newsmakers. In stories on politics and government only 14 per cent of news subjects are women; and in economic and business news only 20 per cent; yet these are the topics that dominate the news agenda in all countries.

As for country specificities, the 2005 Global Media Monitoring Project report (2005) provides data for some South East European countries (Croatia, Bosnia-Herzegovina and Serbia-Montenegro) and for some new EU member states such as Hungary, Estonia, Malta and Romania. In all European countries studied – the study provides data also for Austria, Belgium, Finland, Germany, Ireland, Italy, Netherland, Norway, Portugal, Spain, Sweden, Switzerland and the UK – females were dramatically underrepresented as news subjects; on average, only 21.6 per cent of news subjects were women. The proportion is below 20 in Hungary, Bosnia-Herzegovina, Serbia-Montenegro, Malta, Austria, Italy and Switzerland. As news subjects women were underrepresented in major topic areas, especially in economy and business (18.3 per cent) and politics and government (15.4 per cent), but also in social and legal issues. Here, however, South and Eastern European countries ranked better, especially Romania (52 per cent), Hungary (46 per cent) and Estonia (42 per cent). Among Western European countries only Norway ranked comparably with 43 per cent.

Women were also underrepresented as reporters; only an average of 41 per cent being women. In five countries there were more than 50 per cent of female reporters: Croatia, Serbia-Montenegro, Austria, Portugal and Spain. Newspaper reporters were more likely to be male although the situation for South East and Eastern European countries was much better in this regard: 71 per cent of newspaper reporters are female in Estonia and 54 per cent in Croatia and Romania. The situation was comparable only in Portugal (51 per cent). While in Serbia-Montenegro the proportion was above 40 and in Bosnia-Herzegovina and Hungary above 30, and only 11 per cent for Malta, some Western European countries reported an even worse situation, with the lowest figure in Belgium (6 per cent) (all data based on Gallagher 2005: 118–40).

As newsmakers, women are visibly under-represented in professional categories such as law (18 per cent), business (12 per cent) and politics (12 per cent) while in reality, women's share of these occupations is higher. Overall, male journalists report at the so-called 'hard' or 'serious' end of the news spectrum such as politics and government (where women reporters contribute only 32 per cent of stories). Female journalists are more likely to work on the so-called 'soft' stories such as social and legal issues (40 per cent reported by women). Although many 'soft' news stories are important, they are not always perceived as such in the hierarchy of news values. As a result, the work of female journalists is sometimes under-valued, and women reporters are frequently assigned to stories that are downright trivial – celebrity news (50 per cent reported by women), or arts and entertainment (48 per cent) (Gallagher 2005: 16–21). Also, when women do make the news it is primarily as 'stars' (celebrities, royalty) or as 'ordinary' people. Women barely feature in news stories as authorities and experts. Expert opinion in the news is overwhelmingly male. In 2010 men made up 77 per cent, and 81 per cent of spokespersons. By contrast, women appear in a personal capacity – as eye witnesses (36 per cent) or giving personal views. Also, symptomatically there is hardly any news reporting on gender stereotypes and even among those that do so, more stories are published in all countries that reinforce stereotypes compared to those that challenge them (Gallagher 2010).

Women are also more than twice as likely as men to be portrayed as victims: 18 per cent of female news subjects, compared with 8 per cent of males are portrayed in this way. News disproportionately focuses on female victims in events that actually affect both sexes – accidents, crime, war. In stories on crime, violence or disaster, pictures of women are frequently employed for dramatic effect. In newspapers and on television, the female body is often used to titillate (Ibid.)

The most recent Global Media Monitoring project (Gallagher 2010) reports female news subjects are more than three times as likely as males to be identified in terms of their family status: 18 per cent of women are described as wife, daughter, mother etc.; only 5 per cent of men are described as husband, son, father and so on. Even in authoritative functions such as spokesperson or expert, women do not escape this identification with family. Estonia is an exception, where male family status was more frequently mentioned. Italy, Norway and Austria have differences of up to 50 per cent while in all other countries female family status was mentioned in more than twice as many cases as male (Gallagher 2005). So, while men are perceived and valued as autonomous individuals, women's status is deemed to derive primarily from their relationship to others. It is from these relationships, rather than from her own autonomous being, that a woman draws her authority.

Some positive trends should be noted as well. There has been a steady increase in the proportion of news items reported by women from 28 per cent in 1995, to 31 per cent in 2000, reaching 37 per cent in 2005 and retaining the same share in 2010. Female reporters have gained more ground in radio and television than in newspapers. The press lags far behind the electronic media, with only 29 per cent of stories written by female reporters in 2005 and 33 per cent in 2010.

Domestication in Representation, Gaps in Readership

Taking a long-term view at gender patterns in media representations in Central and Eastern Europe, it appears that political and economic changes have ushered in some 'old' gender stereotypes that did not exist under socialism or were covered by the alleged egalitarianism. The market-oriented shifts in media landscapes that followed 1989 have introduced new stereotypes of women, particularly with respect to the sexualization and exploitation of women's bodies. The capitalist mode of media production seems to have forced women out of their jobs and away from relatively equal positions (EC 1999: 7, 25) – relatively, since equality was largely limited to the sphere of labour, while inequality in the private sphere persisted.

True (1999: 366) notes a shift in the post-socialist countries: in contrast to socialist claims that women are emancipated through labour, the new idiom of emancipation is to express one's femininity. The post-socialist era is marked by the privatization of social policy as well as retraditionalization of family relations. Gender differences are increasingly portrayed by the media as 'facts of nature': post-communist images depict women as consumers in contrast to socialist images of working women. Arguably, a large number of women's magazines has contributed to this trend.

Contemporary media and advertising images in the region tend to address both the socialist past and the capitalist present: the former socialist order where identity was tied to labour is negated, while the new capitalist order of individualism, sexual identity and gender difference is affirmed, manufacturing new gender-specific needs, desires and identities (Ibid.: 367, 373, 379). Portrayals of gender in Bulgarian TV advertisements confirm the trend towards new kinds of gender stereotypes compared to previous images of working and liberated women. Women appear for the most part visually, but not speaking; they're overwhelmingly young, placed in leisure or home setting, and advertising domestic and leisure products, used for self-enhancement and pleasure (Ibroscheva 2007: 414).

Comparative studies of gendered media representations are extremely rare. An exception to the rule is a cross-country comparison of newspaper portrayal of gender roles in Bosnia and Herzegovina, Croatia and Serbia (Isanović 2006). Results show that men appear almost five times more often than women, and there are no significant differences among the nine monitored newspapers or among the three countries. The situation with regard to the persons who have a central role in the article is similar: this position is mostly occupied by men (77.5 per cent of cases) and rarely by women (13.3 per cent). The comparison of the positioning of gender groups in different thematic sections indicates that men dominate in all of them, though less so in the sections culture/art and entertainment. The proportions of men are particularly high in current affairs and politics, sport and economy and business. Men are also 5.5 times more often presented as the primary source of information in all countries. Results also show that men are quoted four to five times more often than women and are also interviewed five times more often than women. In cases when an expert gives an opinion, 89.2 per cent of the time it is a man. What is significant is that the diversity of women's professions visible within the inside pages is smaller than that of men, and that most of the professions seem to be dominated by men.

The distribution of specific gender groups across different occupations show that 3.8 per cent of all women are identified as celebrities, musicians, actors or writers (entertainers and performers), while 18.2 per cent of women could not be linked to any specific occupational category. Unlike women, men are more evenly distributed across different occupations, i.e. they appear as celebrities, musicians, actors or writers, politicians and representatives of government. The research shows that newspapers present women as dominant only in the sex-industry, i.e. as sex-workers, or as homemakers/parents. In all other professions women are represented significantly less frequently than men. Irrespective of occupation, women who appear in articles on inside pages are three times more often identified in terms of their family status or relationships, or with references to family relations, and descriptions and discussions of marital status, parenthood and family life. The analysis of newspaper photographs reached similar results. Among photos published on the inside pages, the majority were photos of men (55.2 per cent) while women were present in roughly a quarter of that (15.7 per cent). In photos published on the front pages, the presence of women was even smaller (Isanović 2006: 58–70).

It is instructive to compare these results to those reached by a comparative study of gender roles in television in some Western European countries, i.e. in Denmark, Finland, Sweden, Netherlands, Norway and Germany. Although the methods of analysis and sampling procedures were too different to allow for a direct comparison, it is clear that the overall results are similar to those seen in Central and Eastern Europe. The data points to a very traditional divide, with most female participation on television associated with topics such as human relations, family, health and social issues. Women are also less likely to be present as experts (17 per cent). The study points out that the concern is not only with the matter of how many women participate, but also with contexts in which they appear, their authority and ways of communication (Eie 1998).

The WomenAction 2000 report (Shivdas 2000) also confirms that the stereotyped media portrayal of women is a worldwide trend. The report also notes a significant increase in media images that perpetuate violence against women, and points to women's lack of access to expression and decision-making in and through the media. With regard to Central and Eastern Europe the report mentions the Czech media arguing that they have managed to maintain traditional, patriarchal views on women that are expressed foremost through advertising. The Croatian media are criticized for the lack of socially responsible and gender-sensitive journalism, as well as for the lack of awareness of the need for gender equality criticized. The media are reproached for publishing decidedly sexist images of women, for not providing programming addressing the problems and status of women, and, among others, for their low regard of women's human rights.

Another trend noted across Europe is the stereotypical characterization of women in power: women's gains at work are presented to be possible only at the expense of domestic failure (EC 1999: 11–12, 14). Women politicians are often masculinized, presented as robust, as strong as men but lacking feminine virtue, or, alternatively, their beauty becomes the subject of media attention. Research for Latvia points out that a woman politician has to prove that she is suitable and professional, and that the media are not forgiving at all in case of mistakes. On the other hand, the media pay attention to their appearance, clothes, style of dress and so on. In contrast, a key attribute for a male politician is his ability to generate ideas. In Estonia, the media were found to reinforce gender stereotypes by emphasizing that women only come to politics thanks to social ties or by chance and that their motivation is self-actualization and ambition but never professionalism or altruism. In a similar vein the analysis of roles that the media attribute to female politicians in television in Italy showed that topics such as job, career, and competence are eclipsed by the topics of family, domestic matters, even cooking abilities. Reports for Latvia, Estonia, Italy and Denmark all show that the media, when dealing with a female politician, pay special attention to her looks, manners and are much more interested in her private life (Kilis 2004). Similar patterns are recognized in the analysis of Bulgarian print media which favour the consumer lifestyle of women in power. Female politicians are represented as beautiful, elegant, devoted mothers and wives, favouring their own private images over their public figures (Danova 2006: 119, 130–131). Studies all over Europe show that while media emphasise the political record and experience of male politicians, female politicians are placed in the context of family or their appearance. These patterns have been confirmed for the Nordic countries, the Netherlands (van Zoonen 2000) and the UK where analysis reveals sexualization, exclusion of women from core political issues, emphasis on domestic and family circumstances, and commodification of their bodies (Ross and Sreberny 2000: 84, 87, 88).

Gender differences also exist in newspaper readership across Europe where the general trend is that men read more than women. The extent of these differences varies significantly between countries. Hallin and Mancini (2004: 24) report there are large gender differences in newspaper reading in Southern Europe while these are small or non-existent in Western and Northern European countries: the gender gap is 35 per cent in Portugal while it hardly reaches 1 per cent in Sweden. These differences are believed to be related to historical developments, they are reflected in the level of literacy, development of the press, and are also connected to the fact that the media in Southern Europe were more closely related to political life that excluded women. In Central and Eastern European countries gender gaps are comparable to the situation in Northern and Western Europe, while the Netherlands, Denmark, Luxembourg and Belgium have larger gaps. Among post-socialist countries the difference is 1.3 per cent in Slovakia, 2 per cent in Estonia, 3.6 per cent in Slovenia, 4.6 per cent in Czech Republic and 4.7 per cent in Hungary, while Poland appears as the only European country with a 'negative' gender gap (0.5 per cent), meaning that women tend to read more than men. In addition, the reading patterns of Slovakia and Poland appear closer to Southern Europe, while Hungary, the Czech Republic, Slovenia and Estonia have fewer non-readers and people spend more time reading (Elvestad and Blekesaune 2008: 432, 435).

Conclusions

Fragmented data prevent us from making conclusions that would systematically point to regional differences within Europe, related to specific media systems in their dealing with gender in news production, representation and consumption. Nevertheless, data presented in this chapter suggests that Central and Eastern European countries share significant similarities. These similarities can be linked to their shared experience of market liberalization and the pluralization and diversity of media ownership in the post-1989 period. They are also rooted in the shared experience of socialism, which was associated with a relatively high level of state support for gender equality, albeit limited only to the labour sector. Of course, differences between individual countries in the region should not be underestimated either. They are related to their previous experiences with the socialist regime and various post-1989 experiences with the changes of political systems and processes of market liberalization.

On the whole, the data discussed in this chapter suggest that over the past two decades, gender inequality in Central and Eastern Europe has worsened, and its patters have come to resemble those familiar from Western, Northern or Southern European states. The various data sets discussed throughout the chapter clearly show a decline in women's employment rates and the lowering level of social provisions that negatively affected women's positions in general, and in the media in particular. The only area where the socialist legacy appears to persist is related to the gendered distribution of labour; generally speaking, Central and Eastern Europe still boasts more women in senior positions and in technical occupations and fewer women in part-time work compared to Western Europe. This means that much of the positive heritage of socialist gender policies was lost. Despite different histories of media development and different paths of political and economic development, European countries are now all characterized by markedly similar patterns of gender inequality, both in the realm of media employment and wages and in the realm of media representations. The exact levels of gender discrimination of course vary from country to country but their overall presence implies similar patterns of gender divide across all parts of Europe.

These similarities can be explained by arguing with Splichal (2001: 33) that Central and Eastern European societies 'were caught up in imitation of West-European practices in economy and society rather than examining the possible contributions of Western media systems to the specific situations in East-Central Europe that would contribute to a radical departure from the previous non-democratic activities under the socialist regimes'. It is thus not surprising that commercialization of media markets in Central and Eastern Europe, increased privatization and foreign ownership as well as increased foreign, especially American, leisure TV programmes introduced new gender stereotypes, related specifically to the sexualization of women. A related characteristic of post-socialist media systems that can explain their pronounced gender inequity is the so-called 'paternalist commercialism', a characteristic of media systems in the region that originally stands for privatization and commercialization of the media and the exercise of political power over the media (Splichal 2001: 52). Media commercialism is paternal towards women and attitudes of 'paternalist commercialism' are seen in various fields of media operation: employment and wage policies that direct women to underpaid lower-ranking jobs, professionalization standards that lack gender sensitive reporting, stereotypical representations of women and so on. This helps explain why frequently the data presented in this chapter points to similar levels of gender inequity in spheres of communication across Europe, specifically in employment of female media workers and in stereotypical mediated representations of women. It thus seems that current efforts of gender mainstreaming will have the capacity to improve women's positions only if they first recognize and deal with paternalist structures on which the liberalization and commercialization of Central and Eastern European media systems are based.

References

Corrin, C. 1992. 'Introduction', in *Superwomen and the Double Burden: Women's Experience of Change in Central and Eastern Europe and the Former Soviet Union*, edited by C. Corrin. London: Scarlet Press, 1–27.

Council of Europe. 1998. *Gender Mainstreaming: Conceptual Framework, Methodology and Presentation of Good Practices*. Strasbourg: Directorate General of Human Rights.

Danova, M. 2006. *Women in politics in Bulgarian newspapers: post-feminism in a post-totalitarian society, in Stereotyping: Representation of Women in Print Media in South East Europe*, edited by N. Moranjak Bamburać, T. Jusić and A. Isanović. Sarajevo: Mediacenter, 111–32.

De Bruin, M. 2000. Gender, Organizational and Professional Identities in Journalism. *Journalism*, 1(2), 217–38.

EC. 1996. *Incorporating Equal Opportunities for Women and Men into all Community Policies and Activities*. Brussels: European Commission.

EC. 1999. *Images of Women in the Media: Report on Existing Research in the European Union*. Luxembourg: Office for Official Publications of the European Communities.

EC. 2008a. *Report on Equality Between Women and Men – 2008*. Brussels: European Communities.

EC. 2008b. *Gender Mainstreaming of Employment Policies: A Comparative Review of Thirty European Countries*. Luxembourg: Office for Official Publications of the European Communities.

EC. 2008c. *Women and Men in Decision-Making 2007: Analysis of the Situation and Trends*. Luxembourg: Office for Official Publications of the European Communities.

Eie, B. 2009. Screening Gender. Who Speaks in Television? A Comparative Study of Female Participation in Television Programmes. Available at: http://yle.fi/gender/whos/whosreport.html [accessed 30 June 2009].

Einhorn, B. 1993. *Cinderella Goes to Market: Citizenship, Gender and Women's Movements in East Central Europe*. London: Verso.

Elvestad, E. and Blekesaune, A. 2008. Newspaper Readers in Europe: a Multilevel Study of Individual and National Differences. *European Journal of Communication*, 23(4), 425–47.

Eurostat. 2008. *Employment Gender Gap in the EU is Narrowing: Labour Market Trends 2000–2007*. Brussels: European Communities.

Eurofound. 2007. *Working Conditions in the European Union: The Gender Perspective*. Luxembourg: Office for Official Publications of the European Communities.

Eurofound. 2008a. *Annual Review of Working Conditions in the EU 2007–2008*. Luxembourg: Office for Official Publications of the European Communities.

Eurofound. 2008b. *Employment Security and Employability: A Contribution to the Flexicurity Debate*. Luxembourg: Office for Official Publications of the European Communities.

Gallagher, M. 1995. *An Unfinished Story: Gender Patterns in Media Employment*. Paris: Unesco.

Gallagher, M. 2005. *GMMP (Global Media Monitoring Project): Who Makes the News?* London: WACC.

Gallagher, M. 2010. GMMP *(Global Media Monitoring Project): Who Makes the News?* London: WACC.

Hallin D.C. and Mancini, P. 2004. *Comparing Media Systems: Three Models of Media and Politics*. Cambridge: Cambridge University Press.

Ibroscheva, E. 2007. Caught between East and West? Portrayals of gender in Bulgarian television advertisements. *Sex Roles*, 57, 409–18.

Isanović, A. 2006. *Media discourse as a male domain: gender representation in the daily newspapers of Bosnia and Herzegovina, Croatia and Serbia, in Stereotyping: Representation of Women in Print Media in South East Europe*, edited by N. Moranjak Bamburać, T. Jusić and A. Isanović. Sarajevo: Mediacenter, 43–110.

Kašić, B. 2005. Feminist Cross-mainstreaming within 'East–West' Mapping: a Postsocialist Perspective. *European Journal of Women's Studies*, 11(4), 473–485.

Kilis, R. 2004. Gender Inequality and Political Governance: Summary of Country Research Reports. Available at: http://www.medijuprojekts.lv/?object_id=427 [accessed 30 June 2009]

Novikova, I. 2004. Gender Equality and Gender Mainstreaming: Achievements and Issues. Sociologija. Mintis ir veiksmas, 3, 6–12.

Pajnik, M. 2008. *Prostitution and Human Trafficking: Gender, Labour and Migration Aspects*. Ljubljana: Mirovni inštitut.

Pascall, G and Manning, N. 2000. Gender and social policy: comparing welfare states in Central and Eastern Europe and the former Soviet Union. *Journal of European Social Policy*, 20(3), 240–66.

Pascall, G. and Kwak, A. 2005. *Gender Regimes in Transition in Central and Eastern Europe*. Bristol: Policy Press.

Ross, K and Sreberny, A. 2000. *Women in the House: Media Representation of British Politicians, in Gender, Politics and Communication*, edited by A. Sreberny and L. van Zoonen. NJ: Hampton Press, 79–99.

Shivdas, M.M. 2000. Alternative Assessment of Women and Media, Report Based on NGO Reviews of Section J, Beijing Platforms for Action. Available at: http://www.womenaction.org/csw44/altrepeng.htm [accessed 17 August 2009].

Splichal, S. 2001. Imitative revolutions: changes in the media and journalism in East-Central Europe, *Javnost–The Public*, 8(4), 31–58.

Stratigaki, M. 2005. Gender Mainstreaming vs. Positive Action: an Ongoing Conflict in EU Gender Equality Policy. *European Journal of Women's Studies*, 12(2), 165–86.

True, J. 1999. Expanding Markets and Marketing Gender: the Integration of the Post-socialist Czech Republic. *Review of International Political Economy*, 6(3), 360–89.

Verloo, M., ed. 2007. *Multiple Meanings of Gender Equality: A Critical Frame Analysis of Gender Policies in Europe*. Budapest: CEU Press.

Witt-Barthel, A. 2006. Putting Journalism to Rights, EFJ-survey: Women Journalists in the European Integration Process. Paper presented at EFJ annual meeting, 7–9 April 2006, Bled, Slovenia.

Zoonen van, L. 2000. *Broken Hearts, Broken Dreams? Politicians and their Families in Popular Culture, in Gender, Politics and Communication*, edited by A. Sreberny and L. van Zoonen. Cresskill, NJ: Hampton Press, 101–19.

Chapter 5

Transnational Capital, Media Differentiation, and Institutional Isomorphism in Central and Eastern European Media Systems

John Downey

Introduction

The purpose of this chapter is to explore at the level of individual firms the nature and extent of transnational media investment in Central and Eastern Europe and to consider the impact of such investment on media systems in the region. Subscribing to a neo-institutional line of reasoning, the central argument will be that transnational media firms export business models successful elsewhere, notably in North America and in other parts of Europe, to Central and Eastern European countries. This is *mimetic* institutional isomorphism based primarily on the *know-how* of transnational media companies operating in an uncertain environment and the possibility of transnational synergies across distinct national markets. The extent of such investment is dependent upon a number of factors, namely, relative affluence and expanding advertising markets in Central and Eastern Europe, relatively permissive media regulatory regimes and stable political regimes, and relative paucity of domestic and international competitors. Such transnational media investments tend to have a moderating effect, for a variety of reasons, on the development of media systems in the region and help to explain why media systems there have not developed straightforwardly into politically polarized systems as we might have expected given comparative analysis of post-authoritarian media systems, especially Hallin and Mancini (2004). Neither, however, do these markets exhibit a 'triumph of liberalism' if we mean by this the development of highly competitive media markets.

The chapter consists of two parts: in the first part the overall theoretical framework and method of the chapter is explained through discussing the competing logics that affect media development and the importance of neo-institutional analysis (that is still unknown in media analysis although widely practised in the adjacent field of cultural sociology) in explaining changes in media systems; in the second part these methods are adopted in order to analyse briefly four important cases of transnational media investment in Central and Eastern Europe.

The Competition of Logics

Hallin and Mancini (2004) in their analysis of North American and Northern, Western and Southern European media systems develop three ideal type models: the liberal or North Atlantic model, the North/Central European or democratic corporatist model, and the Mediterranean or polarized pluralist model. A key feature of the Mediterranean or polarized pluralist model is 'late democratisation' (2004: 68). Most of the states concerned (Greece, Portugal, and Spain) have only recently, in the 1970s, emerged from authoritarian regimes and, of course, Mussolini's Fascist regime in Italy endured for over twenty years in the second quarter of the twentieth century. While Germany has far from a polarized media system, it may be an exception (and an exception that can be readily explained). It may be that, generally, the experiences of authoritarian regimes, after their fall, lead to politically polarized systems. In the politically polarized parts of Europe, the Right still continues to be associated with Fascist dictatorships by the Left and the Right associate the Left with Bolshevism and Stalinism. Both tend to regard media as useful instruments in a continuing civil war by other means.

Given this apparent relationship between authoritarian regimes and the subsequent development of polarized pluralism, it is certainly a reasonable hypothesis that Central and Eastern European states after the fall of state socialism would develop similarly polarized media systems. This would mean states in this region would have media systems with high levels of press and broadcasting political parallelism, low levels of journalistic autonomy and professionalization, high levels of state intervention, and 'savage deregulation', a speedy and sweeping introduction of commercial media. There are clearly some elements here that are common to both Mediterranean and Central and Eastern European post-authoritarian states, most notably savage deregulation and the speedy introduction of commercial media, but does that mean that the region's media systems can be easily categorized as 'polarized pluralist' media systems? While there are some elements of politically polarized media systems in Central and Eastern Europe, they do not fit *neatly* into such a system and this is partly accounted for by the substantial presence of transnational media companies that have had a moderating effect on media systems in the region. While transnational media are the subject of this chapter, it is important to stress at the outset that transnational media investment is not the only or even the major cause of this process. Another major factor is the reality and possibility of European Union membership and the moderating effect that this may have on party political pluralism in the region, which in turn may influence the degree of polarization in media systems.

Mazzoleni (1987) has referred to the structural-functionalist process of media differentiation as the development of an independent 'media logic' as opposed to a 'political logic', where media are subordinate to political interests. Hallin and Mancini refer to this process as the triumph of the North Atlantic or liberal model while admitting the difficulty associated with the concepts of differentiation and 'media logic'. Is media logic, for example, 'essentially a *professional* or a *commercial* logic' (2004: 253). As this ambiguity exists, it is better to speak of *three* logics, not two – the ideological-political, the professional, and the economic – existing in a complex and mutating relationship with one another that is extremely difficult, but desirable for analytical purposes, to disentangle. As I show, however, to understand media developments in Central and Eastern Europe (and elsewhere for that matter) one has to grasp the complicated and undulating relationship between these three forces. Through showing the interplay of these three forces and the rise of transnational media investment in selected post-communist states I will also show that the claim of a triumph of a 'liberal model' is also somewhat premature, to say the very least, in these countries. Many Central and Eastern European media markets are not characterized by high levels of competition and transnational firms have become dominant players. It is difficult to characterize media developments in the region as either the advent of polarized pluralism or as the triumph of the liberal model.

An 'ideological-political' logic is one that sees newspapers as ideally the bearers of a particular set of political positions or ideology that it passes on to readers. It may involve a political party controlling a newspaper or an owner using his newspaper to promulgate his worldview or an advocacy newspaper collectively owned by journalists. The links between controller and editorial position may be indirect, where an editor has some relative autonomy, or more direct where the owner simply picks up the phone to instruct an obedient editor. There can, therefore, be degrees of differentiation between political-ideological and media systems that are often difficult to observe directly and are often intentionally obscured. There may well be tensions within organizations between ideological-political and professional logics.

What is meant here by 'professional logic' is the dominant self-description of journalists in North America and Western Europe namely that it is the job of journalists to report 'objectively', 'neutrally', and 'impartially'. This has also been referred to, in a more critical fashion, as 'depoliticized' journalism (Chalaby 1996). Such journalism is largely achieved through placing before the public the competing positions of political and economic elites without explicit comment. There is a clear separation between reporting and commentary and editorial with separate sections in newspapers and television news programmes devoted to commentary. This professional logic is founded on a notion of the appropriate role for a journalist in a democratic society, usually formulated in terms of the duty of journalists to inform citizens and thus secure democratic institutions. The professional logic is also, therefore, fundamentally a political-ideological logic in that it operates according to a vision of liberal representative democracy but one that seeks to distance itself from the ideologies of competing political elites within such systems. For example, politicians and journalists may share commitments to the establishment of a liberal capitalist democracy but journalists may take distance from social democratic and neo-liberal variants of this ideology. This commitment to liberal democratic institutions means that anti-system parties on the left and right are often either excluded from being reported or, when present, are not seen as part of the sphere in which it is desirable to maintain 'impartiality'.

'Economic logic' views media as instruments of capital accumulation. From this perspective, the higher the profit, the better. The best story here is the one that maximizes profit. Sometimes this may be achieved by an 'objective' approach to journalism, sometimes by becoming associated with a particular elite (for example, when that elite controls state advertising spend).

Whereas ideological-political and commercial logics are often underpinned by considerable coercive and/or economic institutional power, professional logic is often just that or backed by relative weak organizations such as federations of journalists. It may be used, however, to justify commercial ownership and control or the use of media for ideological purposes (for example, the US State Department after the Second World War was eager to spread an American notion of professionalism as a way of combating the spread of communism and/or the return of fascism (Blanchard 1986) and this helps to explain why Germany does not have a polarized pluralist media system). Imagine a case where newspaper journalists protest against an owner who has sacked a critical journalist because the state has threatened to cut its advertising spend with the newspaper. Or another where the owner clearly wishes to further an ideological agenda as well as make profit and hires journalists who share his ideology while claiming that journalists will be autonomous and free from political influence. Sometimes it is clear that a political logic is the driving force, at other times it is clear that commercial criteria are paramount, often there is a complex mixture of motivations that are impossible to disentangle entirely. Professional logics of autonomy and rituals of 'objectivity' may at times work together with commercial logic and at others the two logics may be in conflict depending on economic and political conditions.

Transnational Media and Institutional Isomorphism

Paul DiMaggio and Walter Powell's development of the concept of isomorphism to explain institutional change, in particular the process of homogenization, is essentially a challenge to Weberian explanations of institutional change as a product of rationalization (1991). Following Hawley (1968) they define isomorphism as a 'constraining process that forces one unit in a population to resemble other units that face the same set of environmental conditions' (1991: 66). There are two varieties of isomorphism: a competitive isomorphism and an institutional isomorphism. Competitive isomorphism is where one competitor adopts similar strategies, structures, practices to a competitor because of a perceived competitive advantage of the competitor. While this is a useful concept itself for understanding media development in Central and Eastern Europe it will not be discussed in detail in this chapter. Institutional isomorphism may be broken down into three categories: coercive, mimetic, and normative.

Coercive isomorphism is when pressure is exerted by one organization on another. The pressure can be more or less formal. DiMaggio and Powell point in particular to the activities of states in setting standards, enforcing laws and so on that leads to organizational homogeneity. They also, however, point to softer, more subtle forms of coercion where organizations that are dependent on other organizations change their strategies to appeal to those organizations. This may occur, for example, when a non-governmental organization is dependent upon governmental or quasi-governmental organizations for funding. Pushed further it could also refer to how organizations might adapt to a broader environment, for example, to respond to cultural values such as nationalist or religious beliefs.

Mimetic isomorphism, the second form of institutional isomorphism, is a product of uncertainty. When the environment is a new or difficult one, there is a temptation for organizations to adopt models that were successful previously or in other places. Media environments generally are highly uncertain. It is difficult to know why certain films and music are highly successful and others disastrously unsuccessful. Media environments in Central and Eastern Europe, especially after 1989 but still to a considerable extent today, are highly uncertain environments. Given that the option of copying successful models from the past does not appear to be viable, the obvious approach is to adopt models successful elsewhere. The push in this direction is even greater when we consider transnational firms who may have experience of implementing models successfully elsewhere.

Normative isomorphism is the product essentially of professionalization. Here ideas about what a particular group of professionals, for example, journalists, extend beyond particular organizations and may act as a homogenising force. A central way in which normative isomorphism imposes itself is through recruitment practices where prospective employees are expected to have certain qualifications and so on.

While all three varieties of institutional isomorphism are relevant to the analysis of media development in Central and Eastern Europe, the particular focus here will be on mimetic isomorphism as a way of explaining the behaviour of transnational media companies in the uncertain media environments in the region. In order to illustrate the appropriateness of the concept of mimetic institutional isomorphism the chapter will discuss the activities of possibly the four most significant transnational media companies operating in Central and Eastern Europe: Central European Media Enterprises (CME), Axel Springer, Westdeutsche Allgemeine Zeitung (WAZ), and Ringier. First of all, though, it is important to point to three conditions that appear to be necessary before large scale transnational media investment in the region occurs.

Conditions of Transnational Investment

Relative Affluence and Size

Transnational media companies looking to invest in Central and Eastern Europe are profit-maximizers and will therefore look for markets where consumers are relatively affluent. It is this affluence that permits consumers to spend more of their income on media goods and services and also helps to establish an advertising market where corporations will pay media firms for providing advertising space.

Size of the market is also important as media products have high *first copy* costs and thus there are clear economies of scale. Media firms will be usually unwilling to invest large sums in relatively small markets. The ideal market for media firms is a relatively large, relatively affluent market. This helps to explain growing recent interest in Poland as affluence begins to accompany its size and to some extent the Ukraine as it is a large if not presently an affluent market.

Membership of the European Union should see economic convergence over the long run as Central European countries exploit advantages of place (lower labour costs, proximity to market) to compete effectively in European wide markets. Over the long run, one would expect advertising spend per capita to rise to Western European levels, which makes the region a sound long term media investment.

Permissive Regulation

Membership or prospective membership of the European Union also helps to establish economic and political stability together with a permissive regulatory regime. Media companies stay mostly clear of unstable or uncertain political regimes. Russia, for example, despite being a large and growing advertising market has not attracted a great deal of transnational media investment. To a certain extent this helps to explain the neo-authoritarian character of much Russian media.

Relative Absence of Competition

The third key factor appears to be that the media sector in Central and Eastern Europe is undeveloped in terms of competition in comparison to Western Europe. It has been possible for transnational media firms to make modest investments in the region and yet quickly become dominant players in the market. The lack of domestic competition as a result of inadequate capital and media know-how means that transnational firms can quickly gain *first mover* advantages that serve to concentrate advertising spend and lead to virtuous circles for the companies concerned. It also means that the tendency towards monopoly that is present in all media systems is particularly acute in this part of Europe. Some idea of the importance of this factor may be gleaned from two examples. Ringier has only about 50 of its 7000 employees in Germany (in comparison to 800 in Hungary, Czech Republic, Romania) although one might imagine that a shared language would encourage the Swiss firm to invest in Germany. Its attempts to break into the German market, however, have been largely unsuccessful due to the severity of domestic competition. In 2008 Axel Springer decided not to launch a *Bild* clone in France. Two years previously it had successfully launched a *Bild* clone *Fakt* in Poland. Both markets do not have a tradition of Boulevard newspapers. Even though Western European markets are potentially much more lucrative the combination of good long run prospects together with a lack of competition makes Central and Eastern Europe an attractive investment for transnational media companies.

Although transnational media companies may be diverse in terms of ownership structure (family owned versus publicly listed), country of origin, and political orientation (Axel Springer and WAZ), it is possible to discern common elements in terms of the process by which they invest in the region.

CME and the Confluence of Commercial and Professional Logics

Sparks (1998, 1999) is concerned with the early history of Central European Media Enterprises (CME) from its foundation in 1994 by cosmetic magnate Ronald Lauder to the late 1990s when SBS announced that it had agreed to buy CME. CME's entry into Central and Eastern European markets depended on the extent both of its capital and *political capital* (links with political elites) in different states in order to win licences to broadcast (or not, as in the cases of Poland and Hungary) rather than *know-how* in the television industry. Even in markets where CME managed to gain a national licence, it encountered, according to Sparks, strong competition for limited advertising markets and so, by 1999, he could conclude that 'CME was a casualty of the very logic (*i.e. the commercial*) that it introduced to the region' (1999: 25). Sparks, however, overestimates the extent of competition, particularly in the Czech Republic and Slovakia, and underestimates the ultimate advantages of being a *first mover* in states where national income and consequently advertising revenues are predicted to increase rapidly over the next years and decades to approach Western European levels. Whereas in 1999 CME faced extinction, from the perspective of 2011 its prospects look brighter and it is difficult to see how the company could fail having weathered an extremely turbulent patch. It would appear then that the painful period in the early years of its existence has given way to a situation where CME can finally exploit its *first mover* position in expanding markets for example through price-setting. If Sparks was concerned to explain CME's rise and fall, here I will explain CME's further descent into the abyss and then resurrection. While the business was worth $160mn in 2004 (about 25 per cent of what SBS was willing to pay for it in 1999) by 2007 it was valued at $5bn, a dramatic turnaround prompted initially by a large compensation payment to CME by the Czech state.

Czech TV Nova has been the highest profile CME venture and the Czech Republic provides the most revenue for CME. In 1993 CET 21, a company comprising six Czech former dissidents, including Vladimír Železný, received a licence to broadcast nationally. They contracted with a majority owned CME Czech based subsidiary, Česká nazávislá televizní společnost (CNTS), to provide programming and TV Nova saw the light of day in February 1994. It was quickly a great success – by the end of its first year it had an incredibly high audience share of 70 per cent and it continued to be 'a great success story' until mid-1999 (Sparks 1999). Železný, the Director General of TV Nova was largely credited with its success through his introduction of 'tabloid' television (US imports, domestic versions of international formats, sensationalist news and, notoriously, topless weather), was, however, dismissed from CNTS by CME in April 1999. CME President Fred Klinkhammer accused Železný of using TV Nova as his personal propaganda channel and undermining CNTS (Meils 1999). In response, Železný, as licence holder, continued to broadcast Nova TV but from different premises. CME took Železný to the International Chamber of Commerce Court of Arbitration in Paris. The Czech Council for Radio and Television Broadcasting supported Železný in recognising the licence holder's right to broadcast and in claiming that an exclusive relationship did not exist between CET 21 and CNTS meaning that CET 21 could buy programming and other services from other companies (The Prague Post 1999). This prompted CME to sue the Czech Republic for violating a bilateral trade agreement in Washington DC (an example of coercive isomorphism). CME in November 1999 took out full-page advertisements in the *New York Times* and the *Washington Post*, warning US investors of the difficulties of investing in the Czech Republic and alleging collusion between Železný and the Council for Radio and Television Broadcasting. The Czech Justice Minister Motejl argued that the bilateral agreement did not apply because CME is a Bermuda registered company while Klinkhammer alleged that the support of the Czech government was part of an agreement for TV Nova to support Klaus and the ODS (Dawtrey 2001). Shares in CME dropped from a $37 dollar high in 1997 to $1 in 2000 and the company ceased to be traded on NASDAQ as its value fell below $15mn.

The February 2001 arbitration ruling meant that Železný had to pay $23mn to CME for stock in CNTS but did not have to pay damages to CME (CME had claimed $470mn in damages). The ruling placed Železný in considerable financial difficulty and he continued to be mired in financial scandal in subsequent years. The protracted arbitration between CME and the Czech state was finally settled in May 2003 with the ruling that the Czech state should pay CME a considerable $353mn for failing to protect its investment as it was obliged to do so under a Dutch-Czech bilateral agreement. The ruling prompted the dismissal of the Broadcasting Council and Železný as TV Nova's Director. The sum represented almost two times the then market capitalization of CME and was roughly equivalent to the Czech Republic's annual budget for public health (Green 2003). In December 2004 CME announced, in a move that surprised many, that it had bought 56 per cent of TV Nova from Czech finance company PPF for $642mn, the largest US investment in the Czech Republic and completed deals to take over the whole of the company in May 2005. This means that CME controls the licence that expires in 2017 in contrast to the situation prior to 1999. Michael Garin, CME's CEO at that time, said that the acquisition 'has transformed CME from the leading regional broadcaster into the dominant regional broadcaster' (Jenkins 2005). In June 2005 Ronald Lauder bought Gustav Klimt's portrait of Adele Bloch-Bauer for $135mn and then two months later sold off half of his shares in CME for $190mn (Fabrikant 2006: 1). His initial investment in 1994 was $40mn. It appears that every other business venture of Lauder has failed. This gives some indication of media market conditions in Central and Eastern Europe in comparison to media market conditions in Western Europe.

TV Nova's market dominance in the Czech Republic where it controls about 60 per cent of TV advertising revenue has led the Broadcasting Council to allow public television to continue to sell advertising time and not to grant TV Nova a digital franchise (TV Nova intends to introduce thematic digital channels). TV Nova and Nova Cinema had a prime-time audience share of over 45 per cent in 2010. Its margins are higher than in other states because of a lack of competition in advertising markets. Analysts Atlantik.FT in their prognosis for 2008 'This year TV Nova wants to push up the price of ads by 20 per cent, which should be feasible since there is not much competition in the market'. TV Prima, the only other national commercial broadcaster, is losing ground and has less than half of Nova's market share.

It is clear that Garin's assessment of CME dominance in the Czech Republic and also in Slovakia and Slovenia is correct (TV Markíza in Slovakia has a prime-time audience share of almost 34 per cent in 2010 while Pop TV and Kanal A have a combined prime-time audience share of 48.5 per cent). In the Czech Republic and Slovakia CME faces competition neither from a strong public service broadcaster nor from strong commercial rivals while in Slovenia there is competition for audience share with the public service broadcaster but not with strong commercial rivals. In Slovenia Tomaž Kržičnik, head of acquisitions for Slovenian the Slovenian public broadcaster TV Slovenija, said that the broadcaster 'changed its program schedule within two weeks of Pop TV's launch' (Nadler 1996: 37). In Romania, CME may be leading but not dominant (total prime-time audience share of 31 per cent in 2010). CME sold its Ukrainian station Studio 1 + 1 other operations in April 2010.

Sparks (1999) set out a model of CME development. It is now possible to update that model to show how CME behaves in maturing markets:

Table 5.1   Model of CME development before and after 1999

CME model to 1999	Build war chest → Establish strong national contacts → Develop coherent licence bid → Win licence → Establish station → Defend territory
CME model 2000 onwards	Develop local programming → Focus on target demographic → Develop transnational synergies → Disentangle CME from local partners → Apply policy of equidistance from competing factions of political elite → Establish news and current affairs 'objectivity' → Extend existing licences → Prepare for digital television (theme stations).

When CME entered Central and Eastern European markets many commentators expected a diet of mostly imported US films and series. While there are US imports, the popularity of local production means that 60 per cent of prime-time TV is locally produced in the Czech Republic and 45 per cent in Slovakia. As well as domestic game-shows there are more expensive soap operas. Czech films are aired as well as Hollywood films and series. This strategy was established early on. Vladimir Repčík, General Manager of Markíza, commented 'If we want to be successful, we have to produce more and more in-house programs, even though local production is far more expensive than imported programming' (Andreeva 2000). This strategy was based on commercial imperatives. Already in 1998 the highest rated imported show was Friends at a lowly 47th in the top 100 programmes.

CME stations aim to be mass stations targeted at a younger audience. This mimics commercial broadcasting practice in Western Europe and North America as younger audiences are of greater interest to advertisers as they have greater disposable income and are more ready to spend that income on consumer products.

Garin states that there are sub-regional synergies, for example, between the Czech Republic and Slovakia and between Slovenia and Croatia. Local management means that decision-making is decentralized and marks out CME as different according to Garin. Decision-making is devolved downwards. The Regional News group meets twice a year to coordinate coverage. The Programme Acquisitions Group meets four times a year and develops a coordinated acquisition strategy in order to increase its market power (Jenkins 2005). Although there is a certain amount of decentralization, it is one of CME's objectives to use experience gained in one CEE state to increase profits in another. Adrian Sarbu, for example, originally in charge of Romanian operations was then promoted to oversee Romania, Czech Republic, and Slovakia, and promoted further to the position of Chief Operating Officer of CME in October 2007.

As Sparks points out, the development of local political capital through establishing partnerships with local elites was essential for the initial successes of CME. Such agreements, however, ran into trouble not only in the Czech Republic but also in the Ukraine and in Slovakia. In the Ukraine Rabinovitch was accused of having close connections with organized crime while in Slovakia Pavol Rusko, as General Manager of Markíza used the station's news and current affairs to further his own political ambitions. Both Železný and Rusko have been called the 'Berlusconis' of their respective states. CME recognized this did not represent the optimum strategy either in the short or medium term (loss of audience, difficulties surrounding possible licence renewal, and so on) and sought to remove troublesome local partners from the stations. It has only managed to do so from 2004–5 onwards. Even where local partners have not been troublesome CME have sought to buy out minority shareholders as, for example, in Romania with Pro TV.

In an environment where political elites commonly seek to control news and current affairs output, CME have recognized the value of observing 'objectivity rituals' that are common in North America and in some Western European broadcasting systems (where there is no explicit preference expressed for one political party or position in TV news). This is not only a way of maximising audience share as the news may appeal to people with contrasting political views but also may attract viewers disenchanted with political control of public service broadcasters and other commercial stations. In an adversarial and polarized public broadcasting system it may also help to establish the long run presence of CME as the decision to back one party over another in an opportunistic or even in an ideologically committed fashion may return to adversely affect future licence renewals.

After buying out minority shareholders in TV Markíza in 2005, for example, CME changed the personnel in the newsroom associated with Rusko, introduced a standards' manual for news journalism, and issued statements that the company would seek to establish objective journalism. Ivan Godarsky of Memo 98, a Slovak media watchdog, said that 'This is a good step by CME in that they appear to want to raise the objectiveness in Markíza's news' (Stracansky 2005). Markíza's news audience share was up to almost 80 per cent in 2006 (Gehl 2006: 30) while TV Nova news in the Czech Republic has an audience share of 60 per cent. TV Markíza's licence was extended by 12 years in March 2006. Here professional logics and commercial logics are clearly pulling in the same direction.

CME is preparing for digital television by buying up thematic channels (such as sports) and bidding for digital licences. Their market power in analogue television broadcasting is actually hindering this transfer to digital. For example, in the Czech Republic the Broadcasting Council is proving unwilling to grant CME a digital channel before the shutdown of analogue. This is in order to try to reduce TV Nova's market dominance.

The initial successes of CME in the 1990s were not based either on industry know-how or on significant amounts of capital (Lauder's initial outlay was in the region of $40mn). Konstantin Eikovsky in SME summed it up well 'CME is a successful firm only thanks to the fact that at the right time, it had good judgment about people who had the right political contacts to get exclusive licences for free' (Balogová 2007). What this misses, however, is that CME's recent success is based on disentangling itself, albeit messily, from original partners. With a modest initial outlay and little knowledge of the industry they can now exploit their first mover position in expanding advertising markets.

The future of CME looks extremely promising in that they are the dominant or leading broadcaster in several markets that are likely to see rapid growth in advertising revenue in the next decades. Advertising spend per capita in Western Europe is $75 on average compared to $45 in Slovenia, $38 in the Czech Republic, $31 in Slovakia, $32 in Croatia, $19 in Romania, and $8.5 in Ukraine. With the exception of Croatia and Ukraine all states are members of the EU. Croatia is expected to become a member in 2013. The advertising spend in these EU member states is expected to converge with that of other member states over time. The weakness of CME lies in its absence from Poland, the largest recent entrant to the EU, and from Hungary, up until recently one of the most economically successful.

The highest risk of CME's investments was their operation in the Ukraine. This is a potentially very high growth and lucrative market with a large population of 46 million and undeveloped advertising markets. It is also, however, a highly competitive and fragmented television market as well as being politically unstable. CME in 2008 announced that it was buying out minority shareholders in Studio 1 + 1. While this fits with their strategy in other states there are elements of the Ukrainian situation that mark it out as distinctly different. In summer 2007 it was announced that Ukrainian oligarch billionaire Igor Kolomoisky (personal fortune estimated to be $3.6bn) had purchased 3 per cent of CME's shares and had been invited to join CME's Board of Directors. Kolomoisky is a prominent supporter of Western-facing former Ukrainian President Victor Yushchenko (donating $5mn to the cause of the Orange revolution and $40mn in the last two elections). In 2010 CME sold its Ukrainian operations to Kolomoisky. Given the highly polarized character of Ukrainian politics, there must be serious doubts over whether Studio 1 + 1 will seek to be an 'objective' broadcaster. It may be in this case that ideological-political and commercial logics fit together well.

This brings us to the issue of the extent to which Lauder himself is politically motivated. He is a well-known neo-conservative who rose to political prominence under Ronald Reagan (serving at the Pentagon and later as Ambassador to Austria) and enthusiastically supported Reagan's approach to the 'Evil Empire'. His investment in CME was motivated by his desire to help create capitalist representative democracies in Central and Eastern Europe as well as profits. It is not clear to what extent this conflicts with the goal of news 'objectivity'. It certainly appears that this principle can be overlooked when it is pragmatic to do so (in order to establish partnerships for example) and embraced when it is pragmatic to do so (as in the case of Slovakia).

CME has struggled like most media firms in Central and Eastern Europe during the financial crisis. *Daily Variety* reported in October 2009 that revenues (primarily from advertising) had fallen 33 per cent from the previous year. The fortunes of CME are heavily dependent upon the economic fortunes of the region. While short term prospects are not good, CME maintains its dominant position in media markets. This dominance together with greater investment from Time Warner (who increased their stake in CME to 31 per cent in April 2011) means that medium and longer term prospects are very good.

Axel Springer and the Confluence of Ideological-political and Commercial Logics

Axel Springer has enjoyed spectacular success in Poland over the past seven years. Axel Springer founded the company in 1946 in post-war Germany and it is Germany's largest newspaper publisher and third largest magazine publisher. In 2010 it had revenues of £2.9 bn, was active in 33 countries, and employed almost 10,000 people. Poland is, by far, currently the most important market in Central and Eastern Europe for Springer but it also has operations in Hungary, the Czech Republic, and Russia. In a company presentation in April

2008 'internationalization' was identified as the driver of profitability – a clear recognition not only of the potential growth of markets in Central and Eastern Europe but also the relative lack of competition in those markets in comparison to Western Europe that provides the potential for higher profit margins.

Axel Springer established five socio-political principles for the company in 1967. These are: the integration of Germany into Western and European inter-state organizations such as NATO and the EU; reconciliation between 'Jews and Germans' and support for the state of Israel; the support of alliances with the United States and the support of common values based on freedom; the rejection of totalitarianism in whatever form; and the support of a free social market economy. The ideology of Axel Springer is national-conservative and in favour of free market economics. It is closely linked with the neoconservative movement in the USA. Mathias Döpfner, the chief executive of Springer, has written, for example, criticising the failure of Europe to support George Bush's invasion of Iraq (Döpfner 2004). This ideology informs *Bild*, the largest selling European tabloid, and *Die Welt*, which is Springer's intellectual, and until recently loss-making, flagship. Clearly with *Die Welt* ideological-political logics outweigh short-term economic logics.

Poland is Springer's most important market outside Germany. It is much the largest market of the EU accession countries in this part of Europe in terms of both population and national income although far from the richest on a *per capita* basis.

Axel Springer Polska was established in 1994. There have been four phases to Springer's development in Poland. The first phase from 1994–2000 saw the extension of non-controversial consumer magazines to the Polish market (*Computer Bild, Auto Bild*). This is a common strategy in markets seen to be potentially politically unstable or authoritarian (for example, it is a common strategy in China and Vietnam). The second phase from 2000 to 2002 saw the establishment of Polish franchises of US magazines (*Newsweek* and *Forbes*). The third and most remarkably successful phase from 2003 to 2006 saw the establishment of German 'clone' newspapers, *Fakt* and *Dziennik*, that have seen Springer reach 42 per cent share of national newspaper circulation. The fourth phase saw a blocked attempt by Springer to acquire just over 25 per cent of the shares of Polsat, the leading Polish commercial TV channel. Here the focus will be on third and fourth phases of development.

Fakt was launched in October 2003. It has had an immediate impact on the Polish newspaper market and is now the top-selling Polish newspaper. Circulation has declined, however, from over 500,000 in 2007 to 384,000 in May 2011 (a decline in line with that of other Polish newspapers signalling the importance of Springer's digitalization strategy in Central and Eastern Europe). *Fakt* has a very broad reach. Florian Fels, German managing director of Axel Springer Polska 'our broadest reading circle is 7 million. One in three Polish newspaper readers reads *Fakt*' (Lesser 2005: 29). *Fakt* is similar to *Bild* in that it is aimed at a wide audience and expresses a national-conservative ideology in a populist manner.

There was some concern that *Fakt* would essentially promote German interests and Axel Springer went to some lengths to allay such fears. Only one of *Fakt*'s

500 employees is German. Andreas Wiele, the Axel Springer Board member with responsibility for international business, claimed that 'We place very great value on the editorial autonomy of our journalists. As a German publisher we naturally do not interfere in the daily political questions of Newsweek and we will not do so in *Fakt*' (Wegner, 2003). While this may be accurate, the publisher does set the political principles or ideology of the newspaper. Jankowski, editor in chief, in an interview with *Die Welt* in 2003 'We're making a Polish newspaper that represents a Polish point of view and supports Polish interests. Axel Springer publishes also *Newsweek*: a German publisher publishes a Polish magazine with an American title. *We orientate ourselves to the principles of the publisher.* With the entry into the EU all these borders will lose their importance' (Die Welt 2003).

This shows some of the confusions and contradictions that are presently at large between national and cosmopolitan identities in a time of international integration. *Fakt* explicitly defends what it sees as Polish interests in the face of Germany and the European Union (it supported Kaczyński's 'hard-line' on European negotiations, for example). This national-conservative ideology is, however, a transnational ideology in that it is clearly present across Western states and is expressed in both *Bild* and *Die Welt*. It is this worldview that *Fakt* represents rather than a specifically German ideology. It supports a vision of Europe made up of distinct peoples, of strong nation-states and free markets rather than a federalist system with an emphasis on welfare, it is avowedly anti-communist, and advocates close alliance with the USA.

The support of both *Fakt* and *Dziennik* for the Kaczyńskis did not deter Jaroslaw Kaczyński in an interview in Springer magazine *Newsweek* in March 2008 from claiming that they represent the interests of German capital: 'I have used the term 'German media', to be precise. The issue of German influence on Polish media has even attracted the attention of diplomatic circles...These mechanisms (of control) can be either subtle or primitive. I do not know exactly how they work at your company. What I do know is that capital always has a motherland. In this case the motherland is Germany, which would like Poland to be meek and obedient' (Polish News Bulletin 2003).

Dziennik is ideologically also national-conservative with a liberal approach to economics. It is aimed at the growing younger Polish middle class. It publishes a Wall Street Journal supplement, the key US financial paper and important advocate of neoconservatism.

The launch of both newspapers was accompanied by extensive promotional campaigns and introductory prices designed to attract new newsreaders and to take readers away from the principal competition in the respective markets segments: Super Express in the popular market and *Gazeta Wyborcza* in the 'quality' market. Mariusz Ziomecki, editor of Super Express, accused Springer of price dumping designed to bankrupt Super Express: 'I have myself worked at Springer's. But I hadn't reckoned that they would now want to break my newspaper with a fighting price of 1.20 Zl' (Lesser 2005: 29). Super Express has cut one hundred of 500 employees and has seen a decline in circulation of over 100,000 copies since 2002.

Fakt's success prompted Agora, the publisher of *Gazeta Wyborcza*, to introduce a popular newspaper *Nowy Dzień* in November 2005. The paper only lasted four months selling only 130,000 copies in February 2006. With Springer's swop with magazine publisher *Marquand* of its women's titles for the leading sports newspaper, *Przegląd Sportowy*, in 2007 its domination of the popular newspaper market is ensured. Clearly, Springer has used its know-how in the production of *Bild* to achieve remarkable success with *Fakt*. That *Fakt* represents an ideological position and is considerably stronger than rivals means that there is little media pluralism in this sector of the newspaper market.

The launch of *Dziennik* is a different case. It sought to take readers from *Gazeta* by selling at roughly half its price but it appears that the sales of *Gazeta* have held up well while *Dzennik* may have taken some readers away from *Rzeczpospolita*. Given that the centre-left *Gazeta* was dominant before *Dziennik*'s launch it may be argued that the introduction of a conservative-national paper has actually served to increase pluralism in this segment of the Polish newspaper market. Financially, it appears that *Dziennik* is not as successful as *Fakt* – it stands financially in the same relationship as Die Welt to *Bild*. However, it may well be that Springer see *Dziennik*'s role as being similar to that of *Die Welt* in Germany i.e. not primarily an investment but more of an ideological-political project designed to contest the framing of news. On the first day of publication *Dziennik* contained an editorial written by Robert Krasowki that claimed the newspaper would be independent from individuals and parties but would defend principles of liberty, democracy, the rule of law, the free market and a pro-Western vision.

While the third phase of development has clearly been successful with Springer controlling almost half of the Polish national newspaper market, the fourth phase has so far proved to be a failure. Springer's determination to acquire a stake in Polish commercial analogue and digital broadcaster PolSat was part of a broader transnational move into digital media. Springer in the short term saw cross-promotional opportunities between print and television and in addition recognizes that advertising revenue from paper newspapers and magazines are likely to fall in the longer run and is intent on moving into digital media i.e. Internet newspapers, magazines, portals, digital television stations. Digitalization joins internationalization as Springer two key strategies. Springer sought to takeover ProSiebenSat TV in Germany but this takeover was blocked by the German competition regulator as it would leave private television in Germany essentially in the hands of two multimedia conglomerates – Bertelsmann and Springer.

In December 2007 Springer announced that not only was it selling its 12 per cent stake in ProSiebenSat but also that it had failed to reach agreement with Polish PolSat on the acquisition of PolSat shares. An agreement between Springer and Polsat had originally been announced in December 2006 that Springer would acquire 25.1 per cent of PolSat shares for in the region of £250–300mn. Springer would appoint two members of the eight member PolSat supervisory board and any decision to spend more than Zl100mn would need the approval of both Solorz-Żak and Springer. Springer expected the Competition and Consumer Protection

Office to approve the deal because of the minority nature of the shareholding. In April 2007, however, the UOKiK said that Springer would have to submit a new application because although the shareholding was a minority one, the control given to Springer under the deal was greater than the shareholding would suggest.

In subsequent negotiations Solorz-Żak and Springer were unable to agree a deal. This was in a context of rapidly improving fortunes for PolSat and it was rumoured that Solorz-Żak wished to strike a much harder bargain financially and in terms of receiving shares in Axel Springer Polska. He was also reluctant to lose control over Polsat, which may have been the key stumbling block from Springer's perspective. The December 2007 announcements of the failure of both of Springer's attempts to enter the television market in Germany and Poland respectively were a consequence of regulations and regulatory action but also show the importance once again of being the first mover. Essentially Springer has lost out to Bertelsmann in the German market and to Solorz-Żak in the Polish market by not investing in television in the 1990s. Springer's digitalization strategy then will most likely have to rely on its Internet operations (portals, IPTV and so on).

In contrast to most other media firms Axel Springer has gone from strength during the financial crisis and subsequent recession, achieving record profit margins of over 25 per cent in 2010. In 2010 Springer announced a joint venture in Central and Eastern Europe with Ringier (see below).

WAZ and the Conflict of Logics

Westdeutsche Allgemeine Zeitung (WAZ) is the second largest newspaper group in Germany after Springer. In contrast to Springer, however, it does not own a national newspaper and it traditionally supports the SPD. WAZ's other European interests are particularly concentrated in South-East Europe although it owns around 500 print titles in nine European countries. In Bulgaria and Macedonia, for example, WAZ newspapers have a monopoly position. In 2004 in an interview in *Taz*, Bodo Hombach, who had recently left Gerhard Schroeder's Cabinet to succeed Erich Schumann as Director of WAZ, joked about this situation (Grimberg 2004: 14):

> Question: The whole press in Bulgaria is owned by WAZ?
> Hombach: No. Not all.
> Question: How much of it then?
> Hombach: Almost all of it!

WAZ's control has come through purchases but also through price competition where it can undercut competitors for a period of time in order to drive them out of business or make them ripe for a take-over. This is what happened in Bulgaria in 1997.

WAZ sees itself not merely as a profit-making organization, however. Erich Schumann described the values of WAZ as a human rights charter. The leading principles are 'human rights, no nationalism, no extremism either from left or right, parliamentary democracy' (Frank 2001. Within this broad ideology editors of newspapers can choose their positions. WAZ prides itself in separating clearly the financial and the journalistic sides of the industry and yet it has an established ideology that its papers need to follow.

Hombach claims that WAZ ownership of newspapers in South-East Europe has led to a greater differentiation of press and politics than otherwise would have been the case through preventing newspapers from falling into the hands of criminals or from being subservient to political parties because of financial need. In 2003 WAZ and the Organization for Security and Co-operation in Europe signed an agreement establishing principles to guarantee 'editorial independence'. It has since been signed by only one other company, Orkla from Norway. The agreement, however, does not guarantee editorial independence. It states that a common code of conduct should be established between directors and journalists that should contain at least the following: standing up for human rights, standing up for the UN Charter, democratic rights, the parliamentary system, fighting totalitarian activities of left and right, and fighting 'any nationalist or racial discrimination'. In other words, this agreement was very close to the extensive ideological principles that WAZ already abides by. Far from guaranteeing editorial independence, it strictly limits independence and effectively sanctions intervention if, for example, editors fail to fight 'nationalist or racist discrimination'. The agreement effectively creates a circumscribed space for editorial independence that may be more generous than direct political control but it is still ideological-political control but by more subtle means.

In July 2007 WAZ and the International Federation of Journalists signed an agreement on the defence of press freedom. WAZ is the only company to have such an agreement. The agreement is based on six principles: press freedom and independent journalism; the importance of professional journalists who report accurately, credibly and who follow ethical standards; the duty of journalists to inform while not being subject to undue economic, political or social pressure; the importance of media pluralism; media should support social cohesion and bridge cultural, social and political divides; transnational media should be subject to scrutiny and support editorial independence and pluralism. Again, however, this agreement is caught between wanting journalists to engage in an ideological-political project and observing editorial independence.

It is ironic then that while WAZ was signing this agreement with the International Federation of Journalists it was unaware of the behaviour of its two market leading newspapers in Bulgaria that joined in a campaign aimed at a young Bulgarian-German art historian who had questioned the historical facts surrounding the Batak massacre in Bulgaria. This affair shows the contradictions between ideological-political logics and professional logics as well as the contradictions within the professional logic itself.

As mentioned previously WAZ controls around 80 per cent of national newspaper circulation through its titles *24 Chasa* and *Trud*. Generally these papers follow a moderate pro-European line and are regularly attacked by the radical right in Bulgaria, notably Ataka and a TV station Skat that is closely associated with Ataka. Ataka is highly critical of Bulgarian Rom and Muslims and is critical of the moderate 'German' newspapers and argues that the WAZ newspapers are opposed to them. If this were the case, then the newspapers would be following WAZ, the Organization for Security and Co-operation in Europe, and International Federation of Journalists principles and agreements. Ataka leader Siderow accompanied by activists and a Skat cameraman occupied *24 Chasa* offices at the end of February 2007 after the newspaper had published a story that Ataka had received a large donation from the Turkish minority party. While the newspaper may have been fighting discrimination through opposing Ataka it is difficult to maintain that it was simultaneously providing 'objective' journalism. WAZ wanted to avoid the impression that a Western newspaper company was fighting the radical right in the Balkans. Andreas Rudas, the head of South-East Europe for WAZ commented 'as a matter of principle we do not intervene in editorial matters and we do not comment upon articles' (Mappes-Niedek 2007: 19). While the policy here is stated as one of non-intervention, the situation appeared to change, albeit briefly, only a few months later.

Martina Baleva, a 35 year old art historian, wrote an essay about Antoni Piotrowski's 1892 Massacre at Batak that depicted the massacre of villagers by Ottoman troops in the late 1870s. Baleva claimed that the artist relied upon staged photographs of the event and that the number of victims had been exaggerated. Baleva's work was to be presented at a conference on representations of Islam supported by the Bosch Stiftung, the Deutsches Historisches Museum, and the Freie Universität in Berlin. Baleva's work was met with indignation by the Bulgarian media including WAZ papers and BTV (the dominant TV channel with around 40 per cent audience share owned at that time by News Corporation and now by CME) and a campaign was waged against Baleva that led to the cancelling of the conference. Her photograph appeared in *24 Chasa* while Skat offered £2500 for her address (Kraske and Schmitter 2007: 74). Baleva in fear of her life decided to leave Bulgaria for Germany.

Axel Schindler, the head of WAZ for Bulgaria who is based in Essen and was at the time learning Bulgarian, said that he first heard of this case in November 2007 when *Der Spiegel* broke the story in Germany. As well as the business manager for Bulgaria he understands himself as the 'protector of the values of WAZ' (Kraske and Schmitter 2007: 74). WAZ and the International Federation of Journalists issued a joint press release saying that the WAZ papers had acted unprofessionally and unethically.

Bodo Hombach then proceeded in an interview with *Berliner Zeitung* to compare Bulgarian media unfavourably with the German media. Their behaviour 'would be quite unthinkable here' (Klatt 2007. This may be interpreted as national discrimination on Hombach's part, overlooking the less than unimpeachable behaviour of elements of the German media while tarring all of Bulgaria's media with the same brush. Such behaviour of the WAZ papers in Bulgaria, he continued, would be removed through education. So much for guarantees of editorial independence! Journalists working for the WAZ paper complained of censorship and subsequently an interview with Hombach printed in both papers that WAZ's 'iron principle remains in place – editors decide over the papers' contents' (Oertel 2007: 17).

WAZ's experience in Bulgaria is an interesting case study of the complexity of media development in Central and Eastern Europe as a whole. It seems that simultaneously they wish to advance commercial, professional and ideological-political logics. They are in favour of media pluralism and yet follow a commercial policy that sees them enjoy dominant positions in Bulgaria and Macedonia. Given the values of WAZ it is doubtful whether pluralism is furthered by such market dominance. There is also a contradiction between the ideological-political project of supporting democracy and fighting extremism and the goals of journalistic impartiality and objectivity. There was no apparent need for WAZ to criticize, for example, their papers' approach to Ataka. Finally, there are tensions within the professional logic itself between the principle of editorial independence and 'educating' journalists and newspapers after failing to behave professionally as in the case of Baleva. The fact that Hombach retreated and assured newspaper readers of the editorial independence of WAZ newspapers may have been taken for commercial reasons and/or because of a recognition of the contradiction within WAZ's behaviour. That he took a step backwards, however, also indicates at least some differentiation from a political logic.

WAZ's experience of the financial crisis and recession was much more difficult than Springer's, partly the consequence of WAZ's focus on South-East Europe that was particularly badly hit by the recession (advertising revenues in Romania fell by 70 per cent in 2009). In 2011 WAZ took the decision to leave Serbia claiming that the anti-competitive actions of oligarch Milan Beko make undertaking media business next to impossible. It is also likely that it will divest from Romania. In countries with weak economies it appears that there is little profit to be made because of low advertising revenues and oligarchs exercise considerable political leverage while seeking to control the media.

Ringier and 'Depoliticized' Journalism

Ringier AG is a family owned though not run, Swiss based media company that celebrated its 175th anniversary in 2008. As well as cross-media activities in Switzerland, it operates in Central and Eastern Europe and Asia. Its concerns in Central and Eastern Europe focus on Czech Republic, Slovakia, Hungary, Romania, and Serbia. Almost half of its 7000 employees are based in Switzerland with around 800 in Czech Republic, Hungary, and Romania, and around 300 in Slovakia and Serbia. Ringier was active until it sold *Blik* in Ukraine employing around 100 people. Significantly Ringier has only around 50 employees in Germany and this reflects repeated failed attempts to break into the competitive German media market. Central and Eastern European countries with their projected advertising growth rates and lack of domestic competition offer a much more attractive investment opportunity than the highly developed German market.

Ringier's leading newspaper title is the daily Boulevard newspaper *Blik* with a circulation of 215,000 in 2010 in Switzerland. *Blik* launched in 1959 has a number of clones: *Blesk* in Czech Republic (385,000 circulation in 2010 launched in 1992), *Blikk* in Hungary (191,000 circulation in 2010 launched in 1994), *Blic* and *Alo!* in Serbia (with 146,000 and 113,000 daily circulation respectively in 2010), and *Nový Čas* in Slovakia with 143,000 circulation.

Ringier's business model for newspapers across the region is clear. To launch Boulevard newspapers and magazines that have little or no political content, that are depoliticized, and focus on entertainment, scandal, sex and sport. This also has some synergistic potential as international scandal, sex and sport can be shared across titles that appeal to essentially similar segments of their respective national markets. Slovakian *Nový Čas* and Czech *Blesk* regularly share content.

In 2010 Springer and Ringier announced a joint venture that would see them working together across Poland, Czech Republic, Hungary, Serbia, and Slovakia. Together they control the leading tabloid newspaper in each national market but do not compete directly with each other with the exception of Hungary. Basically each firm can harness the power of the other to cement their dominance of press markets in Central and Eastern Europe. The joint venture was established to share the development of digitalization in the region and finance acquisitions with a view to a stock market listing between 2013 and 2015. The joint venture has been agreed in all countries except Hungary where the Media Council blocked the venture for competition reasons. Even so, it would appear that there is remarkable press concentration across the region with transnational firms playing a key role in this process.

Conclusion

Over the course of the discussion of the four examples a clear pattern has emerged. We can explain the investment by transnational companies in Central and Eastern Europe with reference to three factors: a potentially profitable market to occupy, a regulatory environment that permits transnational investment, and a relative lack of domestic competition. These conditions appear to be necessary ones. As membership of the EU for some states in the region seems to guarantee these economic and political conditions it is likely that we will see further investment by transnational capital in Central and Eastern European media with obvious implications for pluralism and democracy in this part of Europe. No doubt the financial crisis and recession has slowed this process down as it has reduced the profitability of media markets in the region. However, it is likely that it is the transnational firms with greater financial backing behind them that will weather this storm and emerge as dominant players in Central and Eastern European media landscapes.

Transnational companies tend to rely initially on developing close contacts and even partnerships with domestic economic and/or political elites. In the longer term, however, they appear to be eager to loosen ties to particular political elites primarily for commercial reasons. The long run goal of transnational investors appears to be operating autonomy from particular elite fractions and complete ownership of media enterprises.

The transnationally owned media companies tend to adopt the same strategic approach to content through developing clones or near clones of products that they have had success with elsewhere, a mimetic isomorphism that is a response to the uncertainty of media markets in Central and Eastern Europe together with the opportunities of synergies of both organization and media content. They appear to adopt content models that have worked for them in the past. This allows them to use their know-how in new markets and also offers the possibility of synergies across markets. Ringier has introduced 'depoliticized' tabloids modelled on the Swiss *Blick* in a number of states in the region while Springer has introduced the nationally conservative *Fakt* modelled on *Bild* in Germany. CME now appears to follow a course of maintaining equidistance from political elites and the production of 'objective' journalism. WAZ appears intent on encouraging at once both a professionalized journalism and one that it committed to social democratic and pro-European values. The experience of WAZ, however, has often been difficult with conflicts arising between WAZ and national political elites and oligarchs. Both WAZ and Springer have a clear set of distinct political values that their papers are supposed to embody. Within that framework there is relative autonomy for editors. All companies use their power to shape content whether it is the 'objective', 'depoliticized' content of CME or Ringier or the clearly more ideological-political goals of Springer and WAZ.

The issue of foreign ownership of media is certainly contentious in a number of Central and Eastern European states. There are claims that the region's media has been 'Americanized' and 'Germanified'. These claims are often part of nationalist discourses and do not shed much light on media transformations. It is much more illuminating to focus initially on particular companies and analyse the strategies that they employ and then attempt to discern commonalities in approach. As transnational companies have come to be dominant players in Central and Eastern European markets, this means that the media systems, although displaying characteristics of polarized pluralist systems (for example, political parallelism in broadcasting), also are shaped by the concerns of the transnational firms themselves that are not at home in a polarized pluralist system. As I have shown these logics are complex – they tend to be a mixture of economic, professional and political-ideological logics. All three logics, however, tend to operate as a moderator of polarized pluralism. Economic logic in the longer run tends to mean that companies try to disentangle themselves from a particular political elite and a professional logic of public service is regularly used to legitimate such a move.

That is not to say that political-ideological logics are absent. If we examine the cases of Springer and WAZ we clearly see that their Central and Eastern European newspapers tend to follow the political principles of the company. These competing principles, however, belong within the orbit of liberal representative democracy and so they too tend to moderate possible tendencies towards polarized pluralism in the region's media systems.

As Central and Eastern European media systems do not neatly fit into the polarized pluralist model, it is perhaps tempting to describe them as a combination of liberal and polarized pluralist elements. Such a judgment, however, would be in danger of underestimating the degree of market power that some transnational companies enjoy in these markets making it unwise to consider them to be truly competitive markets. The joint venture between Springer and Ringier that aims to harness their market power in five countries in the region is hardly a good omen for the development of competitive, pluralistic press markets.

References

Andreeva, N. 2000. Local TV thrives in old country: Ex-Soviet bloc nations look inwards for original programming. *The Hollywood Reporter*, 4 October 2000 (accessed via Nexis UK 19 July 2011, no page number).

Balogová, B. 2007. Right time, right place. *Slovak Spectator*, 23 July 2007. Available at: http://spectator.sme.sk/articles/view/28481/11/right_place_right_time.html (accessed 19 July 2011).

Blanchard, M. 1986. *Exporting the First Amendment: The Press-Government Crusade of 1945–52*. New York: Longman.

Chalaby, J. 1996. Journalism as an Anglo-American invention: A comparison of the development of French and Anglo-American journalism 1830s–1920s. *European Journal of Communication*, 11(3), 303–26.

Dawtrey, A. 2001. US mogul Czech-mated. *Variety*, 23 January 2001. Available at: http://www.variety.com/article/VR1117792401?refCatId=22&query=dawtrey+ODS [accessed 19 July 2011].

Die Welt. 2003. 'Tabus brechen'. *Die Welt*, 22 December 2003. Available at: http://www.welt.de/print-welt/article281403/Tabus_brechen.html [accessed 19 July 2011].

DiMaggio, P. and Powell, W., eds. 1991. *The New Institutionalism in Organizational Analysis*. Chicago: University of Chicago Press.

Döpfner, M. 2004. Europe – dein Name ist Feigheit. *Die Welt*, 20 November 2004, Available at: http://www.welt.de/print-welt/article353728/Europa_-_dein_Name_ist_Feigheit.html [accessed 30 June 2009].

Fabrikant, G. It's not a Klimt, but the Eastern European TV venture is sweet. *New York Times, Business Day* supplement, 16 October 2006, 1.

Frank, A. 2001. Der bose Onkel vom Rhein. *Die Tageszeitung*, 14 November 2001, 22–3.

Gehl, C. Slowakischer Medienmarkt Lohnende Nischen in Visier. *Media und Marketing* 4 May 2006, 30.

Green, P. 2003. Czech Republic pays $355 million to media concern. *New York Times*, 16 May 2003. Available at: http://www.nytimes.com/2003/05/16/business/czech-republic-pays-355-million-to-media-concern.html?src=pm [accessed 19 July 2011].

Grimberg, S. 2004 Mit Boss Bodo im Nahkastchen. *die Tageszeitung* 25 March 2004, 14.

Hallin, D. and Mancini, P. 2004. *Comparing Media Systems: Three Models of Media and Politics.* Cambridge: Cambridge University Press.

Hawley, E. 1968. Secretary Hoover and the bituminous coal problem 1921-1928. *Business History Review*, 42, 247–70.

Jenkins, B. 2005. Organic growth in Central Eastern Europe is CME's goal. *Video Age International* (Online), 25(4). Available at: http://www.videoageinternational.com/articles/2005/06/article1.html [accessed 30 June 2009].

Klatt, T. 2007. Hasstiraden im Sudosten. *Berliner Zeitung*, 22 November 2007, 34.

Kraske, M. and Schmitter, E. 2007. Terror um ein Bild. *Der Spiegel*, 19 November 2007, 74.

Lesser, G. In Polen tobt ein ruinoser Zeitungskrieg. *Tages-Anzeiger*, 18 May 2005, 29.

Mappes-Niedek, N. Bulgarian brutalities. *Frankfurter Rundschau*, 19 March 2007, 19.

Mazzoleni, G. 1987. Media logic and party logic in campaign coverage: the Italian general election of 1983.' *European Journal of Communication*, 2(1), 81–103.

Meils, C. 1999. CME prexy removes Zelezny. *Variety*, 25 April 1999, http://www.variety.com/article/VR1117493619?refCatId=18 [accessed 19 July 2011].

Nadler, J. 1996. Pop goes Slovenian TV. *Variety*, 5 August 1996, 37.

Oertel, B. 2007. Verleung um eine Losung. *TAZ*, 28 November 2007, 17.

Polish News Bulletin. 2003. Jaroslaw Kaczynski: Self-proclaimed elites, oligarchs, and foreign capital still in control (transcript of interview), *Newsweek Polska* 23–7, 28 February 2003 [accessed via Nexis UK].

Prague Post. 1999. CME takes on Broadcast Council. *Prague Post*, 25 August 1999. http://www.praguepost.com/archivescontent/30600-cme-takes-on-broadcast-council.html [accessed 19 July 2011].

Sparks, C. with Reading, A. 1998. *Communism, Capitalism, and the Mass Media.* London: Sage.

Sparks, C. 1999. CME in the former communist countries. *Javnost/ the Public*, 6(2), 25–44.

Stracansky, P. 2005. Ownership raises freedom issues. *Inter-Press Service*, 8 November 2005, Available at: http://ipsnews.net/news.asp?idnews=30919 [accessed 19 July 2011].

Wegner, R. 2003 'Was Lesern gefaellt, setzh sich durch'. *Horizont*, 23 October 2003, 34.

Chapter 6

Transnational Media Regulation in Central and Eastern Europe

Alison Harcourt

Beginning in the late 1980s, policy experts from international organizations, company associations, foundations, non-governmental organizations and national governmental departments (e.g. US Agency for International Development, UK Department for International Development, Swedish International Development Cooperation Agency) were a common sight in the capital cities of Central and Eastern European states. They provided key expertise on the drafting of media laws, codes of practice and the setting up of national associations. International pressure to adopt regulatory systems was used through exclusion sticks (e.g. World Trade Organization/ European Union membership) and aid carrots. States in the region largely based regulatory models upon those in Western Europe. Although European models were adopted on paper (provision of public service broadcasting and quotas and subsidies for independent and national production), there was at the same time tremendous pressure from the US, international organizations and large media companies to move towards a more liberal regulatory framework. Hence, in practice, a more liberal market model similar to that of the US is in place in Central and Eastern Europe today.

This chapter will examine this phenomenon and draw conclusions for media systems theory with case studies on press and broadcasting regulation in the region. Scholars seeking to categorize Central and Eastern European states have tended to identify them with the polarized pluralist media system. Although these states certainly share characteristics and tendencies with the polarized pluralist model, the system actually in operation resembles a much more liberal model. The chapter argues that Central and Eastern European media systems have been shaped more by external factors rather than factors which are usually seen in the literature to carry greater weight such as behavioural adaptation, cultural factors, or post-communist legacy. The main argument in the chapter is that the move towards the liberal model is part of a wider isomorphic process wherein media systems are beginning to homogenize globally. The chapter will draw upon DiMaggio and Powell's (1991) framework of institutional isomorphism to explain this process.

Institutional Isomorphism

Originally derived from scientific disciplines, the term isomorphism was adopted by social scientists to explain how populations in a given set begin to resemble populations in other sets facing the same external conditions (Hannan and Freeman 1977, Meyer and Rowan 1977). DiMaggio and Power (1991) applied the framework of isomorphism (meaning 'the tendency to become alike') to organizations looking at factors which promoted greater homogenization. This framework works well when looking at media policy as states in Central and Eastern Europe are exposed to the same international pressure as states in Western Europe. This chapter argues that although Europe as a whole is under similar pressure for liberalization from market competition and globalization of the industry, Central and Eastern European states are more susceptible to this pressure due to the fact that they are smaller and financially weaker than their Western counterparts and the US. For this reason, the movement towards a more liberal model is progressing more quickly in this part of Europe than it is even in Western European states, which are better able to resist this pressure.

DiMaggio and Powell identified two processes, namely institutional and competitive isomorphism. Under competitive isomorphism, organizations faced with open competitive markets will adopt the most efficient solutions to suit their needs. They argue, however, that institutions do not assimilate merely due to reasons of efficiency but also for reasons of legitimacy. They demonstrated how institutions hoped to attract staff, resources and ease of interaction with other organizations by mimicking institutional practice. The same can be observed in the case of Central and Eastern European states. The chapter will demonstrate that these states have adopted European policy models – on paper – in order to attract resources and interact with policy makers at the European level. However, a different model is operating in practice.

DiMaggio and Powell's model looks at sources of institutional isomorphic change identifying coercive, mimetic and normative change. Coercive change is usually in response to external (such as governmental) pressure; mimetic change (or imitation) is usually occurs as a political strategy when institutions are seeking legitimacy and normally occurs under conditions of uncertainty; normative change refers to a much more complex learning process which incorporates the transfer of norms or procedures. In this chapter, it will be argued that institutional change and regulatory adoption has been both coercive and mimetic, but seldom normative. Mimetic change has clearly taken place in Central and Eastern European states with policymakers having adopted regulatory frameworks that have been successful elsewhere. However, in practice, a more liberal market model is in place which is operative due to coercive change. In some cases is it apparent that normative change has taken place where policy makers have engaged in complex learning, or engaged in analysis and self-reflection on indigenous political systems or policy regimes.

Media Systems Theory

Much of the early literature on media transition focuses on policy choices made by Central and Eastern European states. These invariably lay between the more 'liberal' US model and the European 'social responsibility' model (Sparks 1997, Harcourt 2003, Jakubowicz 2004). The United States is often seen as an example of a libertarian or liberal model (Oates 2008). Under this model, public policy has a very limited role to play, emphasis is on transparency, access and market self-regulation and content is largely not regulated. There are no production or content quotas, no rules on relationships between owners and editors, no broadcasting boards and few media ownership restrictions. Public service broadcasters draw a small audience and are mainly funded by private donations. By contrast, the European social responsibility model has expressed a need for greater public regulation and the provision of a state broadcaster specifically to guarantee social goals. In many European countries there is strong support for public service broadcasting, and a more interventionist approach to regulation in both press and broadcasting, including ownership legislation, content quotas and the subsidization of production and distribution of newspapers.

Before transition, the countries of Central and Eastern Europe were seen to be operating under a 'Soviet model' under which, according to which Siebert et al. (1956), the media were state rather than privately owned. The media were meant to convey a Marxist-Leninist view of the world. Modern media scholars point out that the media systems in Central and Eastern Europe were much more nuanced than US scholars made it out to be. There was mixed adaption to the Soviet model throughout Central and Eastern Europe with varying degrees of media professionalism expressed by those coping with constraints put upon them by the political systems (Jakubowicz 2001, Lauk 2008). In any case, this model ceased to exist with the collapse of the Soviet Union although certain tendencies continue.

More recent theory has sought to develop new criteria when comparing media systems within Europe. Building upon Siebert et al.'s original model, Hallin and Mancini (2004) developed the liberal, democratic corporatist and polarized pluralist models. Similar to Siebert et al.'s model, the 'liberal' model denotes a system in which the private media dominate markets and there is a relatively small role for the state. Hallin and Mancini categorize US and Canada, the United Kingdom and Ireland in this way. Characteristics of the model include the presence of a strong commercial press, minimal political affiliation by newspapers, division of the press into 'quality' and 'tabloid' markets and a high level of industry self-regulation. This chapter argues that Central and Eastern European states resemble the liberal model. The chapter utilises three of Hallin and Mancini's four measurements, namely: the measure of media markets, political parallelism, and the degree of state intervention in media system. It does not look at levels of professionalism in journalism, which may be a weaker fit but is beyond the scope of this chapter.

Hallin and Mancini's democratic corporatist model is one in which there is a historical co-existence of private and state-owned media, with organized state media links to social and political groups. Statutory law guarantees a large role for the state in including a high level of support for public service broadcasters, press subsidies, and a strong role for the courts. Political affiliation and political parallelism is relatively high. This model is present in the countries of continental Northern Europe such as Belgium, the Netherlands, Austria, Switzerland and the Scandinavian countries and has developed historically with its roots in (neo-) corporatism. These countries share similar media development histories such as a high mass circulation of the press from the early nineteenth century; press freedom guaranteed in constitutions from the nineteenth century, industrialization and high media literacy resulting from the Protestant Reformation. Although political affiliation and political parallelism within newspapers is high, limitations on state power are guaranteed in state Constitutions. The Central and Eastern European states do not fit well into this model.

The Polarized Pluralist model is one in which there is integration of the media into party politic systems, a weaker development of the commercial media and a stronger role for the state but, unlike in democratic corporatist states, few limits on state power. Under this model, press circulation is comparatively low. The newspaper market consists primarily of politically parallel 'quality' titles with weak tabloids. According to Hallin and Mancini, this model represents the Mediterranean countries of Southern Europe: Italy, Greece, Spain, Portugal, and also France. Even with developments in media literacy and economic development, numbers of newspaper readers in these countries never caught up with northern Europe. Instead, the broadcast media filled this vacuum and there is consequently a greater reliance on television as a source of news in Southern Europe.

Some scholars have examined whether the Polarized Pluralist model theory can be applied to Central and Eastern Europe (Wyka 2008, Jakubowicz and Sükösd 2008: 27). Wyka concludes that states in the region fit well into this model due to high levels of political parallelism. However, this premise is questionable. As will be shown in the chapter, although there is a high level of state control of public service broadcasting in Central and Eastern European states, other criteria for categorising political parallelism do not apply. Successive governments have attempted to control public broadcasting output, but they have had little influence over the private broadcast media and even less over press markets. This is particularly so given that public broadcasting providers have low audience shares in most states in the region with the exception of Poland. Overall intervention in private broadcasting in Central and Eastern European states is clearly low compared to France, Italy, Greece, Portugal, and Spain. This is because affiliation between domestic political parties and international media groups which dominate press and broadcasting markets in the region is negligible.

Hallin and Mancini also emphasize that politically parallel media systems experienced a weak development of the mass circulation press in the nineteenth century. This is not necessarily the case in Central and Eastern European states particularly in Hungary, Poland and the Czech and Slovak Republics where markets up until the Second World War were similar in development to Western

Europe. Similarly, readership is (comparatively) high in Central and Eastern Europe compared to Southern European states.

Jakubowicz and Sükösd (2008) ask whether Central and Eastern European states are in an earlier stage of media development, closer to Northern Africa, than the countries of Southern Europe as they have more catching up to do. This is, however, doubtful given that the countries of Central and Eastern Europe are ranked, according to Freedom House, as having a 'free' press (whereas northern African states do not) and they have, at least on paper, adopted Western regulatory models. Northern African states by contrast remain generally under heavy control and dominated by the state media. In fact, Central and Eastern European states rank higher than Southern Europe in the Index with most states ranked close to countries such as the UK and France (the Czech Republic even having even surpassed France). Central and Eastern European states have rather leap-frogged stages of media development and moved much closer to a liberal model particularly in regulation due to external pressure.

This is a regulatory model (the liberal one) which the whole of Europe in general is moving towards, not just Central and Eastern Europe. During the last twenty years there has been a move away from the social responsibility model in all European states and a move towards a market based approach. All of Europe is witnessing a pattern of increased survival costs in broadcasting and press markets (due to new technologies), industry concentration, and a decrease in programme diversity due to competition for advertising. Public service broadcasters usually follow suit, competing with private broadcasters for advertisers, and depending increasingly on government funding as costs rise, which creates cosier relationships between public broadcasters and successive governments in power. Hence, even though these pressures exacerbate state control of public broadcasting, media systems in Central and Eastern Europe cannot be catagorized as 'polarized pluralist' as a whole. Rather, this phenomenon can be seen as a general European trend. Public service broadcasters through Europe are losing their independence from governments as their market share declines. This is particularly apparent in France and Italy. The weakness of public broadcasting in Central and Eastern Europe can be seen to be a more accelerated process of this, rather than a result of political parallelism as such. All of Europe is moving towards a lesser role for the state and greater role for the market.

Coercive Change in Central and Eastern Europe

When Central and Eastern European countries liberalized their media markets at the end of the 1980s and the beginning of the 1990s, they were immediately caught up in a longer term battle on going between the US and the then European Community over the liberalization of audiovisual media services under the General Agreement on Trades and Services. This battle has a long history. When negotiations began back in 1947, only a small number of countries were participant to the General

Agreement on Tariffs and Trade. Discussions took place between Western Europe, Australia and the US. At that point in time, liberalization only covered goods. European countries achieved an exception for screen quotas for cinema film under Article IV of the General Agreement on Tariffs and Trade to preserve the European industry, which had been decimated during the war. Europe extended this opt-out to television programming in the 1960s. Opt-outs for subsidies and quotas were acquired in supplementary protocols to the Organization for Economic Co-operation and Development in 1961.

In 1974, broadcasting policy was given additional protection European law. When the cable operator Giuseppe Sacchi brought the public service broadcaster Radiotelevisione Italiana to a tribunal court in Biella, Piedmont over a monopoly in advertising, the Italian court referred the case to the European Court as it might have a European dimension. Television signals could cross borders and there could be obstacles to the sale of 'goods' from other Member States. The Italian court queried whether the movement of *goods* within the common market applied to television signals. The European Court took the opportunity to define television signals as *services* rather than *goods*. Hence, the Court effectively took broadcast signals out of the realm of the General Agreement on Tariffs and Trade which covered goods only at that time, effectively protecting European broadcasting policies from challenge from the US under the Agreement.

Ten years later in 1986, the Uruguay Round began to extend trade agreements in goods to those of services so the liberalization of audiovisual trade was put back onto the agenda. By this time, European Member States were represented both individually and as part of the 'European Communities' under the Article 133 Committee, which is a subcommittee of the Council of Ministers. The European Community campaigned heavily for a general exemption for cultural services. It lost. When the Uruguay Round eventually ended in 1994, audiovisual services had been included in general obligations. This opened the path for liberalization of audiovisual services markets internationally.

The US has, therefore, effectively won the battle in opening up markets. However, the European Community did manage to negotiate on behalf of its members an exemption to the Most Favoured Nation agreement. Detailed notes for each of these mention specific subsidy and quota specifications for European Community member states. Exemptions are granted for a period of ten years and are reviewed every five years. Many member states listed exemptions in the audiovisual sector. As a group, member states were effective in warding off US pressure to open their media markets. However, first and second round accession states in Central and Eastern Europe were not members of the European Community at this point in time. They were not protected by the European Community at the General Agreement on Trade in Services table and did not receive exemptions in the audiovisual field.

During the General Agreement on Trade in Services negotiations, an intense battle was fought between the US and Europe over the adoption of media policy models in Central and Eastern European states. Two issues were particularly contentious: the establishment of public service broadcasters (as opposed to privatization) and the subsidization of European content in programming. The US supported privatization of state broadcasters and opposed the adoption of European-style quotas and content laws. Europe pressed for the establishment of public broadcasting and the subsidization of content. The US and the European Community were clearly seeking support of their respective positions on the world trade platform.

Teams of experts were sent to Central and Eastern European states to provide advice on policy models. The 'liberal' model was promoted through a number of US organizations. The US Agency for International Development and the American Bar Association, through its arm Central and East European Law Initiative (now renamed the Europe and Eurasia Program) specialized in advice on press laws. They were flanked by international organizations such as the International Media Fund, the International Press Institute, the International Research and Exchanges Board, the World Association of Newspapers, and the World Press Freedom Committee and other US organizations such as Time Inc., the Knight Foundation, the New York Times Foundation, the Rockefeller Foundation, the Ford Foundation, the MacArthur Foundation, ProMedia, the Washington Initiative, and the Carnegie Foundation. US advisors had by far the most influence on regulation of the press in Central and Eastern Europe. Organizations pushed for guarantees for press freedom under national constitutions and the strengthening of corporate transparency. Other fora, such as the US Commission on Radio and Television (backed by US television networks), Radio Liberty, Radio Free Europe, Voice of America, Internews and the International Research and Exchanges Board supported the privatization of state broadcasters. The key goal was the separation of the media from the state and the opening of markets to foreign investment.

The 'European' model was chiefly promoted through the Council of Europe and the European Broadcasting Union. These organizations were flanked by European government aid agencies, the Swedish International Development Agency and the Dutch National Committee for International Cooperation and Sustainable Development, and the UK Department for International Development, and political parties in Germany, namely the Social Democratic Party, the Free Democratic Party and the German Christian Democrat Union Party. Other international organizations naturally played a role such as the European Initiative for Human Rights and Democracy, Independent Journalism Foundation, International Federation of Journalists, and non-governmental organizations such as the Open Society Initiative, Article 19, the Bertelsmann Foundation, the Friedrich Ebert Stiftung, the Friedrich Naumann Stiftung, the Konrad Adenauer Stiftung, Norwegian People's Aid, Medienhilfe, the Oestreicher Freedom Forum, Deutsche Welle, and the Guardian Foundation. The European Union did not send expertise until the late 1990s due to a lack of treaty competence in the field and the fact that the accession process had not yet begun.

The European Broadcasting Union assisted with the transition of state broadcasters to public service broadcasters, a model adopted across Central and Eastern European states. This choice can be seen as an example of mimetic change as states in the region were seeking legitimacy for existing large state enterprises. The French model was largely drawn upon for regulation, which included the appointment of political party representatives to broadcasting boards. The exceptions are Hungary and Slovenia that adopted the German model of establishing a broadcasting council with representatives from a wide range of societal groups.

While the Uruguay Round was under way, the Council of Europe's Convention on Transfrontier Television and the European Community's Television without Frontiers Directive were enacted in 1989. They served to provide an additional layer of protection for quotas and subsidies within Europe by requiring that the majority of transmission time and a certain percentage of programming budgets was reserved for 'European works'. However, during the mid-1990s, Central and Eastern European states found themselves both under pressure to adopt European quotas with a view to EU accession and under pressure not to introduce quotas and subsidies from US in preparation for the General Agreement on Trade in Services/ World Trade Organization membership. They largely adopted European models on paper. This adoption can be seen as coercive as states needed to adopt the Television without Frontiers Directive in particular to qualify for accession.

The Council of Europe's programme, the Development and Consolidation of Democratic Stability, was established in 1989 to assist Central and Eastern European states in implementation of the Convention. Signatories to the Convention needed to implement rules on: the freedom of expression, reception, and retransmission; right of reply; prohibition of pornography, limitation of television violence, prohibition of incitement to racial hatred, youth protection; the screening of European works (for a majority of screen time); the screening of cinema films (two years after first showing – one year in the case of films co-produced by the broadcaster); advertising standards (for example, prohibition on the advertising of tobacco and medicines and medical treatments available only on prescription, restrictions on the advertising of certain products such as alcoholic beverages); advertising time (not more than 15 per cent of daily transmission time and not more than 20 per cent of any one hour period); advertising breaks (for example twice during a 90 minute feature film, none during a news or current affairs programme lasting less than 30 minutes); and programme sponsorship rules. These provisions were very similar to those of the Television without Frontiers Directive.

However, accession states were under great pressure from the US not to implement many of the Convention's provisions through US opposition to World Trade Organization membership. This pressure was particularly severe in the Baltic States when they joined in 1999–2001. As Johnson and Rollo explained:

> The US perceives EU cultural policies as protectionist and has mounted a concerted effort to prevent candidates from adopting EU policies ahead of membership. This is perhaps intended to enable the US to ask for compensation for reduced access to candidates' audio-visual markets, to the extent that the WTO General Agreement on Trade in Services permits that; or at least to gain some leverage over an EU policy on enlargement (2001:8).

Despite having implemented the EU Directive by 1995, the Czech Republic, Hungary, Poland, Slovenia and Slovakia were admitted to the World Trade Organization and Bulgaria joined in 1996. Estonia and Latvia joined in 1999 with Lithuania joining in 2001. Although the 'European' requirements were adopted on paper, they were not necessarily implemented in practice.

The EU's role came into being only in the late-1990s, post-World Trade Organization membership. Accession criteria were divided into the 'acquis' criterion (complying with existing EU law) and political criterion. The only statutory requirement under Chapter 20: *Culture and Audiovisual Policy* (established in 1998) of the *acquis communautaire* was the implementation of the 1997 Television without Frontiers Directive (EC 1997a) as a condition of accession. Politically, the Copenhagen criteria included the requirements of 'stability of institutions guaranteeing democracy, the rule of law, human rights and respect for and protection of minorities' (EC 1997b). Although freedom of the media was not a requirement of the accession negotiations, it was covered in the European Commission's Regular Reports and in the Accession Partnership agreements of the Council of the European Union as a part of political criteria.

This was flanked with funding carrots (particularly under the MEDIA programme), and European Commission-run projects on media professionalism in Central and Eastern Europe. Advice ranged from reform of public service broadcasters (boards and funding) to the improvement of professional journalistic practice and the strengthening of transparency. However, what can be concluded from this period is that the most effective instrument was the coercive pressure to implement the Directive under the *acquis*. The aid package and pressure to improve media standards were minimal by comparison and had arrived too late. EU accession did not take place until 2004, when the Central and Eastern European states of Estonia, the Czech Republic, Hungary, Latvia, Lithuania, Poland, Slovenia and Slovakia joined the EU. Romania and Bulgaria became EU members in 2007. Programmes on media professional were also funded by the Council of Europe by the mid-2000s through its medium term training programme and the International Federation of Journalists through its Civil Society Project funded by the Ministry of Foreign Affairs of the Netherlands. However, by this time, the media system had consolidated itself and a liberal model was in operation.

Mimetic Change in Central and Eastern Europe

When looking at policy adoption in Central and Eastern Europe, most statutory adoption is mimetic. States in the region adopted European policy models on paper but they have not worked well in practice. Hence, although the European model seems to have prevailed over the US model, in practice, a more liberal market model has emerged. Audience share for public service broadcasters in the region is very low (with the exception of Poland). Government efforts to control private media have been largely unsuccessful. Political influence as a whole can be seen to be minimal as a consequence. Indeed, as small states in a global economy, Central and Eastern European media markets are more prone to influence from economic pressure and globalization factors (such as concentration in ownership and cross-border broadcasting) than state control.

Czech Republic

Czechoslovakia was the first state in the region to introduce broadcasting legislation post-1989. It was strongly influenced by the US Trans-Atlantic Dialogue on European Broadcasting. Czech law guarantees freedom of expression under its Charter of Fundamental Rights and Freedoms which was based on the US Bill of Rights. These were incorporated into Article 17 of the Czech 1993 Constitution. The 1991 Federal Broadcasting Law reflects 'hands off' approach to commercial broadcasters. Media ownership rules were not put in place and the Television without Frontiers Directive's content requirements were not initially introduced. Czech civil servants were also advised by experts from the European Institute for the Media, but the European model for both press and broadcasting was largely put aside.

The US Ambassador to Hungary put pressure on the Czech Republic not to introduce quotas stipulated in the Television without Frontiers Directive (BBC Monitoring World Media 2000). Consequently, when the 2001 Act on Radio and Television Broadcasting (WIPO 2001) was agreed, the minimum European works quota was not introduced. A looser regulatory framework whereby requirements are placed on commercial broadcasters at the time of licensing was introduced rather than statutory requirements. The media law was never updated and further laws, namely the 2005 Electronic Communications Act (which implements EU's 2002 Directives under the regulatory framework for communications) and the amendments to the Broadcasting Acts in 2006 and 2007, never introduced the quotas. During negotiations for the 2007 Audiovisual Media Services Directive, Czech delegates supported the most liberal policy proposals mostly backing the UK position within the Council.

Post-transition, the public service broadcaster, Czech TV was never privatized but turned into a public service broadcaster. Academics at the time argued that the adjustment would have been too sudden given the large number of staff (circa 4,000) working for the state broadcaster at the time. However, Czech TV was never able to develop properly as a public service provider with decreasing audience and funding cuts. Audience share has been consistently low. State control may be responsible for low audience in addition to lack of investment. The Council for Radio and Television Broadcasting which regulates Czech TV was modelled on the British regulator, the Independent Transport Commission. However, its appointment procedure reflects the French/Italian model with representatives distributed amongst political parties in the Chamber of Deputies (the lower House of Parliament). Although political control has lessened in recent years (EUMAP 2008), there has been no effort to grant the authority independence from parliament. In sum, although political pressure on public service broadcasting is evident, there is little alliance between private operators and the state. Political parallelism is thus not pronounced. Rather there is a high degree of dominance by the private market and self-regulation particularly in press markets.

Hungary

On paper, Hungary, borrows heavily from the 'European' model. This reflected both coercive and mimetic change. Even though European models were adopted on paper, implementation has been problematic. The private broadcast media in Hungary are generally seen to be aiming exclusively for mass audiences with little regulatory oversight and there has always been weak support for public service broadcasting culminating in the removal of the licence fee in 2002.

Council of Europe 'missions' were dispatched to Budapest from the Council of Europe to assist in the drafting of broadcasting laws in 1990 and 1994. The 1996 Radio and Television Act law borrows heavily from the 'European' model, and implements media ownership limits recommended by the Council of Europe. The law covered both public service broadcasting and the issue of private commercial licences. However, by this time, 1996, the television market had largely developed in a regulatory vacuum and the regulatory provisions were rendered almost impossible to implement retrospectively.

As documented by Lengyel (1998: 22) 'legislators were at pains to ensure that the 1996 Media Act was largely 'European compliant'; in keeping with western European broadcasting policy'. The 1996 Act, however, failed to implement a number of Television without Frontiers provisions into Hungarian law. For this reason, Chapter 20 of the acquis, which was opened in 1998, did not close until September 2002. To add pressure to adopt the Television without Frontiers Directive, the European Union excluded Hungary from the Media programme, which is clearly a case of a coercive mechanism being employed to produce change (as defined by DiMaggio and Powell 1991). The 2002 Media Act consequently included the minimum of 50 per cent European works and a further 25 per cent Hungarian works according to Television without Frontiers requirements. It also banned false advertising; included restraints on alcohol advertising, advertising to minors and separation of advertising and programming. Further Television without Frontiers provisions limiting advertising to 15 per cent of broadcasting time and 10 per cent of programming resources for EU content production or independent producers, including an additional 5 per cent towards Hungarian content, were also added. However, implementation has been not been successful (Attentional 2009).

As in the Czech Republic, the public service broadcasting was not privatized. Sparks argues that privatization of the public broadcasting was discounted due to its then low advertising revenue, the dominance of the state broadcaster by political parties and the importance of nationalism in Hungary (Sparks 1998: 144–6). Despite the adoption of the European public broadcasting model, Hungary does not seem to be aiming at providing public service or securing goals of pluralism. Adaption was thus mimetic in that the German model of appointing societal and political representatives to the public broadcasting regulator fit well with Hungarian needs.

Government control in public broadcasting programming has been heavy handed particularly between 1994 and 1998 and between 1998 and 2002 when respective left and right governments were awarding licences and election periods. When the market consolidated, domestic owners sold to international groups. Public broadcasting control remained heavy handed and, although it indicates perhaps a tendency towards political parallelism, private broadcasting is largely divorced from state ties. Hungary abolished the licence fee for its public service broadcaster in 2002, which has been consistently in deficit and is trying to play catch-up with its private counterparts. Audience share however remains very low.

Poland

Poland provides an exception to our case study, in that its media market resembles those of Western Europe. Press and broadcasting companies are largely domestically owned and there is a dominance of audience share by the public service broadcaster Telewizja Polska. Telewizja Polska is financially healthy and popular maintaining the highest level of viewing of any public service broadcaster in Europe (EUMAP 2008). This is most likely due to the high level of funding it receives considering it operates from both licence fee income and advertising. In 2004, the public broadcaster was permitted to establish new channels and assume ownership of public television archives created before 1994. Private groups have complained that public service broadcasting is distorting the market and it has been criticized for falling under political control.

The media system resembles a 'polarized pluralist' system, similar to that of France, due to closer ties between the state and political spheres. Oversight of the public service broadcaster resembles the French model. Members of the National Broadcasting Council, which regulates television programming and an advisory board for the public service broadcasting, are drawn from political parties who are appointed by parliament (four by the Diet, two by the Senate, three by the President) for six year terms. The Council Chair was elected by Council members since 1997.

Transparency of media ownership is weak in Poland and ownership restrictions were never introduced. Any changes in ownership should be reported to the National Broadcasting Council but this has not worked in practice. However, the National Broadcasting Council reserves the right to revoke broadcasting licences if there is a change in the control structure. Restrictions on foreign ownership of the media were introduced post-accession. These were not compatible with EU legislation and the *acquis*, and were eventually removed in 2004. Poland did not fully adopt Television without Frontiers provisions until 2004. For this reason, European quotas were not introduced until 2004 but have never worked in practice.

Slovenia

In Slovenia, a similar pattern to most other Central and Eastern European states can be observed. Public broadcasting audience share remains low and the market is dominated by the large US group Central European Media Enterprises (CME). Output in the private sector is highly commercial and seen to be dominated by low-quality production and imports. This scenario has meant minimal overall political parallelism between the state and the private media but successive government control over public broadcasting. The 2006 law on Radio and Television Slovenia increased the role of government in public broadcasting governance. Audience share is not expected to rise and may in fact drop further as a result.

Slovenia was more receptive to the West pre-transition and its press sector was less constricted than in other Central and Eastern European states. Academic exchanges during the 1980s with the US via the American Cultural Center in Ljubljana increased exchanges of ideas on press freedom and legal approaches to freedom of expression as grounded in the First Amendment of the US Constitution. The Slovenian journalists' association was in favour of a hands-off approach to regulation and greater transparency measures, particularly those relating to Freedom of Information. However, legislation covering the press included in the 1994 Slovenian media act (which regulated both press and broadcasting) was largely influenced by *Länder* press laws, particularly in relation to the German ideas of *Tendenzschutz* under which newspaper owners have greater influence over editorial line of newspapers.

Transparency was introduced in company law with the requirement of publication in accounts in the *Official Gazette of the Republic of Slovenia*. A Freedom of Information Law was not agreed until much later in 2001. Before the 1994 Media Act was agreed much of the press market in Slovenia had been privatized. Owners of the new press groups were initially former Slovene journalists and editors. However, as in Hungary, the market was since taken over by large, mainly Austrian, publishing groups. Stringent media ownership restrictions on broadcasting and press were introduced in 1994 but never worked well in practice. They were eventually dropped in 2001. The 2001 Media Act also implements the Television without Frontiers Directive which mandated quotas. Quotas however are clearly not enforced in Slovenia (Attentional 2009), and a more liberal framework is operating in practice. The 2001 Media Act established an independent authority for both media and telecommunications, the Agency for Post and Electronic Communication which widened market definitions. This Act was followed by the 2004 Law on Electronic Communication. Like the Czech Republic, Slovenia has proactively supported deregulatory initiatives at the European level.

Croatia

In Croatia, the media are regulated by three Acts: the 2003 Electronic Media Act; the 2004 Media Act, and the 2004 Competition Act. Regulatory bodies are the Croatian Competition Agency and the Council for Electronic Media. Restrictions are in place to limit shares of one broadcaster in another to 25 per cent of capital. This is lowered to a 10 per cent share if the other broadcaster also publishes daily newspapers of over 3,000 copies distribution. The Media Act prohibits newspapers and periodicals belonging to one owner reach 40 per cent all the sold copies in the Republic. Company information is to be reported to regulatory authorities.

However, these ownership restrictions do not apply to broadcasts from abroad – namely the foreign owned Nova TV (Central European Media Enterprises) and RTL (Bertelsmann) channels which, along with the state broadcaster channels HTV1 and HTV2, take up the majority of audience share. This is because, with a view to EU membership, Croatia has implemented the EU's Television without Frontiers Directive (now the Audiovisual Media Services Directive) which stipulates that a broadcaster can only be regulated in the country of transmission, not reception. The EU's Television without Frontiers Directive allows foreign broadcasters to bypass national restrictions – including ownership restrictions.

The state broadcaster, HRT, is financed by a mixture of advertising and licence fee revenues. In an attempt to maintain independence from political control, the state broadcaster HRT assigned politically unaffiliated professionals to top positions in 2004, including the appointment of two women at that time. The quality of news programming and local production has improved since this time. Subsidies are provided to broadcast programming for public information, representation of national minorities, promotion of cultural creativity, and development of education, science and arts.

Estonia

In the Baltic states European policy models are also evident on paper but strong liberal models prevail in practice. Financially strapped public service broadcasting, dominance by private media and self-regulation is in operation with the state unable to maintain any real regulatory oversight. The Estonian 1994 Broadcasting Act gave legal recognition to private and commercial television and broadcasting licences were issued by the Ministry of Culture. The National Communications Board of the Ministry of Transportation and Communication is responsible for issuing licences to Cable-TV operators. By 2000, broadcasting regulation was brought into accordance with the Television without Frontiers Directive and Articles 4 and 5 on quotas were adopted into national law. The Estonian Broadcasting Act stipulates that the broadcasters shall ensure that at least 51 per cent of the annual transmission time excluding the time appointed to news, sports events, games, advertising, teleshopping and teletext services is reserved for European works, at least 10 per cent for the European works created by independent producers and at least 10 per cent of the monthly transmission time for the own production. These quotas requirements have been adhered to more rigorously in Estonia compared to other CEE states, on both state and private channels.

The public broadcasting is overseen by the Broadcasting Council. The public service broadcaster, Eesti Televisioon, has been experiencing serious funding difficulties. Several unsuccessful attempts were made to achieve stable and sufficient funding. Due to commercial pressure, advertising on Eesti Televisioon was stopped from 1998. In exchange, commercial broadcasters agreed to pay an annual compensation to Eesti Televisioon's budget.

A Press Council was established in 1991 but split in 2002 due to internal disagreement. There are now two Press Councils operating simultaneously in Estonia. One is funded by the Broadcasting Association and includes members from the broadcasting association, the journalist's association and academics. The second is funded and run by the Estonian Newspaper Association.

Lithuania

As in other Central and Eastern European states, Lithuania has adopted EU legislation on paper, but, in operation, represents one of the most liberal frameworks in Europe with a hands off approach to the regulation of content. There are no ownership restrictions, and markets are overseen by competition law in Lithuania. In addition, the 1996 Law on Provision of Information to the Public of the Republic of Lithuania contains a number of provisions. A broadcaster is required to inform the Radio and Television Commission of Lithuania about: changes in ownership of above 10 per cent; transfers in licence ownership.

Transparency measures are more stringent for the media sector. The Ministry of Culture of the Republic of Lithuania every year collects data from newspapers, journals and information society media. These are published annually on 15 May in the *Informaciniai Pranešimai* (Information Bulletin) to the official gazette *Valstybės Žinios*. Information on ownership by public officials is also published in this issue. On 30 March of each year, companies are required under Article 24 of the Law on Provision of Information to the Public to provide the government with data on shareholders who control at least 10 per cent of shares; the names and surnames of shareholders; and their personal identification code. They are also obliged to provide property information and cross-media ownership details.

Latvia

In Latvia, the broadcast market is regulated with the 1995 Law on Radio and Television. The National Broadcasting Council allocates frequencies. Transparency remains a salient problem in Latvia. Information on ownership is not publicly accessible. The Broadcasting Council requires disclosure of ownership but anonymous off-shore companies present a particular problem to Latvia.

Coercive Pressure: The World Trade Organization and International Agreements

The establishment of the World Trade Organization did not lesson US pressure on content subsidies and quotas globally, but the umbrella of the EU-protected Central and Eastern European states from direct pressure. After the establishment of the World Trade Organization, third (non-EU) states came under pressure from the US over quotas and subsidies which are common to Europe. Canada was challenged by the US under World Trade Organization dispute settlement procedures over press distribution subsidies and Turkey was challenged over domestic film quotas. The dispute settlement panels of the World Trade Organization decided in favour of the US in both cases. In its conclusions, the deciding body stated 'we would like to stress that the ability of any Member to take measures to protect its cultural identity was not at issue in the present case' (WTO 1997: 21). New Zealand was later challenged over quotas for local radio news in 2001. The US Trade Representative threatened that news quotas violated New Zealand's commitments under the General Agreement on Trade in Services and they were subsequently never introduced (Bernier 2005: 769, Hahn, 2006: 542). Similarly, the Republic of Korea was required to reduce screen quotas for domestically-produced films in 2006 in order to comply with a Korea-US Free Trade Agreement.

There was great concern in Europe that the US might bring a World Trade Organization case against quota or subsidy systems for content within Europe or a challenge to public broadcasting. This threat, coupled with internal pressure from private media conglomerates, led certain EU member states to seek protection for public broadcasting and quotas/subsidies within the United Nations Educational, Scientific and Cultural Organization (UNESCO). In November 2005, 148 nations signed the UNESCO Convention on the Protection and Promotion of the Diversity of Cultural Expressions was approved by UNESCO on 20 October 2005. The Convention guarantees rights to domestic quotas, subsidies and distribution, across the sector: Article 6 on the Rights of parties a) protects 'regulatory measures aimed at protecting and promoting diversity of cultural expressions'; h) protects 'measures aimed at enhancing diversity of the media, including through public service broadcasting'; and Article 7 of the Convention guarantees the right to 'create, produce, disseminate, distribute and have access to their own cultural expressions'.

Conclusion

It is clear that policymakers in Central and Eastern European states engaged in mimetic change due to reasons of efficiency and legitimacy. Although European policy models were adopted on paper which included provision of public service broadcasting and subsidies for independent and national production, states in Central and Eastern Europe faced coercive pressure particularly from the US and the private media not to adopt these provisions but to follow a 'liberal' market model. The result is that, although on paper regulatory models resemble those of Western Europe, in practice a more liberal market model is operating in these states. Normative change is not in evidence. Due to efficiency reasons, it is expected that the liberal model will continue to dominate. Central and Eastern European states do not have the resources in terms of civil servant numbers nor the finances to cover the regulatory cost of implementation of the European model. This was evident in submissions on consultation to the 2007 Audiovisual Media Services Directive and 2009 regulatory framework for communications.

In practice, Central and Eastern European states have shown preference for 'liberal' market models on international platforms and little home support for public service broadcasting. This was most evident with the recent revision of the Audiovisual Media Services Directive (formerly Television without Frontiers Directive) in 2007. When under revision, Central and Eastern European states supported the most 'liberal' proposals on the European table. This liberalising Directive extends cross-border broadcast of on-demand services and greatly liberalizes rules on content and advertising breaks including the introduction of new forms of advertising (such as US style split-screen, virtual and interactive advertising and product placement); abolishes the daily limit on television advertising; and drops all restrictions on teleshopping. Hence, the whole of Europe is converging into a similar liberal model for broadcast regulation with Central and Eastern European states greatly supporting this move. Similar moves towards greater deregulation were introduced with the 2009 regulatory framework for communications package.

All of Europe, not just Central and Eastern European states, are under pressure for market liberalization by the US and the World Trade Organization. Internal pressure for deregulation also comes from within from large media conglomerates operating within Europe. Western European states may be merely more robust to this pressure than their smaller and financially weaker counterparts in the East.

References

Attentional. 2009. *Study on the application of measures concerning the promotion of the distribution and production of European works in audiovisual media services (i.e. including television programmes and nonlinear services*. Final Report for the European Commission (DG Information Society and Media), 28 May 2009.

BBC Monitoring World Media. 2000. Czech Republic: Media law to define share of European production. BBC Monitoring World Media, 16 November 2000.

Bernier, I. 2005. Trade and Culture, in *The World Trade Organization: legal, economic and political analysis*, Volume 2, edited by P. Macrory, A. Appleton and M. Plummer. New York: Springer, 747–94.

DiMaggio, P.J. and Powell, W.W. 1991. *The New Institutionalism and Organizational Analysis*. Chicago, IL: University of Chicago Press.

EC. 1997a. 'Television without Frontiers' Council Directive of 3 October 1989 updated by Directive 97/36/EC of 19.06.97 amending Directive 89/522/EEC on the co-ordination of certain provisions laid down by law, regulation or administrative action in Member States concerning the pursuit of television broadcasting activities.

EC. 1997b. Report to the General Affairs Council of the Luxembourg European Council meeting on 9 December 1997. Doc. 13241/97 of 10 December 1997.

EUMAP. 2008. Television across Europe: More Channels, Less Independence. Follow-up Reports. Budapest: Open Society Foundation.

Hahn, M. 2006. A clash of cultures? The UNESCO *Diversity Convention* and international trade law, *Journal of International Economic Law*, 9(3), 515–52.

Hallin, D. and Mancini, P. 2004. *Comparing Media Systems*. Cambridge: Cambridge University Press.

Hannan, M.T. and Freeman, J. 1977. The population ecology of organizations. *American Journal of Sociology*, 82(5), 929–64.

Harcourt, A. 2003. The regulation of media markets in selected EU Accession states in Central and Eastern Europe. *European Law Journal*, 9(3), 316–40.

Jakubowicz, K. 2001. Media in transition: The case of Poland, in *Media Reform: Democratizing the Media, Democratizing the State*, edited by M. Price, B. Rozumilowicz and S. Verhulst. London: Routledge, 203–31.

Jakubowicz, K. 2004. Ideas in Our Heads: Introduction of PSB as Part of Media System Change in Central and Eastern Europe, *European Journal of Communication*, 19(1), 53–74.

Jakubowicz, K. and Sükösd, M., eds. 2008. *Finding the Right Place on the Map: Central and Eastern European Media Change in Global Perspective*. Bristol: Intellect Books.

Johnson, M. and Rollo, J. 2001. EU Enlargement and Commercial Policy: Enlargement and the Making of Commercial Policy', Sussex European Institute Working Paper 43.

Lauk, E. 2008. How will it all unfold? Media systems and journalism cultures in post-communist countries, in *Finding the Right Place on the Map: Central and Eastern European Media Change in Global Perspective*, edited by K. Jakubowicz and M. Sükösd. Bristol: Intellect Books, 193–213.

Lengyel, E. 1998. The art of careful power balancing: Hungary, in *The Development of the Audiovisual Landscape in Central Europe since 1989*, edited by European Commission/ Eureka Audiovisuel. New Barnet: John Libbey, 81–5.

Meyer, J. and Rowan, B. 1977. Institutionalized organizations: Formal structure as myth and ceremony. *American Journal of Sociology*, 83(2), 340–63.

Oates, S. 2008. *Introduction to Media and Politics*. London: Sage.

Siebert, F.S., Peterson, T. and Schramm, W. 1956. *Four Theories of the Press: The Authoritarian, Libertarian, Social Responsibility and Soviet Communist*

Concepts of What the Press Should Be and Do. Urbana, IL: University of Illinois Press.

Sparks, C. 1997. Post-communist media in transition, in *International Media Research: A Critical Survey*, edited by J. Corner, P. Schlesinger and R. Silverstone. London: Routledge, 96–122.

Sparks, C. 1998. *Communism, Capitalism and the Mass Media*. London: Sage.

WIPO. 2001. Act No. 231/2001 of 17 May 2001 on Radio and Television Broadcasting. Available at: http://www.wipo.int/wipolex/en/text.jsp?file_id=197933 [accessed 16 June 2011].

WTO. 1997. Canada – Certain Measured Concerning Periodicals. Report of the Panel. Available at: http://www.worldtradelaw.net/reports/wtopanels/canada-periodicals%28panel%29.pdf [accessed 16 June 2011]

Wyka, A. 2008. In search of the East Central European media model? The Italianization model? in *Comparing Media Systems in Central Europe: Between Commercialization and Politicization*, edited by B. Dobek Ostrowska and M. Głowacki. Wroclaw: Wroclaw University Press, 55–69.

Chapter 7

Back to the Local?
Transnational Media Flows and Audience Consumption Patterns in Central and Eastern Europe

Václav Štětka

Introduction

It is textbook wisdom that processes of economic liberalization and privatization, which were at the heart of the general systemic changes in Central and Eastern European countries after 1989, created favorable conditions for gradual transnationalization[1] of their media systems as well. The conventional narrative is that, following the removal of ideological and legal constraints, the media markets and audiences in the region soon became a primary target for Western media companies and their products, resulting in a massive influx of foreign investment as well as Western media content, particularly visible in the audiovisual sector. With the overcoming of technological gaps and barriers, especially in the introduction of satellite and cable broadcasting in the early 1990s, the Central and Eastern European media landscapes have become a fully-fledged part of the global media system and have been pushed into the midst of transnational communication flows.

However, the comparative research on media transformation of this part of Europe has so far predominantly focused on the structural-economic aspects of this process, particularly on changes in media policies and regulation, including harmonization of national laws with the European *acquis communautaire* (see Paletz and Jakubowicz 2003, Sükösd and Bajomi-Lázár 2003, Harcourt 2003), as well as on ownership structures, particularly issues of concentration and internationalization of media markets (see Hrvatin and Petković 2004). In comparison to this rather advanced scholarship, what seems to be neglected within the academic investigation of media change in post-communist countries is the character, intensity and direction of the communication flows, as manifested

---

1 In this chapter, we follow the definition of media transnationalization as 'the increasing transborder flow of services and programmes and the increased exposure of audiences to an imported media culture, combined with the growing participation of nonnational entities in broadcasting' (Esser 2002: 14, quoting McQuail, 1995: 159).

through changing programme structures, amount and origin of audiovisual imports/exports, television programme production and consumption (not to mention audience reception). These kinds of processes and issues have been a focal point of global/international communication research for several decades, with growing popularity in the recent years (Tunstall 2008, McMillin 2007, Straubhaar 2007, Thussu 2006), however without almost any attention paid to the Central and Eastern European media landscapes and audiences. Aside from various case studies, looking at selected aspect of audiovisual (in)flows and audience behaviour in a particular national media landscape (Milosavljević 2008, for Slovenia; Peruško and Popović 2008, for Croatia; Havens 2007, for Hungary; Halawa 2005, for Poland; Štětka 2008, for the Czech Republic), so far there has been no systematic, pan-regional comparative study that attempts to look beyond a couple of national markets and the mere description of the situation.

Bridging this research gap, this chapter has two main interrelated goals. First, it aims to map the development and current state of audiovisual flows and audiences' preferences in Central and Eastern Europe, particularly with respect to the question of the competitiveness of the local audiovisual entertainment vis-à-vis imported programmes. Second, it attempts to explore the intra-regional differences and similarities in the amount and popularity of domestic programming in relation to a set of economic factors that enable analysis of data from a broader research perspective and answer the question as to why some countries have been more successful than others in challenging the inflow of audiovisual imports, gradually replacing them with locally produced content that is equally or even more attractive for the domestic audiences.

Communications Flow Research: From Cultural Imperialism to Cultural Proximity

Just as research on Central and Eastern European media systems and their transformation appears to neglect issues of transnational media production, circulation and consumption, countries in the region constitute uncharted territory on the map of communication flows, which have been drawn by scholars working in the field of international communication research (see McMillin 2007). During the 1970s and 1980s, the dominant description of international/global communication flows can be characterized by the metaphor of a 'one-way street' (Nordenstreng and Varis 1974), highlighting structural inequality in media production and distribution capacities among the world's countries, with the United States clearly dominating global information and cultural traffic (Tunstall 1977) and their products (Schiller 1969, Boyd-Barrett 1977, McPhail 1984), homogenizing local media forms and contents as well as the cultural tastes, values and identities of local audiences around the world. Studies of communication flows conducted in these decades mostly agreed that the majority of television and film content traded globally came from the United States: as Joseph Straubhaar summarizes the received wisdom 'most countries then imported most of their television programmes, mostly from the United States' (Straubhaar 2007: 61).

Already, however, during the heyday of the cultural or media imperialism thesis, some researchers started to point to the growing attractiveness of domestic media products for domestic audiences and predicted that the alleged supremacy of US media industries could not last forever. As Ithiel de Sola Pool stated at the end of the 1970s, 'In general, it seems that the American lead is eroding, as indeed someday it must' (de Sola Pool 1977: 143). According to him, it was only a matter of time until local television producers would be able to create their own programmes, modeled after successful foreign imports, which would then be ultimately disadvantaged against them in competition for an audience as they would have to overcome what de Sola Pool named 'barriers of culture':

> Domestic products portray characters eating the food the people eat, wearing the clothes they wear, celebrating the events they celebrate, and gossiping about the celebrities they follow ... Foreign works of art have jokes that are harder to get, stereotypes that do not ring a bell, situations that do not come from daily life. (de Sola Pool 1977: 143)

This thesis stays at the core of the so-called 'cultural proximity theory', which was developed along with the growing popularity of domestic audiovisual production – not just in Europe but in other parts of the world, confirming to a large extent de Sola Pool's prediction. According to Joseph Straubhaar, one of the main advocates of this concept, cultural proximity refers to the 'seemingly common attraction audiences feel for cultural products, such as television or music, that are close in cultural content and style to the audience's own culture(s)' (Straubhaar 2007: 26).[2] As Straubhaar reminds us, this attraction does not have to be limited to nation-bound cultural products, but can apply equally to local or regional cultures, with language being 'the clearest line of demarcation in cultural proximity' (Straubhaar 2007: 26). Elaborating on this idea further, some authors (Straubhaar 1997, Sinclair et al. 1996) have proposed the theory of 'geolinguistic' or 'geocultural' media markets, stating that media products which have the opportunity to cross borders are usually successful in markets where the audiences

---

2   As Straubhaar further explains, this tendency is not homogeneous but closely related to differences in social class and cultural capital, with the elites – sharing globalized cultural capital – more attracted towards the US imports while 'most audiences of the lower middle class and below are more interested in cultural products, particularly television and music (but seemingly not necessarily film), which are as culturally relevant or proximate as possible' (Straubhaar 2007: 27). This connection between cultural capital and cultural choices breaks down further by genre: the most popular US genres are the least demanding of cultural knowledge about the United States (action-adventure, cartoons, and physical comedy).

share certain cultural or linguistic characteristics similar to the audiences that the products were originally designed for.[3]

The empirical evidence from various parts of the world, as recently summarized by Straubhaar (2007) and Tunstall (2008) confirms the inclination towards domestic or culturally proximate production, at least among television audiences. As Tunstall puts it, 'the majority of audience time goes to national media. In larger population countries the national, regional, local and across-the-border media typically achieve audiences between six and 12 times those of global or American media' (Tunstall 2008: 10). Nothing probably illustrates this trend away from cultural imperialism as a dominant paradigm of international communication studies better than the titles of the two books written by Jeremy Tunstall and separated by over thirty years: *The Media Are American* (1977) vs. *The Media Were American* (2008), clearly recognizing the declining global hegemony of the US media industries.

The fact that most of the world's media content remains national does not, however, undermine the position of the US as the leading media exporter, still maintaining what Jean Chalaby (2006) calls 'US cultural primacy'. Hollywood feature films dominate most worldwide box offices as well as television screens, leading Joseph Straubhaar to repeat Tod Gitlin's observation that ' US popular culture is now second culture of most people in the world' (Straubhaar 2007: 89). In Western Europe, US TV products still outnumber local production in the genre of television fiction (Figure 7.1, measured by total programming hours).

However, as Tunstall notes, even at the height of American programming inflow in Western Europe in the mid-1990s (see De Bens and de Smaele 2001),[4] European audiences preferred domestic shows and other programmes. According to Tunstall, 'there was not one Hollywood TV series in these top-rated shows' (Tunstall 2008: 275).[5] This preference for domestic products has been reflected by the programming strategies of European television stations, which have been scheduling domestic fiction in prime-time, while the US (and other, most notably Latin American) imports have more often filled the off-prime time programme windows. Michael Buonanno (2001)

---

3   Although Straubhaar's initial categorization (Straubhaar 1997) was slightly different, in his recent account (Straubhaar 2007) he categorized the main world's 'cultural-linguistic regions' as following: Spanish (Latin America), Chinese (East and Southeast Asia), Arabic (Middle East), German (Europe), Hindi and Tamil (South Asia), and Malay (Southeast Asia). However, other authors might draw different geocultural 'maps' of the global media trade; see for example Tunstall (2008).

4   According to Tunstall, American TV exports in Europe have undergone several waves. Until the mid-1980s, there were only few commercial stations and the amount of American imports remained low. The next decade witnessed a significant growth of both commercial channels and, consequently, American programming hours across Europe. However, by the early 2000s, the imports started to decline, as European televisions started making their own popular programs (Tunstall 2008: 250).

5   In 1994, only one Western European country had more US television fiction programs than national ones among the top ten, as measured by audience ratings: that country was Italy (Television – European Key Facts 1995).

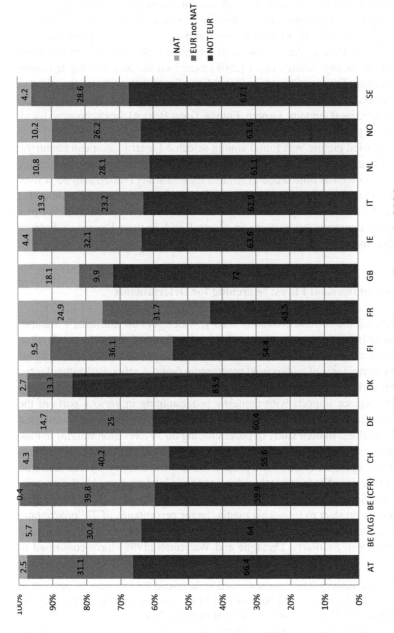

Figure 7.1   Origin of fiction broadcast by TV channels in Western Europe in 2006

Data source: European Audiovisual Observatory Yearbook 2007.

analyzed the programme schedules of five major European countries and found that, while television fiction of domestic origin comprised anywhere from 19 per cent (Italy) to 47 per cent (United Kingdom) of total programming, it accounted for the majority of prime-time programming.[6] Similarly, Sabine Trepte (2003) discovered that although the majority of fiction programming in five European countries originated in the United States, almost all top-rated series in each country were produced domestically. Andrea Esser (2009) examined the origin of top ten series in fifteen Western European countries in 2004 and found that, with the exception of Austria and southern Belgium, most of the series were domestically produced, and in several countries (Germany, Greece, France, Great Britain) they accounted for all of the 10 most popular series broadcast that year.

A more varied picture was found among selected Eastern European countries; however, these findings are difficult to generalize from due to the limited geographical as well as time scope of Andrea Esser's study (which is to be praised for at least including Central and Eastern European countries). It is clear that in order to get a more comprehensive picture of the nature of audiovisual flows and audience consumption patterns in Central and Eastern Europe, a broader comparative analysis is necessary.

Patterns of Audiovisual Flows: Searching for Determinants

Complementing the cultural proximity theory, which sees the audience's 'natural' affinity towards local programming as the driving force of domestic production, more economically oriented perspectives have been suggested when searching for particular determinants of audiovisual programme flows. Analyzing the imbalances in international film and television programming trade as well as the growing tendency to replace imports with domestic programming in various parts of the world, researchers have tested explanatory models based on various economic and structural variables. In their study of programming on 34 television stations in nine East Asian countries, Waterman and Rogers (1994) observed positive correlations between the proportion of domestic production and the country's gross domestic product and the size of broadcast television economic infrastructure.[7] In their words, 'in countries that are wealthier and/or devote relatively large proportions of their gross domestic product to broadcast media, larger percentages of TV programme hours are domestically produced, particularly drama programs' (Waterman and Rogers 1994: 89). Similarly, Dupagne and Waterman (1998) have confirmed in

---

6   The only country where domestic fiction accounted for less than 50 per cent in prime time in 2000 was Italy (43 per cent); in France, on the other hand, the share of domestic fiction was 75 per cent in prime time (Buonnano, 2001).

7   Broadcast television economic infrastructure was understood by the authors as 'an estimate of total economic resources available to the television broadcast system of each country' (Waterman and Rogers, 1994: 5).

their analysis of 61 television stations in 17 Western European countries that the percentage of US television fiction imports tends to decrease with gross domestic product and the broadcast television economic infrastructure (BTEI). In addition, the percentage of private stations in a national television market was found to be an important predictor of the US imports. The impact of the size of national economy and the audiovisual market (as measured by the amount of television advertising spending) on the ratio between domestic and imported audiovisual content were further corroborated by Chmielewski-Falkenheim (2000) in his study of television programming structure in ten South American countries,[8] as well as by Lee (2007) in his longitudinal analysis of foreign programme imports on South Korean television stations.[9] In some of these studies, the authors include other variables but with negative or inconclusive results, such as English language fluency (see Dupagne and Waterman 1998, Fu 2006) or presence of broadcasting quotas (Dupagne and Waterman, 1998).

Even though each of these studies have used slightly different methodologies either for evaluating the level of domestic/foreign content or for determining its relationship to the above mentioned factors, their findings unequivocally support the general thesis according to which the wealthier countries with stronger television markets have a better chance to produce more competitive domestic films and television programmes. As Sangoak Lee (2007: 176) puts it:

> In other words, as more resources become available to be invested in domestic production, the quality of domestic programs improves, at least from a commercial standpoint. Once domestic television programs attain a level of quality that is comparable to that of imports due to enlarged production budgets, viewers become attracted more strongly to domestic programs that tend instinctively to better reflect and incorporate their values, views, and cultural traditions. This results in the strengthening of the competitiveness of domestic programs in the ratings race, which, in turn, results in extended and escalated investments in domestic production.

---

8   As Chmielewski-Falkenheim (2000) has documented, in most South American countries the proportion of domestic programming is higher than programming originating either in the US or in other countries from the region. The countries with the largest gross domestic products and the largest populations (Argentina, Brazil and Columbia) rely on imported programming the least of all, and are also the strongest programming exporters themselves. The smaller states, on the other hand, still compete for dominance on their domestic markets with other regional and global players (Chmielewski-Falkenheim 2000).

9   Lee (2007) conducted a time-series analysis using 25-year longitudinal data on Korean television programming. He observed declining proportion of imports and rising domestic program content over the entire period, correlating with the growth of Korean economy as well as its television advertising market.

In this chapter, this presumed relationship which has been underpinned by the data from Western Europe, Latin America or Asia will be tested against the empirical background of the Central and Eastern European audiovisual markets, utilizing some of the economic indicators used in the above studies.

Historical Context of Audiovisual Imports Central and Eastern Europe: Before and after 1989

Before turning to comparative analysis, it is necessary to contextualize the issue of transnational media flows in Central and Eastern Europe by providing a brief insight into the recent history of audiovisual imports – as it is quite obvious that both films and television programming started to cross borders in this region long before the fall of communism. As Karol Jakubowicz (2007: 331) reminds us,

> Before 1989, media system internationalization in Central and Eastern Europe took the form of an influx of media and media content from the Soviet Union and other 'fraternal' countries, with a media policy dedicated to exposing the population to news, views, ideas, propaganda, and other things coming from other socialist countries.

According to Tapio Varis's study (Varis 1986), in 1983 Eastern European countries imported on average 27 per cent of their TV time (Soviet Union being an exception with only 8 per cent). However, it was not just imports from the East – it is useful to note that, contrary to the myth of the impervious Iron Curtain, media landscapes in Eastern Europe were being legally penetrated by Western contents already before 1989 (Jakubowicz 2007: 331), as can be illustrated with the following examples. During the more liberal period of the communist regime in Czechoslovakia in the late 1960s, Czechoslovak television started importing some popular French and British TV series (most notably the *Forsythe Saga*). In the communist German Democratic Republic, the share of US feature films broadcast on GDR television almost tripled during the 1980s, and this change was most prominent in prime time (altogether 56 per cent of films broadcast on TV came from capitalist countries in 1988; in 1980, there were only 35 per cent – see Stiehler 2004). In Romania, according to a rather anecdotal story, the US crime series *Columbo* almost caused an uprising in the late 1970s, when, after having seen the first 45 episodes, the audience believed the state television censored broadcasting further sequels (Kruml 2001). The last example from the pre-1989 period demonstrates that it was not just Western or US American programming that was being imported in the 1980s: by far the most popular recurrent television programme in the history of Polish state television, Telewizja Polska, was the Brazilian telenovela *Escrava Isaura* (*Niewolnica Isaura*), which became not just a media event but a social phenomenon in Poland in 1985, known as 'Isauromania': the 15 episodes of this series were watched on average by 81–92 per cent of the Polish TV population (Maciejewski 2005).

Nevertheless, the gates for the massive inflow of Western, especially US television and film products truly opened only after 1989. The same pattern was repeated in most of the post-socialist countries: 'The rising proportion of imported programmes, the sharp drop in the number of Soviet/Russian programmes, and the rapid growth of American ones' (Jakubowicz 2007: 331). The situation at the beginning of 1990s certainly justified the metaphor of 'Dallasification', coined by Els De Bens already in the late 1980s (see De Bens et al. 1992), as the most famous US soap operas such as Dallas and Dynasty were ruling over television programmes and audience ratings in many Central and Eastern European countries. In Czechoslovakia, *Dallas* became the most watched TV programme when first introduced in 1992; it was followed by an average of 75 per cent of television audience (Pitterman et al. 2002). In Poland, *Dynasty* achieved 80 per cent audience ratings in the same year (Halawa 2005). As is clear from Table 7.1 US series continued to dominate audience television ratings across the Central and Eastern European region throughout the first half of the 1990s. It is important to stress that, contrary to the prevailing opinion that associates the inflow of American programming with the commercialization of the TV sector, these series were first introduced by public service or even state television stations, not the commercial ones, which had not been established in many countries in the region at that time. However, the first signs of successful domestic production started to appear in 1996 as well – in the Czech Republic and in Poland, the public service TV stations managed to produce soap operas (*Život na zámku* and *Matki, Żony i Kochanki*) that attracted on average the highest number of viewers in that respective year.

Table 7.1   Most popular TV series in selected Central and Eastern European countries in the mid-1990s

	1994	1996
Bulgaria	(no data available)	E.R. (Kanal 1, 32%)
Czech Republic	Back to Eden (CT1, 71%); Covington Cross (CT1, 64%)	*Život na zámku (CT1, 45%)* Dallas (TV Nova, 41%)
Hungary	Dallas (TV1, 52%)	E.R. (MTV1, 55%); Dallas (MTV1, 52%)
Latvia	Covington Cross (LTV1, 35%)	(no data available)
Lithuania	Santa Barbara (Tele 3, 46%)	(no data available)
Poland	(no data available)	*Matki, Żony i Kochanki (TVP1, 45%)*; Dr. Quinn (TVP1, 45%); Angel Falls (TVP1, 43%)
Slovakia	Matlock (STV1, 75%); Beverly Hills 90210 (STV1, 73%) Baywatch (STV1, 60%)	Derrick (STV1, 67%); Dempsey and Makepeace (STV1, 60%) Manuela (STV2, 52%)

Source: IP-RTL: Television – European Key Facts 1994 and 1996

*Note*s: The percentages indicate audience ratings. Titles in Italics stand for domestically produced programmes.

Methodology of the Study

In order to meet the above stated research aims, namely to test the assumption about gradual increase and success of local film and television production at the expense of foreign imports in Central and Eastern Europe, and to search for factors which influence this process and account for differences across the region, I conducted secondary data analysis, which was designed as comparative and longitudinal. The need for a comparative approach is obvious, as this part of Europe, although sharing common history and a post-communist legacy, is far from being culturally homogeneous, and its particular national media systems also differ significantly (see Czepek et al. 2009; Jakubowicz and Sükösd 2008), which can arguably have an impact on the differences in the character of audiovisual flows and audience behavior. Correspondingly the longitudinal design was necessary for tracking the dynamics of audiovisual flows as well as the possible changes in audiences' preferences in time.

The construction of the sample was largely driven by data accessibility. Since the selected method was secondary data analysis, the study relied fully on publicly or semi-publicly available sources, particularly on the series of film and television yearbooks published by the European Audiovisual Observatory and the RTL Group (*Television – International Key Facts*).[10] Unfortunately, neither of these two types of publication contains comprehensive data on Central and Eastern European audiovisual markets that would enable comparison across the entire region and across the entire time period – the two decades of transnationalization of media markets in this part of Europe. In order to enable for longitudinal comparison, the sample needed to reach as far back as possible, and yet contain the countries included for the most recent period (the farther back the fewer the number of Central and Eastern European countries in the yearbooks). Following these criteria, two time points were established, 1999 and 2007, and the number of countries was determined to be 14 in the case of the television sample and 11 in the case of the sample for film production and distribution. In both samples, all the new EU members states were included (Czech Republic, Slovakia, Poland, Hungary, Slovenia, Bulgaria, Romania, Estonia, Lithuania and Latvia), plus Croatia and three post-Soviet countries (Belarus, Ukraine, Russia) as a background for comparison with the new EU member states.

While the database of film production and distribution, as recorded by the European Audiovisual Observatory, was fairly comprehensive, the television yearbooks unfortunately did not contain satisfactory data regarding the exact volume of television programme imports and the amount of national television production in Central and Eastern Europe, which are the measures most often used and referred to within the field of television flow studies (as reviewed in

---

10   I am indebted to ARBOmedia, the Prague-based PR and marketing company, for generously enabling me to retrieve data from the 'Television – International Key Facts' Yearbooks, which are otherwise not publicly available in the Czech Republic.

the previous section of this chapter). Therefore, a different measure had to be used, namely the audience preferences for domestic/imported programming, as measured by the geographical origin of programmes in the top ten television programmes according to audience ratings figures. Nevertheless, it could be argued that audiences' television preferences in regards to the geographical origin of the programming can be in fact regarded as more subtle indicators of the direction of audiovisual flows than the simple statistics concerning the amount of imported/ exported content, since these figures do not tell us whether and to what extent the imported programming really appeals to domestic audiences – which is, after all, the hidden assumption behind the old cultural imperialism thesis. Apart from this, the ranking of the most popular programmes indirectly reveals information about broadcasters' programming strategies as well (and thereby about the actual character of the flows), since the programmes with the highest ratings are usually scheduled in prime time (particularly the fictional genres).

In order to have at least an approximate figure about the differences in programme flows within the sample, this study uses the proportion of European content on television screens in each country, as monitored within the frames of the European Commission's 'Television without Frontiers' directive. This number, measured on the basis of average transmission time reserved for European programmes (excluding news, sports events, games and advertising) on nation-wide TV channels, does of course not fully replace the exact statistics about national production and the extent of imports, but since the biggest proportion of European content usually consists of domestic programmes (Štětka 2008), it is reasonable to assume that there is an inverse relationship between the level of European content and the level of imported programmes.

In an attempt to search for factors influencing the character of audiovisual flows and the inclination of audiences towards either domestic or imported programming, and with the aim to elucidate the presumed similarities and differences within the region, four independent variables were included in the analysis. Inspired by empirical studies on determinants of audiovisual flows (Lee 2007, Dupagne and Waterman1998; Waterman and Rogers 1994), following economic measures were selected: 1. gross domestic product as an indicator of the country's economic power (complemented by gross domestic power per capita adjusted for purchasing power); 2. the total operating revenue of television companies in the respective national market, indicating the size of that television market as well as the amount of financial resources potentially available to invest in domestic programming; 3. the amount of state support for domestic audiovisual production and distribution (used in the analysis of film production); and 4. the market position of public service broadcasting. The latter variable was essentially incorporated as a substitute for the percentage of private stations on a particular national television market, as used by Dupagne and Waterman (1998), because this number was difficult to obtain for the sample in this study; it can be argued that the market position of public service broadcasting is an alternative indicator for the same concept. Moreover, since public service broadcasting has historically been bound with the nation-building project and support for national culture (Scannell and Cardiff 1991, Van den Bulck 2001), it can be hypothesized that countries with stronger public service television will also be among those with relatively more successful domestic production.

It is, however, necessary to note that, despite introducing new variables, this study does not aim to test a new explanatory *model* of transnational audiovisual flows and audience behavior. The nature of the available data and especially the limited size of the sample do not allow more in-depth statistical analysis that would be necessary for such a task. Analytical instruments for this study have, therefore, been limited to frequency tables and bivariate correlations, complemented with a more qualitative interpretation of the observed similarities and differences within the sample. In consequence, the presented relationships should be regarded as indicative rather than conclusive. They nevertheless open doors for further empirical testing.

The Silver Screen: Hollywood's Undisputed Realm?

At first glance, the data about film distribution in the Central and Eastern European markets, as collected by the European Audiovisual Observatory, confirm the persistence of Hollywood's exceptional distribution power. In 2007, the proportion of US feature films in the countries in the sample stretched from 50 per cent (Hungary) to 70 per cent (Bulgaria) of all the films distributed that year in the countries' cinemas. Nevertheless, a trend of strengthening national production can be observed from these statistics as well, as is clear in the case of the Czech Republic, Estonia or Hungary, where the number of domestic films within the selected time period has grown relatively more than the number of US imports. Even more significant seems to be the growth of films from other European countries, which have more than doubled in number in Bulgaria, Estonia, Romania or Slovenia between 2002 and 2007.

Despite growing numbers, market shares of US films actually slightly dropped in five out of six national film markets in the sample during the monitored period. As the following Table 7.2 demonstrates, this drop is explained by the simultaneous growth of the domestic film industries and their market success – in other words, by their ability to attract larger audiences. This trend is most visible in the Czech Republic, which released about 30 per cent more feature films in 2007 (29 films) than in 2002 (21 films) with their market share almost tripling (from 12 per cent to 32 per cent); the US market share dropped to below 50 per cent in 2007. In Poland, 25 films were released in both years; yet in 2007 they accounted for 25 per cent of the market share, while five years earlier for only 17 per cent. Also, there is an almost perfectly negative correlation ($r = 0.943$) between the market share of US and domestic films, which means that the domestic film shares grow at the expense of Hollywood imports.

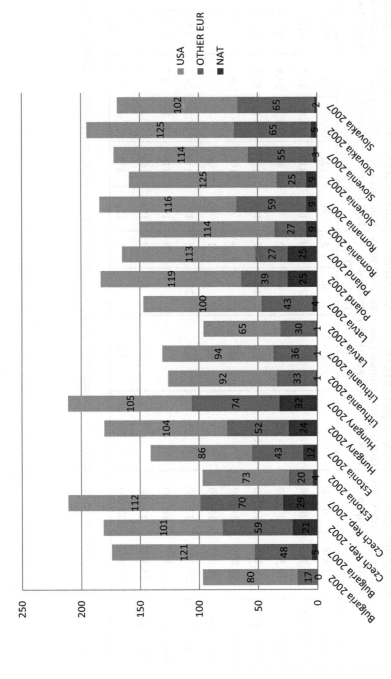

Figure 7.2   Origin of first release feature films in Central and Eastern Europe, 2002–2007

Data source: European Audiovisual Observatory Yearbook 2003 and 2008

Table 7.2 Summary of indicators/contextual variables for film production/distribution in Central and Eastern Europe, 2007

	GDP (2007, million EUR)	GDP (PPS) per capita	State support (2004, million EUR)	STATE support per capita (EUR)	Number of domestic films released 2002 / 2007		Number of US films released 2002 / 2007		Market share of domestic films (%) 2002 / 2007		Market share of US films (%) 2002 / 2007	
Bulgaria	28,898	9,500	-	-	0	5	80	121	0.02	1.5	78.3	71.2
Czech Rep.	133,283	20,200	1.9	0.2	21	29	101	112	11.8	31.7	61.4	47.4
Estonia	15,546	17,600	3.2	2.4	4	12	73	86	10.3	14.4	74.3	69.1
Hungary	100,153	15,700	19.9	2.0	24	32	104	105	8.1	12.2	71.6	67.1
Latvia	19,859	14,400	1.1	0.5	1	4	65	100	-	0.2	-	77.3
Lithuania	28,017	15,000	1.1	0.3	1	1	92	94	-	-	-	-
Poland	320,712	13,300	3.5	0.1	25	25	119	113	17.1	24.7	54.5	56.3
Romania	111,557	10,100	-	-	9	9	114	116	11.1	4.7	72.7	76.4
Slovakia	55,107	17,000	0.7	0.1	5	2	125	102	-	-	-	-
Slovenia	33,542	22,000	2.3	1.2	9	3	125	114	-	0.2	-	71.7

Data sources: Cambridge Econometrics et al. 2008; International Monetary Fund 2009; European Audiovisual Observatory Yearbook 2008.

Analyzing possible relationships between domestic/imported films and the structural-economic factors presented in the Table 7.2, it can be said that the production capacities of domestic film industry seem to be related to the country's overall economic performance, expressed by the gross domestic product. Despite the relative strength of this correlation ($r = 0.643$)[11] a closer look at individual countries demonstrates that there are some exceptions to this seemingly linear relationship, namely Hungary which managed to produce about 20 per cent more films in 2007 than Poland, whose economy is three times as big. One possible explanation for this particular case could be the amount of state financial support for domestic audiovisual production and distribution,[12] which – itself being relatively independent from the size of national economy ($r = 0.133$) – has reached almost 20 million Euros in 2004 in Hungary, which is the highest amount in the sample. On the other hand, in the Czech Republic, which on average produces a comparable amount of films, the filmmakers do not seem to profit from the state's support as much as in Hungary (the amount granted in 2004 to the audiovisual sector in the Czech Republic was only 1.9 million Euros); however, they can evidently rely on the support of their home audience, who buy a lot more tickets to see domestic movies than do the audiences in the neighboring countries.

Central and Eastern European Television Markets: Revival of the Local

Although far from being detailed or complete, the information contained in the yearbooks provide a relatively comprehensible picture about the development of television audiences' preferences across Central and Eastern Europe in the last decade. The first tendency which is clearly observable from the data is the growing popularity of locally produced television programmes within the selected time frame, as is shown in Figure 7.3.

It can be seen that in almost all the countries in the sample, the majority of programmes in the top ten were domestically produced in 2007. For most of the countries the same was true already in 1999, while a few others – most notably Bulgaria and Latvia – experienced a dramatic reverse of the ratio between the popularity of domestic and foreign programming during this time period. Six countries – the Czech Republic, Lithuania, Latvia, Slovakia, Slovenia, Russia and Estonia – managed to fill the entire top ten chart of the most popular programmes just from local sources in 2007. The only countries whose television audiences in

---

11   In this analysis, all the Pearson's correlation figures are presented without testing the level of statistical significance, because of the very small number of cases in the sample, and because of the fact that the analysis does not aim for generalizations beyond the scope of the sample.

12   The correlation between state's financial support for audiovisual production (2004) and the number of domestic films released (2007) is $r = 0,639$.

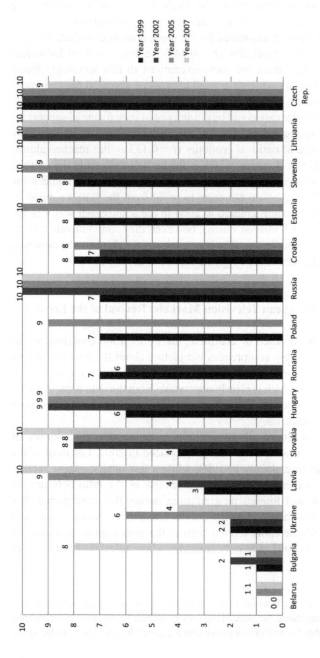

Figure 7.3　Number of domestically produced TV programmes in the top ten, 1999–2007

Source: IP-RTL: Television – International Key Facts 2000, 2003, 2006 and 2008 (based on TV audience ratings; excluding news, extraordinary events and sports programmes).

2007 still preferred imported programming over the local one were Belarus and Ukraine, both importing their most watched shows from Russia.

However, these rather crude statistics do not tell us too much about what the audiences are actually watching, and need to be analyzed in a more detailed way. Table 7.3 presents an overview of the recurrent programmes which achieved the highest ratings in 2007 across the sample:

Table 7.3   Most popular recurrent TV programmes in Central and Eastern Europe in 2007

Country	Channel	Programme title	Genre	Origin	Audience ratings	Audience share
Belarus	ONT	Not born to be a beauty	Soap opera	Russia	36.1%	69.6%
Bulgaria	*BTV*	*Slavi's Show*	*Variety show*	*Domestic*	*34.6%*	*72%*
Croatia	HTV 1	What is a man without a moustache	Comedy series	Domestic	32.7%	57%
Czech Rep.	*Nova*	*Surgery in the pink garden*	*Soap opera*	*Domestic*	*27%*	*52.4%*
Estonia	*Kanal 2*	Dancing with the stars	Variety Show	Domestic	32.1%	57.1%
Hungary	RTL Klub	A star is born	Variety	Domestic	27.3%	51.1%
Latvia	TV3	Dancing with the stars	Variety Show	Domestic	26%	68.2%
Lithuania	*LNK*	*Duets of stars*	*Music Show*	*Domestic*	*25.5%*	*53.9%*
Poland	TVP 2	'L' for love	Soap opera	Domestic	31.2%	59.5%
Romania	TVR 1	Surprise-Surprise	Variety Show	Domestic	17.5%	35.1%
Russia	Perviy	Saboteur. The end of the war	Action series	Domestic	17.4%	54.4%
Slovakia	*Markiza*	*Neighbours II*	*Sitcom*	*Domestic*	*29%*	*58.6%*
Slovenia	*POP TV*	*Victors*	*Variety Show*	*Domestic*	*24.8%*	*57.8%*
Ukraine	Inter	Tatyana's Day	Soap opera	Russia	20.6%	44.3%

Source: IP-RTL: Television – International Key Facts 2008.

*Note*s: The figures for audience ratings and shares indicate the highest achieved values for the particular programme (excluding news, sports and extraordinary media events). Rows in Italic indicate commercial channels.

In almost all the countries the most popular recurrent programmes (reality/ variety/music shows, soaps, sitcoms, talk shows etc.) were produced domestically in 2007; only in Belarus and Ukraine they were imported from the neighboring country, Russia. Also, the majority of the number one programmes were broadcasted on commercial televisions, with the exception of Poland, Romania and Croatia, where the public service channels achieved highest ratings for their shows, as well as Belarus and Russia, where the best rated recurrent programmes came from state owned TV stations.[13] However, the most interesting fact is that in several countries the highest rated shows, even though domestic by production, were actually local adaptations of global TV formats – *Dancing with the Stars* in Estonia and Latvia (originally a BBC format *Strictly Come Dancing*) and *A Star is Born* in Hungary (adaptation of the Simon Cowell's *Got Talent* format).

A closer look in the television yearbooks within the larger time frame reveals that the popularity of television formats has by no means been limited either to the selected year or to these three countries. In 2002, the globally popular quiz show *Who Wants to be a Millionaire* was the highest rated show in altogether five Central and Eastern European countries – Croatia (where it reached an astonishing 65 per cent audience share), the Czech Republic, Estonia, Hungary and Slovakia. Three years later, it still dominated the ratings in Croatia and Hungary, while in other countries the viewers went for reality TV instead – the number one programme in the Czech Republic and Slovakia was *Pop Idol*, and the Bulgarian audience devoted most attention to *Big Brother*. Although none of these shows reached the top position in audience ratings in 2007, they were still among the most followed ones in several countries, complemented by newer formats such as *Dancing with the Stars*, *Got Talent*, *Strictly Come Dancing* or *Wife Swap*. In fact, in ten out of 14 countries in the sample, there was at least one global TV format in the top three recurrent programmes in 2007. This finding certainly puts the previously presented data about the predominance of domestic programming in popularity charts across Central and Eastern Europe in a better perspective; even though these programmes cannot be denied domestic origin, they can hardly be regarded an illustration of the creative power of domestic audiovisual industries, succeeding in a battle for audience popularity with the imported content.

Breaking the statistics down to selected fiction genres, the picture of the alleged hegemony of the national production seen in Figure 7.3 becomes even more blurred. A brief look at the geographical origin of the most popular feature films (see Figure 7.4) reveals that despite the nation's most watched programmes being of domestic origin, in the genre of film Hollywood still maintains its firm grip over the Central and Eastern European television market, just as it does on the

---

13   Regardless of the type of television, none of these programs managed to attract nearly as much audience as the US series in the mid of the 1990s. The best series and shows barely achieved more than a third of the television audience, which can nevertheless be attributed to the fact that the television market is now substantially more fragmented than it was a dozen years ago.

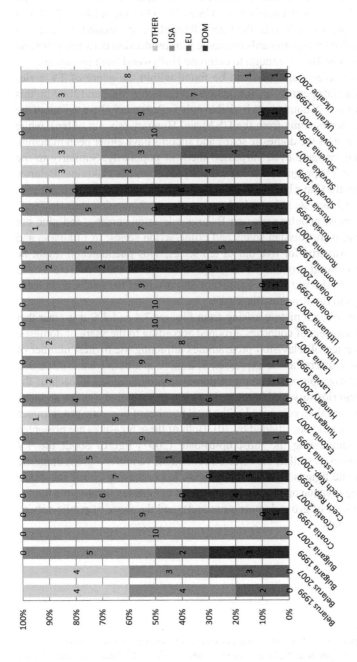

Figure 7.4 Origin of the top ten TV films in Central and Eastern Europe, 1999 and 2007

Source: IP-RTL: Television – International Key Facts 2000 and 2008 (based on TV audience ratings).

silver screen. The only exceptions from the US dominance in this field are Russia (eight out of ten most successful TV films were domestic in 2007) and Poland (with the ratio of six domestic against two US and two European films). Still, in a couple of other countries (Croatia, the Czech Republic and Estonia) the rankings witnessed a positive change towards domestic film production between 1999 and 2007, although not sufficient enough to dethrone Hollywood from its position.

A much more diverse situation can be found within the genre of TV series (unfortunately, the data permit only the comparison between 2002 and 2007 for this genre in the sample). US dominance is visible only in Bulgaria (where ten out of the ten most popular series come from the USA) and Hungary (six out of ten), while in most other countries the domestic soaps and sitcoms have either been matching the imported one, or have even surpassed them in popularity. Similarly to the overall ranking of TV programmes, the post-Soviet countries (Ukraine, Belarus, Latvia, and Lithuania) have been subject to a significant inflow of television series from Russia, which are steadily ranked among the most popular ones. In 2007, eight out of ten most popular series on Belarus television screens, and nine out of ten in Ukraine, were Russian soaps and crime/action series; in Lithuania and Latvia the same was true for five out of ten series. This phenomenon might be attributed to the cultural proximity / language factor (particularly in Belarus and Ukraine) but also to the fact that a significant proportion of the audience in these countries belongs to the Russian minority.[14]

Looking at the overall picture arising from Figures 7.4 and 7.5, it is clear that there are several clusters of countries, grouped according to the share of domestic content in the top ten of television programmes attracting the highest number of audiences. These clusters can be expressed in a more qualitative way (through a three-layer categorization of the share of domestic programming in each of the three top ten categories surveyed here), or in a more quantitative way (as an index of domestic programming, composed of the total number of domestic programmes across the three top ten lists, divided by 30). Both of these measures are presented in Table 7.4, summarizing the most up-to-date (2007) figures about the TV audience preferences as well as the selected contextual variables – gross domestic product (in absolute figures as well as per capita in purchasing power standard), the total operating revenue of nationwide television companies (in absolute figures as well as in per cent of gross domestic product), and the share of public service broadcasting channels.

---

14   The proportion of Russians living in these countries is as follows: Latvia – 6,3 per cent; Lithuania – 29,6 per cent; Belarus – 11 per cent; Ukraine – 17,3 per cent (Der Fischer Weltalmanach 2008, data from the last census).

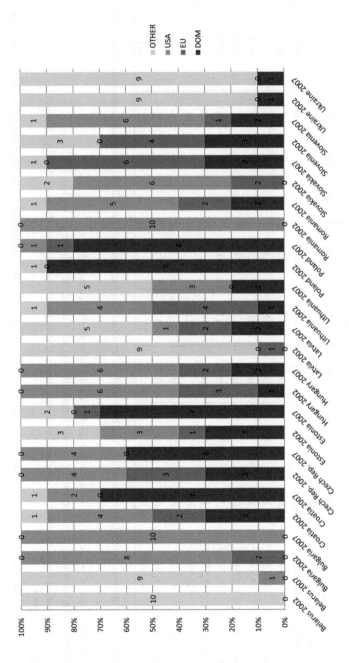

Figure 7.5   Origin of the top ten TV series in Central and Eastern Europe, 2002 and 2007

Source: IP-RTL: Television – International Key Facts 2003 and 2008 (based on TV audience ratings).

Table 7.4   Summary of indicators and contextual variables for TV audience preferences Central and Eastern Europe, 2007

	Gross domestic product (GDP)		TV operating revenue		PSB market share[1]	European content (%)	Domestic programs in the top ten			Index of domestic programming[2]
	Mil. EUR	Per capita in PPS	Mil. EUR	As % of GDP			All	Films	Series	
Belarus	32,494	7,920	-	-	(62.2)[3]	-	1	0	0	0.03
Bulgaria	28,898	9,500	166	0.57	15.1	72.83	8	0	0	0.27
Croatia	37,442	13,900	253	0.67	51.1	-	8[4]	4	7	-
Czech Rep.	133,283	20,200	506	0.38	29.7	79.92	9	4	6	0.63
Estonia	15,546	17,600	51	0.33	17.2	62.73	9	3	7	0.63
Hungary	100,153	15,700	456	0.46	18.3	76.93	9	0	2	0.37
Latvia	19,859	14,400	44	0.22	16.1	62.49	10	0	2	0.40
Lithuania	28,017	15,000	53	0.19	14.2	46.98	10	0	2	0.40
Poland	320,712	13,300	1384	0.43	41.4	81.08	9	6	8	0.77
Romania	111,557	10,100	496	0.44	16.9	57.95	-[5]	1	2	-
Russia	941,732	10,670	-	-	(47.8)[3]	-	10	8	10	0.93
Slovakia	55,107	17,000	118	0.21	23	62.27	10	0	3	0.43
Slovenia	33,542	22,000	158	0.47	32.6	52.28	9	1	2	0.40
Ukraine	90,908	5,040	-	-	(2.1)[3]	-	4	0	1	0.17

Data sources: European Audiovisual Observatory Yearbook 2008; Television – International Key Facts 2008; European Commission 2008, TWF 2006.
Notes:

(1) Audience share of public service broadcasting (combined shares of all PSB channels)

(2) Σ domestic programmes in the top ten + domestic films in the top ten + domestic series in the top ten) / 30

(3) Numbers in parenthesis stand for the combined audience shares of state television channels (Belarus, Russia, Ukraine)

(4) Data from 2005

(5) Almost all of the top 20 programmes in Romania in 2007 were sports events, so the comparable figure for domestic programs is missing.

Economic Context of Localization

The qualitative grouping as well as the quantitative index of domestic programming lead to similar results, dividing the sample into three basic clusters (unfortunately, some of the countries had to be excluded because of the gaps in the data). The first one is composed of countries that scored highly in at least two of the three top ten categories surveyed in 2007. On the very top of this cluster there is Russia (index 0.93) whose TV audiences clearly prefer domestic programming regardless of the genre, followed by Poland (0.77), lagging behind slightly in the number of domestic TV series and films, which nevertheless still make up for more than a half of the top ten in the respective genre categories. The following two members of this first tier are Estonia and the Czech Republic, both scoring 0.63 on the index of domestic programming and having over 50 per cent home produced TV series in the top ten, but less than half of domestic TV films; this genre is therefore still dominated by foreign (mainly US) production.[15] Both Poland and the Czech Republic also belong to the countries with the highest proportion of European content on television screens – 81 per cent and 80 per cent in 2006 (see Table 7.4); only Estonia does not fit into this equation, as it occupies a spot in the middle of the sample with only about 63 per cent of European programming.[16]

The second cluster consists of six countries whose national production only scored highly in the overall top ten category, mainly because of domestic variety/music/quiz shows and reality TV programming, while the most successful programmes in both the specific genres analyzed here (TV films and series) are of a foreign origin. Countries falling within this cluster are Slovakia (index 0.43), Slovenia, Latvia and Lithuania (0.40), Hungary (0.37) and Bulgaria (0.27). The average proportion of European programming within this cluster of countries reaches from 49 per cent (Lithuania) to 73 per cent (Bulgaria). In case of Lithuania, the low percentage of European works (which has been the subject of criticism by the EU, see European Commission 2008) is mainly caused by the programming strategies of private channels LNK and TV3, which in 2006 filled only 42 per cent

---

15   From the figures in Table 7.3, Croatia would be part of the first cluster as well, scoring high in general programming category as well as in TV series genre. However, the data for the first mentioned category were taken only from 2005, as in 2007 the base of programs in top ten was not big enough to calculate the ratio between domestic and foreign programming, as most of the items were sports events and news.

16   The reasons for this difference are difficult to uncover without having more information about the geographical origin of programs broadcasted on Estonian TV stations. It cannot be, however, attributed to the high number of Russian language cable channels broadcasting Russian programs (accounting together for over 22 per cent of Estonian audience) as those are regarded 'local' by the Estonian broadcasting law and as such are not part of the monitoring of the application of Articles 4 and 5 of Directive 89/552EEC 'Television without Frontiers'. In other words, the 63 per cent of European content is calculated as an average of European programming broadcasted in 2006 on three Estonian national TV stations, ETV, Kanal 2 and TV3 (European Commission 2008).

and 36 per cent of their air time with European programmes. In Bulgaria the relatively higher percentage has been skewed primarily through the almost 100 per cent of European works broadcasted on the state-owned BNT 1, which nonetheless has not managed to succeed with one single programme in the audience's top ten, while the market leader, Rupert Murdoch's station bTV (sold in 2010 to CME), reserved only 56 per cent of its time to European works (European Commission, 2008), including several reality TV formats which belong to the most watched shows overall; however the genre of TV series is filled almost entirely with US soaps and crime series (Television Key Facts 2008).

The last cluster collects the two ex-Commonwealth of Independent States countries whose domestic programmes are a minority in all the three top ten categories (or which are not present there at all), which is the case for Ukraine (0.17) and Belarus (0.03). Television audiences in these countries consume predominantly imported programming, in both cases coming mainly from Russia.

The clustering of course does not explain why certain Central and Eastern European television markets are obviously more successful in producing competitive television programmes than others. In order to better understand the above described differences in the attractiveness of domestic television programming for local audiences, we need to examine them in relation to the selected variables that place the audiences' preferences in a wider context of television production in the particular country.

A closer look at the table above suggests that there is a correlation between the 'usual suspects', the country's economic performance measured by the gross domestic product, as well as the size of its television economic infrastructure (measured by the television operating revenues) and the popularity of local production. The strength of the correlation of the gross domestic product with the index of domestic programming is fairly high for the selected sample ($r=0.714$), however if gross domestic product (in purchasing power standards) per capita is used instead of the absolute figures, the relationship weakens a bit ($r=0.404$). Similarly, the absolute sum of a country's television operating revenues correlates quite positively with the combined figure for the most popular domestic TV programming ($r=0.438$), but if we look at the operating revenues as percentage of the gross domeestic product, the previous relationship disappears ($r= -0.193$).[17] These results suggest that it is not so much the countries' living standards or the relative proportion of economic resources allocated within the TV market but the sheer size of both the country's economy and its

---

17   The same positive correlation was found between the gross domestic product and percentage of European content broadcasted on average in each country ($r=0.627$), as well as between TV operating revenues and the European content ($r=0.640$). Analyzed by the relative figures (gross domestic product per capita / TV revenues as per cent of gross domestic product), correlation is diminished ($r=0.452$ in case of TV revenues) or even inverted ($r= -0.123$ in case of gross domestic product per capita).

television companies that creates favorable conditions for local programming. Both findings are in line with the thesis presented in the first part of the chapter, namely that large economies and stronger television markets can generate more financial resources to be used for the production of more expensive domestic programming which, due to the cultural proximity factor, can then succeed in competition with foreign imports.

Nevertheless, it is clear from these results that this relationship is not entirely linear and there are exceptions to the above mentioned 'rule'. The most obvious one is Estonia: despite being a small-size economy and having a small television market, it produces entertainment which in general beats the imported content, both in the overall ranking as well as in the top ten of television series. However, the reason for this anomaly might lie in the relatively higher segmentation of the Estonian TV market, where the three main Estonian channels account for only about 57 per cent audience,[18] resulting in the fact that even the most successful domestic series do not manage to attract as high shares of viewers as in the Czech Republic or Poland.[19] In light of this information, the apparent success of domestic production in Estonia, as recorded in the top ten rankings, is relative (although certainly not completely undermined).

The other external variable included for the purposes of this study, the audience share of public service broadcasting, show similarly positive correlations with the presence of domestic programming among the most popular TV entertainment across the region. Again, Estonia is an outlier in this otherwise nearly linear relationship, according to which the stronger the position of public service television on the particular television market, the more likely it is that audiences will prefer domestic programming over the imported one. However, this correlation might be slightly misleading, because public service television does not necessarily beat its commercial opponents in the popularity of locally made programmes. As the figures in Table 7.3 suggest, it is more often the commercial television stations that produce the most successful domestic entertainment. Table 7.5 takes a closer look at three selected television markets with a different position of public service broadcasting, displaying mixed patterns.

---

18   The rest is divided between for Russian language channels (having over 20 per cent audience share combined) and smaller, predominantly satellite and cable channels (Television Key Facts 2008).

19   In 2007, the top five domestic television series in Estonia had an average audience share of 31 per cent. In both Poland and the Czech Republic, the same figure was 41.3 per cent (Television Key Facts 2008).

Table 7.5   Number of domestic programmes in the top ten according to the type of TV station, selected cases

PSB		Domestic		Imported	
		Private	PSB	Private	Private
Poland	All	9	-	-	1
	Film	5	1	3	1
	Series	6	2	1	1
Czech Republic	All	2	7	-	1
	Film	-	4	-	6
	Series	2	4	-	4
Hungary	All	-	8	-	2
	Film	-	-	-	10
	Series	-	2	-	8

While in Poland, where the public service television has over 40 per cent market share, its domestic programmes literary rule the top ten ranking, in Hungary, where public service television has only about 18 per cent share, imported programming dominates the genres of film and series but the general ranking is occupied by domestic programmes from the production of commercial stations. In the Czech Republic, with public service television at about 30 per cent, domestic programmes broadcast on private stations share the same or even higher rankings than the imported ones. The analysis further revealed that the share of public service television is strongly related to both the gross domestic product (r=0.779) as well as to the sum of operating TV revenues (r=0.768), which means that this variable functions rather as a proxy for the total financial resources available to support domestic television production.

Conclusions: Beyond Domestic and Foreign

Looking at the development of audiovisual flows and audiences' preferences in Central and Eastern Europe in the past two decades, we can see a general trend characterized by the initial inflow of foreign (mainly Western) imports that started to be gradually countered by the growth of domestic production, particularly television programming. The first signs of this transition were already visible in the second half of the 1990s in some countries, notably the Czech Republic or Poland, and by the turn of the century this trend has spread to most of the other countries in the region. Even though there are still significant differences between the countries as well as particular genres (the largest part of the most watched programmes consists of domestic variety shows, soap operas and reality TV programmes, while foreign imports still rule among the films and partially also serials) we can conclude that almost all the countries in the sample are currently producing television entertainment generally capable of attracting the largest part of the audience and successfully compete with foreign imports.

In this respect, the trend in audiences' preferences largely corresponds to Terhi Rantanen's conceptualization of different stages of media globalization that a country in transition usually goes through. According to Rantanen (2001), the process starts with an 'emerging globalization', characterized by gradual globalization of contents, of technology and of consumption; it is followed by an 'increasing globalization', when there is a sharp increase in the consumption of global media products, and concluded by the stage of 'declining globalization', witnessing emerging nationalization of contents and a partial turn to national products in consumption. Even though Rantanen illustrates this process using the example of Russia, which has certainly a specific position, the empirical evidence presented and analyzed in this chapter suggests it could be valid for most of the Central and Eastern Europe, albeit the timing of particular stages might differ from country to country.

Searching for causes that could stand behind the differences in the state of audiovisual production and consumption among the sample, the country's economic capacity and the size of its television market appear to be the most likely factors to explain the amount and audience success of domestic production, which is in concord with previous research in this area (Waterman and Rogers 1994, Dupagne and Waterman 1998, Lee 2007). This finding leads to the conclusion that the more wealth is being generated, both on a national as well as on particular film/television companies' level, the more resources are available to be invested in higher quality production (either through the system of public funding or through the growing advertising revenues) which is then able to attract bigger shares of audience already accustomed to the quality standards of Western (particularly US American) film and television entertainment. As the ever richer commercial television companies, which originally gained their market advantage largely through the sought-after foreign imports in the 'emerging globalization' phase, sense there is potentially more profit to be made in the domestic programming, the circle – which has already occurred in Western European television markets two decades ago – closes.

Even though this study did not look specifically at the issue of television ownership and its relation to domestic production and programme flows, it could be argued on the example of television stations owned by the Central European Media Enterprises across the region (see Downey's chapter in this book) that even the transnational companies, stereotypically portrayed as envoys of cultural imperialism, nowadays heavily invest in local production and are among the engines of the current growth of popularity of domestic programming within this region. To invest in local production at least in some Central and Eastern European states is the profit-maximizing strategy followed by national and transnational media firms alike.[20]

---

20   In Croatia (Nova TV), the Czech Republic (TV Nova) or Slovakia (Markiza), CME's television stations have fill their prime time mainly with domestically produced soap operas, sitcoms and comedy shows in 2007 (Television Key Facts 2008).

The investment activities of transnational media companies, establishing their local branches and/or commencing their broadcasting in local languages,[21] suggest that despite the predominant trend towards localization of production and consumption, the audiovisual flows and audiences' tastes in the region are still being heavily shaped by a variety of transnational processes. The most visible of them is the spreading of global television formats, which has already been discussed earlier in this chapter. As so-called glocalized cultural products (Moran and Malbon 2006), formats leave space for local adaptation and cultural differences but retain the generic form according to which the local adaptations are shaped, making the programme clearly distinguishable regardless of the national context. The question, however, remains what is more important: whether the shared structure, plot and/or idea on which the format is built, or the subtle differences in their particular national appropriations. In spite of their indisputable potential to give prominence to local cultural representations or even symbolically integrate national audiences (as in many instances of the *Pop Idol / Popstars* contests), it should not be forgotten that they represent a type of light entertainment which reinforce processes of depoliticization of the public sphere, pushing other kinds of genres, programmes and topics out of the prime time and (therefore) out of the centre of mainstream audiences' gaze. Regardless of the local variations, it can hardly be disputed that the recent popularity of formats leads to a certain structural homogenization of programme schedules of the Central and Eastern European television markets and contributes to spreading commercial media logic.

Apart from these systemic aspects, the diffusion of television formats has implications for the analysis of audiovisual flows in the region in general, as it illustrates the insufficiency of the exclusively nation-centered approach, which most of the studies of media flows and consumption patterns have been anchored in. The validity of the binary opposition between 'domestic' (national, local) vs. 'foreign' (imported) which serves as basic conceptual tool for analyzing the character of media flows and systems in the contemporary world has indeed been increasingly challenged by processes and agencies which do not fit the traditional understanding of a nation-state as a primary unit of cultural production and consumption (Curtin 2003, Chalaby, 2005). In a condition of an 'electronic bricolage' (Barker 1999) created by an ever more expanding number of media outlets and rapidly growing exchange of ideas, symbols and representations across global mediascapes, it is becoming difficult to ascribe audiovisual products an

---

21   Central and Eastern European media markets are becoming ever more attractive for the transnational companies as their value grows in time. For example MTV, one of the very symbols of cultural globalization in the 1980 (under the slogan 'One Planet, One Music') and glocalization since the 1990s (with the motto 'Local Music, Local People'), currently broadcasts in eleven languages. National Geographic is available to audiences in nine Central and Eastern European countries in their language versions, and the Walt-Disney based network Jetix (formerly Fox Kids) operates seven different local channels (and their respective online portals) in the region (source: corporate websites).

unambiguous identity, bound with a specific nation state and national culture. As Andrea Esser reminds us, 'the uniqueness of the originally national broadcasting markets has been watered down. Television has gradually become less national, more transnational; and this is true despite the newly found popularity of locally produced programmes' (Esser 2002: 26–7). Therefore, further explorations in the contemporary character of media flows should take this issue into account and attempt to look beyond the narrow dichotomy of domestic/foreign production/ consumption, even though this binary still dominates the official statistics, reports and indeed public and political debates on the state and the future of national cultures.

References

Barker, C. 1999. *Television, Globalization and Cultural Identities*. Buckingham, Philadelphia. Open University Press.

Boyd-Barrett, J.O. 1977. Media imperialism: Towards an international framework for an analysis of media systems, in *Mass Communication and Society*, edited by J. Curran, M. Gurevitch and J. Woolacott. London: Edward Arnold, 116–35.

Buonano, M. 2001. *Eurofiction. Television fiction in Europe*. Report. Strasbourg: European Audiovisual Observatory.

Cambridge Econometrics 2008. *Study on the Economic and Cultural Impact, notably on Co productions, of Territorialisation Clauses of state aid Schemes for Films and Audiovisual Productions. A final report for the European Commission, DG Information Society and Media*. Brussels: European Commission.

Chalaby, J.K. 2005. From internationalization to transnationalization. *Global Media and Communication*, 1(1), 28–33.

Chalaby, J.K. 2006. American cultural primacy in a new media order: A European perspective. *The International Communication Gazette*, 68(1), 33–51.

Chmielewski-Falkenheim, B.J.C. 2000. Asymmetries reconfigured: South American television flows in the 1990s. *Canadian Journal of Communication*, 25(2), 285–306.

Curtin, M. 2003. Media capital: Towards the study of spatial flows. *International Journal of Cultural Studies*, 6(2), 202–28.

Czepek, A., Hellwig, M. and Nowak, E., eds. 2009. *Press Freedom and Pluralism in Europe. Concepts & Conditions*. Bristol, Chicago: Intellect.

De Bens, E. and de Smaele, H. 2001. The inflow of American television fiction on European broadcasting channels revisited. *European Journal of Communication*, 16(1), 51–76.

De Bens, E., Kelly, M. and Bakke, M. 1992. Television content: Dallasification of culture? In *Dynamics of Media Politics*, edited by K. Siune and W. Truetzschler. London: Sage, 73–100.

Der Fischer Weltalmanach 2008. Frankfurt am Main: Fischer Taschenbuch Verlag.

Dupagne, M. and Waterman, D. 1998. Determinants of US television fiction imports in Western Europe. *Journal of Broadcasting and Electronic Media*, 42(2), 207–20.

Esser, A. 2002. The transnationalization of European television. *Journal of European Area Studies*, 10(1), 13–29.

Esser, A. 2009. Trends in television programming: Commercialization, transnationalization, convergence, in *Media in the Enlarged Europe. Politics, Policy and Industry*, edited by A. Charles. Bristol: Intellect, 23–36.

European Audiovisual Observatory 2007. *Yearbook 2006. Film, Television and Video in Europe. Vol. 2: Trends in European Television*. Strasbourg: European Audiovisual Observatory.

European Audiovisual Observatory 2008. *Yearbook 2007. Film, Television and Video in Europe. Vol. 2: Trends in European Television*. Strasbourg: European Audiovisual Observatory.

European Commission. 2008. *Communication from the Commission to the European Parliament, the Council, the European Economic and Social Committee and the Committee of the Regions. Eighth Communication on the application of Articles 4 and 5 of Directive 89/552/EEC 'Television without Frontiers', as amended by Directive 97/36/EC, for the period 2005–2006*. Brussels: European Commission.

Fu, W.W. 2006. Concentration and homogenization of international movie sources: Examining foreign film import profiles. *Journal of Communication* 56(4), 813–35.

Halawa, M. 2005. Opery mydlane: opowiesc w 5. odcinkach, in *30 najważniejszych programów TV w Polsce*, edited by W. Godzic. Warszawa: Wydawnictwo Trio TVN S.A., 93–110.

Harcourt, A. 2003. The regulation of media markets in selected EU accession states in Central and Eastern Europe. *European Law Journal*, 9(3), 316–40.

Havens, T. 2007. The hybrid grid: Globalization, cultural power and Hungarian television schedules. *Media, Culture & Society*, 29(2), 219–39.

Hrvatin, S. and Petković, B. (eds.) 2004. *Media Ownership and its Impact on Media Independence and Pluralism*. Ljubljana: Peace Institute.

International Monetary Fund. 2009. Available at: www.imf.org [accessed 15 June 2009].

IP/RTL Group 1995. *Television – European Key Facts 1994*. Köln: IP and RTL Group.

IP/RTL Group 1997. *Television – European Key Facts 1996*. Köln: IP and RTL Group.

IP/RTL Group 2000. *Television – International Key Facts 2000*. Köln: IP and RTL Group.

IP/RTL Group 2003. *Television – International Key Facts 2002*. Köln: IP and RTL Group.

IP/RTL Group 2006. *Television – International Key Facts 2005*. Köln: IP and RTL Group.

IP/RTL Group 2008. *Television – International Key Facts 2007*. Köln: IP and RTL Group.

Jakubowicz, K. 2003. Social and media change in Central and Eastern Europe: Framework for analysis, in *Business as Usual. Continuity and Change in Central and Eastern Europe*, edited by D.L. Paletz and K. Jakubowicz. Creskills: Hampton Press, 3–44.

Jakubowicz, K. 2007. *Rude Awakening. Social and Media Change in Central and Eastern Europe*. Cresskill: Hampton Press.
Jakubowicz, K. and Sükösd, M., eds. 2008. *Finding the Right Place on the Map. Central and Eastern European Media Change in a Global Perspective*. Bristol: Intellect.
Kruml, M. 2001. Televizní seriály. Drogy z obrazovky. Živel 14. Available at: http://www.zivel.cz/index.php?content=article&id=284 [accessed 14 July 2011].
Lee, S. 2007. A longitudinal analysis of foreign program imports on South Korean television, 1978–2002: A case of rising indigenous capacity in program supply. *Journal of Broadcasting & Electronic Media*, 51(1), 172–87.
Maciejewski, L. 2005. Byłem Isaurą. Niewolnica Isaura, czyli stan wojenny w telewizji, in *30 najważniejszych programów TV w Polsce*, edited by W. Godzic. Warszawa: Wydawnictwo Trio TVN S.A., 159–71.
McMillin, D. 2007. *International Media Studies*. Malden, MA: Blackwell Publishing.
McPhail, T. 1981. *Electronic Colonialism: The Future of International Broadcasting and Communication*. Newbury Park: Sage.
Milosavljevič, M. 2008. Can technical needs dictate cultural and public interests? Public service programming and the digital age in Slovenia, in *Public Service Television in the Digital Age. Strategies and Opportunities in Five South-East European Countries*, edited by M. Sükösd and A. Isanovic. Sarajevo: Mediacentar, 39–98.
Moran, A. and Malbon, J. 2006. *Understanding the Global TV Format*. Bristol: Intellect.
Nordenstreng, K. and Varis, T. 1974. Television traffic, a one way street? A survey and analysis of the international flow of television programme material. *Reports and Papers on Mass Communication*, 70, Paris: UNESCO.
Paletz, D.L. and Jakubowicz, K., eds. 2003. *Business as Usual. Continuity and Change in Central and Eastern Europe*. Creskills: Hampton Press.
Peruško, Z. and Popović, H. 2008. Media concentration trends in Central and Eastern Europe, in *Finding the Right Place on the Map. Central and Eastern European Media Change in a Global Perspective*, edited by K. Jakubowicz and M. Sükösd. Bristol: Intellect.
Pitterman, J., Saturková, J. and Šnábl, V., eds. 2002. *(Prvních) 10 let České televize*. Praha: Česká televize.
Pool, de Sola I. 1977. The Changing Flow of Television. *Journal of Communication*, 27(2), 139–49.
Rantanen, T. 2001. Old and the new: Communications technology and globalization in Russia. *New Media and Society*, 3(1), 85–105.
Scannell, P. and Cardiff, D. 1991. *A Social History of British Broadcasting. 'Serving the Nation, 1923–1939'*. Oxford: Blackwell.
Schiller, H. 1969. *Mass Communication and American Empire*. Boston: Beacon Press.
Sinclair, J., Jacka, E. and Cunningham, S., eds. 1996. *New Patterns in Global Television. Peripheral Vision*. New York: Oxford University Press.

Štětka, V. 2008. Promoting diversity, or protecting national culture? Television without Frontiers Directive in the context of the Czech television landscape, in *Comparing Media Systems in Central Europe. Between Commercialization and Politicization*, edited by B. Dobek-Ostrowska and M. Głowacki. Wroclaw: Wydawnictwo Uniwersytetu Wrocławskiego, 165–84.

Stiehler, H.-J. 2004. Disappearing reality: The end of East German television. *Historical Journal of Film, Radio and Television*, 24(3), 483–9.

Straubhaar, J. 1997. Distinguishing the global, regional and national levels of world television, in *Media in Global Context*, edited by A.Sreberny-Mohammadi, D. Winseck J.McKenna and O. Boyd-Barrett. London: Arnold, 284–98.

Straubhaar, J. 2007. *World television: From Global to Local*. London: Sage.

Sükösd. M. and Bajomi-Lázár, P., eds. 2003. *Reinventing Media: Media Policy Reform in East-Central Europe*. Budapest: Central University Press.

Thussu, D.K. 2006. *International Communication: Continuity and Change*. London: Arnold.

Trepte, S. 2003. *The Intercultural Perspective: Cultural Proximity as a Key Factor in Television Success*. Paper to the International Communication Association Conference, San Diego, CA, June 23–7.

Tunstall, J. 1977. *The Media Are American: Anglo-American Media in the World*. London: Constable.

Tunstall, J. 2008. *The Media Were American: US Mass Media in Decline*. New York, Oxford: Oxford University Press.

Van den Bulck, H. 2001. Public service television and national identity as a project of modernity: The example of Flemish television. *Media, Culture & Society*, 23(1), 53–69.

Varis, T. 1986. Trends in international television flow. *International Political Science Review*, 7(3), 235–49.

Waterman, D. and Rogers, E.M. 1994. The economics and television program production and trade in Far East Asia. *Journal of Communication*, 44(3), 89–111.

Conclusion

John Downey and Sabina Mihelj

The field of comparative media research has a history that stretches back over 50 years. It is a sporadic history, however. It is a history marked by a number of landmark books, of which Hallin and Mancini (2004) is simply the latest. This book has undoubtedly inspired a revival of interest in comparative media, which is very welcome and we hope is sustained over the coming years. As with all landmark books subsequent research tends to position itself in relation to it: for it, against it, for it and against it. The danger of this is that other approaches and other questions may be overlooked. The best way to sustain the development of comparative media as a field, we believe, is not to slavishly follow Hallin and Mancini's work but think through theoretical and methodological problems associated with doing comparative media research (borrowing from comparative analysis in humanities and social sciences). We can judge if progress has been made because of the coherence of the concepts and methods and whether they help us to do empirical research.

Despite the relatively long history of comparative media research, it is not clear that much progress has been made to explain why we have the media we have and how the media, in turn, influence attitudes and behaviours of audiences. What we take from Hallin and Mancini is the insistence that comparative media should refocus its efforts towards the task of explanation. It is not that we believe in value-free social science, that normative judgements should not be made, but rather the concern is that normative judgements in the field have tended to crowd out explanation and analysis. Normative judgments about what media institutions should be like and the role they should play in society are of crucial importance but the task of explanation should remain central. There can be no emancipation, as Elder-Vass (2010) argues, without explanation.

In this book we have taken to heart the task of explaining why we have the media we have. Tied up with this is necessarily a critique of mediacentrism. If we wish to explain why the media are as they are we need to look outside of the media as well as inside. How do economic, social, cultural and political structures shape media institutions? How much autonomy do media institutions have from extra-media structures? Media institutions are not mere reflections of extra-media structures, they can be more or less autonomous. This approach certainly does not deny media institutions causal powers. They do influence attitudes and behaviours but again the critique of mediacentrism is important here. Media institutions do not influence attitudes and behaviours in isolation from extra-media structures that have their own causal powers. If we wish to understand why people believe the things they do and act in particular ways we need to situate media as one cause amongst others.

The above comments are rather programmatic in nature, suggesting if not articulating a general approach. However, all academic work involves a division of labour and so it is encumbent upon us to explain what we think this book has contributed to the collective endeavour of comparative media analysis.

As editors we requested authors to write chapters that focused primarily on a single explanatory variable (the economic, the cultural, the political, and so on). The focus here is on explaining why the media are as they are rather than examining the causal powers that media institutions themselves possess. It is not that we think the latter do not exist or they are unimportant but it is not the focus of this book. We asked authors to concentrate on one causal variable not because we believe in monocausal explanations, far from it. The intention here was two-fold. First, by asking authors to focus on a particular causal factor we hoped not only that the strength of that factor as a cause would be substantiated theoretically and demonstrated empirically but also that the limits of that factor as a cause would become apparent because that factor alone fails to furnish a complete explanation. This is evident in a number of chapters. Sparks, while arguing for the primacy of the economic, suggests that we need to consider the interplay between economic and political factors. Jakubowicz, while arguing for the primacy of the political, notes the importance of cultural factors in shaping political attitudes that in turn shape media institutions. Second, we hoped to set up a dialogue between the chapters or a contest of causes where the relative strengths of causes and their relationships to one another would become apparent to the reader. What we hope to have produced is a recognition that the media are as they are because of a complex causation where there are multiple causes that sometimes work antagonistically and sometimes in harmony.

For comparative media analysis to develop and mature we must interrogate the assumptions that are often made about space and units of analysis. When we talk of media systems in the region of Central and Eastern Europe are we not in danger of assuming that the space within this region is homogenous? If we move to a slightly more sophisticated level and point to differences between states in the region, are we not in danger of assuming that the space within individual states is homogeneous? Are we not committing a methodological nationalism when we simply line states up for comparison? The alternative to methodological nationalism that we offer here is not to ditch the nation-state. States remain important actors and national identities persist. However, we must situate the nation-state in both transnational and local contexts. States are subject to transnational forces and local forces as are media institutions themselves. If we take Downey and Štětka's chapters, we see in the case of the Czech Republic that a transnational media company CME is clearly the dominant force in broadcasting but that much of Czech prime-time is made up of domestically-produced content albeit based on transnational formats. To understand what is going on in the Czech Republic we need not only to grasp the importance of transnational forces and cultures (the dominance of the profit-motive in explaining both CME's investment and the decision to offer national content based on transnational formats) but their interplay with national identities, which persist despite, and perhaps because of, those transnational forces. If we take Mihelj and Pajnik's chapters on ethnic diversity and gender, we can see the importance of cultural factors on media landscapes in Central and Eastern Europe. To speak of national media systems in the face of such manifest ethnic and gender inequalities is, at best, myopic. On both counts, the countries of CEE have seen wide-ranging transformations – for instance the decline of female participation in the labour force, the disintegration of socialist federations, and the rise of new nation-states – that have reverberated in the media sector as well. We would argue that our turn towards explanation and consideration of a broader range of causes should be of interest to those wishing to build more inclusive or egalitarian media systems. While there has been substantial work done on ethnicity and the media there is very little on gender and media in Central and Eastern Europe and we hope that Pajnik's ground-breaking contribution does encourage others to look at the consequences of social change for women in media industries. We are aware that there are whole areas of culture that we did not touch on (social class, sexuality) and would encourage others to consider cultural factors.

Karol Jakubowicz's contribution concentrated on the links between media systems and political systems. The chapter developed three inter-related arguments. First, it demonstrated that the scope of political and administrative control over the media depends on whether a country is democratic, semi-democratic, or autocratic. Second, it showed that specific institutional solutions adopted at the level of the political system are likely to be replicated at the level of the media. Third, it demonstrated that the extent of media freedom and independence depends crucially on the behaviour and normative attitudes among the political elites and the general population, specifically on their attitudes to democratic values and behaviour vis-à-vis democratic institutions. Even in democratic post-communist states political elites control public service broadcasting directly. A change in government is followed by a change in public service broadcasting personnel and political position. This is generally accepted not only by elites but by populations who expect broadcasting to be used in an instrumental fashion by the powerful. The culture of the communist legacy prevents the development of a relatively autonomous public service broadcaster. It is also reasonable to expect this to endure as a newly elected government is unlikely to grant public service broadcasters greater autonomy precisely when they have achieved a position to ensure that their views are promoted. Here cultural factors and political factors combine to encourage stasis.

That media institutions in Central and Eastern Europe enjoy little autonomy comes as no surprise to Colin Sparks. The central insight of his chapter, written from a political economy perspective, is that the economies of Central and Eastern Europe are generally too poor to sustain media institutions that are relatively autonomous either from capitalists or the state. The weakness of media markets explains this lack of relative independence in comparison to media institutions in advanced capitalist societies. From this perspective, the development of relatively autonomous media is dependent upon economic growth, increasing disposable incomes, and advertisers keen to persuade consumers to buy their products. The creation of wealth means that markets for media products can develop and thrive. They become less reliant on owners as they do not need to be bank-rolled constantly. This is the precondition for the development of a more autonomous journalism and greater professionalism. Journalist re-education programmes, Sparks argues, are bound to fail in present economic circumstances. There is plenty to be said for this materialist economic analysis of the state of capitalism, and hence of media institutions, in Central and Eastern Europe rather than a more idealist approach. Sparks' chapter also represents, with its emphasis on the transnational analysis of capitalism, the first significant departure from existing comparative frameworks. As capitalism develops in the region (at contrasting rates) we would expect to see the rise of media institutions that are profit-making and thus more independent from either political elites or the political beliefs of individual capitalists. The myth of journalistic objectivity may well have a future in Central and Eastern Europe.

Sabina Mihelj turned to another aspect that has so far remained largely absent in *comparative* media research, namely the relationship between media systems and ethno-cultural diversity. This means that work on ethnic diversity has missed out on the explanatory power that comparative analysis can provide. Her chapter distinguished between national political strategies that involve the eradication of differences and strategies premised on the accommodation of differences. These broader strategies are to be found within media policy: while some countries opt for a media system segmented along ethno-cultural lines, others establish an integrated one. Mihelj then explained the adoption of the respective models with reference to domestic and international factors. Three factors were identified as being particularly influential: the ethnic composition of the domestic population, historical factors such as the trajectory of nation-state building and recent inter-ethnic conflicts, and the presence of a kin-state and kin-state media that are perceived as a threat.

There is some convergence in explanation evident here if we consider Jakubowicz's and Mihelj's chapters together. While not dismissing the role that political causes play, they both see cultural factors as being of primary importance as these are the terrain on which political actors operate. Cultural factors enable and constrain the room available for political manoeuvre, they provide the cloth out of which the suit is cut. This has quite profound implications for comparative media analysis generally in that the political is often taken to be primary and sometimes the only cause. The lesson from Jakubowicz and Mihelj is that we need to investigate broader historical and cultural reasons if we are to explain why media are as they are. Comparative media analysis has borrowed up to now extensively from comparative political analysis but there are many other fields of comparative analysis (history, religion, sociology, and so on) that are largely untapped and surely fertile sources for developing the field of comparative media analysis. In the face of such possibilities, it is hard to avoid the conclusion that we have barely scratched the surface of what the comparative study of media could become.

European countries – East, West, North and South – also differ significantly in their gender policies as well as in the level of women's participation in the labour market and political decision-making. It is reasonable to assume that these differences will also have their counterpart in the gendered structures of media systems. In the post-WWII period, communist countries made significant progress in fostering women's employment, including employment in the media sector: planned economies required a large workforce, and the state encouraged women's participation through family-related supports and benefits, including paid maternal leave, family allowances and free health services. Mojca Pajnik's chapter developed and tested an analytical framework that combined the analysis of the gendered structures of media systems with an examination of relevant contextual factors, in particular gender mainstreaming policies and labour market participation. The position of women in CEE societies generally and in media industries in particular has been shaped by the decision to imitate Western European societies after the 1989 revolutions and the break-up of the Soviet Union instead of seeking a more radical, democratic alternative to state socialism that would have produced greater gender equality rather than greater gender inequality. As a result, the position of women in labour markets generally and in media work, in particular, has worsened. In addition, the representation of women has shifted dramatically towards sexual objectification (an observable if less dramatic trend in Western Europe). It is remarkable that so little research has been undertaken as yet in this area. We hope that Pajnik's chapter opens up a new avenue of enquiry and inspires a new generation of researchers to consider the gendered media industries and texts of CEE.

John Downey's contribution was the first of three that focused on the impact of transnational factors. His chapter drew on neo-institutional analysis of DiMaggio and Powell that has been widely used in the sociology of organizations and sociology of culture but has yet to be applied in comparative media analysis (and is thus one instance of how comparative media analysis can benefit from a broader engagement with other humanities and social sciences). It is argued that the concepts of institutional isomorphism are helpful in analysing media change in CEE. To demonstrate this, the chapter focused on the strategies and tactics adopted by transnational media companies that invest in CEE media and explained why transnational companies invest in some parts of CEE but not others. Downey's contribution complements that of Sparks. While Sparks engages in more macro-analysis of capitalism, Downey examines the behaviour of individual firms. The unit of analysis is not the nation-state but rather the individual firm. Firms will invest in media markets where there are prospects of profits. While this is obviously related to a country's GDP this is not the sole factor in play. CEE is a potentially attractive site of investment because of a lack of competition in media markets in contrast to other European regions. Firms tend to roll out similar products across territories as they have experience in producing products of a certain type. The use of transnational formats reduces costs (pooling of resources, saving on management costs) and risks but firms also recognise the importance of developing local content and employing local journalists to produce content for the format.

Alison Harcourt's chapter addressed another important transnational force shaping the recent transformation of CEE media, namely transnational regulatory pressures. CEE states largely based regulatory models upon those in Western Europe, including the provision of public service broadcasting and subsidies for independent and national production. At the same time, however, policy makers from the region were also under a tremendous pressure from the US and international organizations to move towards a more liberal regulatory framework. As a consequence, although on paper regulatory models resemble those of Western Europe, in practice a more liberal market regulatory model influenced by the US prevails. Harcourt argued that smaller and financially weaker CEE states are in a weaker position to contest the policies of liberal globalization advocated by the USA and the WTO. The weak position of public service in many CEE states bears this out. Many public service institutions are resource poor and lack popular trust in comparison to a number of Western and Northern European PSBs, which in turn means they are more susceptible to commercialization. Such circumstances, however, only create the preconditions for commercialization, of course. The extent to which it occurs depends not only on media policy but on media economics. It should be noted that a liberal approach to regulation does not necessarily produce competitive markets and some transnational firms have built a striking dominance in different markets in CEE. There are clear tendencies to monopoly at work.

Václav Štětka explored the dynamics of transnational communication flows in CEE. Following the removal of ideological and legal constraints after 1989, the CEE media markets and audiences soon became a primary target for Western media companies and their products. This has resulted in an influx of foreign investment as well as Western media content, particularly visible in the audiovisual sector. The comparative research on media transformation of CEE countries has so far focused predominantly on the structural-economic aspects of this process, in particular changes in media policies and regulation and ownership structures. In contrast, shifts in the intensity and direction of the transnational communication flows, manifest through changing programme structures, amount and origin of audiovisual imports/exports and so on, have not received much attention. While some single-country studies do exist, comparative research in this area is virtually non-existent. This chapter began to fill this important area of study. First, it mapped the development and current state of audiovisual flows and audience's preferences in the CEE region, particularly with respect to the question of competitiveness of the local audiovisual entertainment vis-à-vis imported content. Second, it explored the intra-regional differences and similarities and identifies in a set of spcio-economic factors that help answer the question why some CEE countries have been more successful in challenging the inflow of audiovisual imports than others. What we find is that a country's GDP is very important in determining whether domestic content is widely available on prime-time. Higher levels of GDP permit higher levels of investment in content that allow domestic programmes to compete more successfully with foreign imports.

The findings of Štětka's chapter fits well with both the importance of the economic stressed by Sparks and the importance of the cultural emphasised by Mihelj. It also sits nicely with Downey's chapter on transnational firms and formats. Much of the domestic production that takes place in CEE uses transnational formats and is broadcast on networks owned by transnational firms. Thus domestic production is often a 'glocal' phenomenon and to understand it we need to understand the relationship between transnational and national forces.

Such an example brings us to a conclusion and a call for more comparative media analysis. In order to understand developments in CEE media systems over the last twenty years we need to grasp the importance of complex causation, of multiple determination. It is not the economic or the political or the cultural or the transnational or the national that by themselves determine the character of the media system but the interaction of a number of factors. Sometimes these factors push in the same direction, at other times they stand in an antagonistic relationship. There are, in other words, factors that encourage change and factors that encourage stasis (for example, the development of a capitalist economy and higher levels of GDP will promote change; the persistence of communist legacy thinking with respect to the instrumental use of media promotes stasis). It is, of course, one thing to say that we must consider complex causation and quite another to show how and when this occurs. To do so we must rethink how we do comparative media analysis (Downey and Stanyer 2010). Methodological innovation must be backed by detailed empirical investigation. It is only then that we can truly make headway in explaining why the media are as they are.

References

Downey, J. and Stanyer, J. 2010. Comparative media analysis – why some fuzzy thinking might help: applying fuzzy-set qualitative comparative analysis to the personalization of mediated political communication. *European Journal of Communication*, 25(4), 331–47.

Elder-Vass, D. 2010. *The Causal Power of Social Structures: Emergence, Structure and Agency*. Cambridge: Cambridge University Press.

Hallin, D. and Mancini, P. 2004. *Comparing Media Systems: Three Models of Media and Politics*. Cambridge: Cambridge University Press.

Index

For Product Safety Concerns and Information please contact our
EU representative GPSR@taylorandfrancis.com, Taylor & Francis
Verlag GmbH, Kaufingerstraße 24, 80331 München, Germany